RETELLING TRICKSTER
IN NAAPI'S LANGUAGE

RETELLING

Trickster

IN NAAPI'S LANGUAGE

Nimachia Howe

UNIVERSITY PRESS *of* COLORADO
Louisville

© 2019 by Nimachia Howe

Published by Utah State University Press
An imprint of University Press of Colorado
245 Century Circle, Suite 202
Louisville, Colorado 80027

 The University Press of Colorado is a proud member of
the Association of University Presses.

The University Press of Colorado is a cooperative publishing enterprise supported, in part, by Adams
State University, Colorado State University, Fort Lewis College, Metropolitan State University of
Denver, Regis University, University of Colorado, University of Northern Colorado, University of
Wyoming, Utah State University, and Western Colorado University.

∞ This paper meets the requirements of the ANSI/NISO Z39.4-1992 (Permanence of Paper)

ISBN: 978-1-60732-977-0 (hardcover)
ISBN: 978-1-60732-978-7 (paperback)
ISBN: 978-1-60732-979-4 (ebook)
https://doi.org/10.5876/9781607329794

Library of Congress Cataloging-in-Publication Data

Cataloging-in-Publication data for this title is available online at the Library of Congress.

Cover illustration © John Nieto, 1936–2018. "Coyote." 48″ × 60″. Reproduced with permission.

For the Niitsítapiiksi,
and Allen

Contents

Preface and Acknowledgments

Who is Naapi, the so-called Trickster of the Blackfoot People[1] of the Northwest Plains?

For almost two-and-a-half centuries, visitors to the Blackfoot homeland, which was traditionally in the Northwest Plains and currently still spans Alberta, Canada, and the US state of Montana, have heard about Naapi and his comparable characters in other Indigenous Peoples' traditions. A diverse set of collectors gathered Naapi stories, an important genre that is part of a large array of stories outlined in the Blackfoot creation cycles. This study looks as some of the features and uses of Blackfoot language in Naapi story contexts as he connects the land to the People; Naapi predates the arrival of the People and, as a child of Sun and Moon, has an entire genre of stories devoted solely to his episodic creativity. Naapi stories explain how he established the landscape with help from Iihtsipáítapiiyo'pa, "the one through whom we live,"[2] and Á'pistotooki, "the one who made us";[3] universal energies coordinated with atmospheric and astral forces, often called "spirits" in English. All are considered Persons proper in Blackfoot because they are infused with creative power, the same power Naapi uses to shape and bring forth life to the homeland so People and other beings may live in it. People repeat the knowledge of this space and of the entire landscape where Naapi stories occur to mark out a home perfectly created for them.

Naapi also connects Peoples' land to life values. In Naapi stories, his actions also inform and shape Peoples' values, humor, creativity, ethics, morals, codes, and

DOI: 10.5876/9781607329794.c000

potential futures with which People can identify and can claim. Naapi's interactions with other living Beings include a multiplicity of actions with a range of Beings, such as birds, bears, winds, waters, spirits, rocks, seeds, mountains, and berries, to name but a few. He is the mediator among Peoples, plants, animals, and the elemental forces of creation, the accounts of which are told in story. When and where these stories occur is of paramount importance because in each, he creates spaces for all forms of living Beings in situ and thus connects original Peoples to the beginnings of time, as it is re-created over time *in a place*; this is the definition of the homeland. Hereto is the source of why many Indigenous languages identify humans as "original" People; it is an expression to distinguish us from all the rest of the surrounding life forms and not to mean *the* People in an ethnocentric sense, for the emphasis should be on the *People* instead as a distinguishing fact. All other forms of life are alive and thus share with People intelligence and will, so stars, winds, and thunder, for instance, "speak" to People, and Naapi is an important go-between as these forces reach out to communicate with us. Blackfoot and other Algonquian/Algonkian languages use oral tradition styles, devices, and speech acts that demonstrate a human interest in, and a desire to receive and comprehend, these messages.

This study of Naapi stories is an effort to decode some of these methods or systems, guided by a few questions. How, or do, Naapi stories and the ways Blackfoot use language *about* Naapi express core values that emerge from these land-based experiences? What do Indigenous Plains Peoples' and Algonquian/Algonkian Peoples' stories have in common with the homeland? How is the traditional Indigenous land ethic taught with Naapi stories? What, if any, relevance does Naapi's name have in this? How are universal energies of creativity, adaptation, and change, accounted for, if they are? This study reviews storytelling occasions and also questions extralinguistic material. It combines some story analyses with a consideration of the metaphysical aspects of Naapi, as reported and expressed in the Blackfoot language. Naapi story analysis is an extensive subject that deserves its own book, so only a few examples are explored in this discussion. Statements put forth about Naapi stories are nonetheless drawn from a much larger body of Naapi stories and are thematically and linguistically consistent with them. As such, this study is organized around themes that introduce readers to the physical and metaphysical dimensions of Naapi and considers how these dimensions are expressed in the Blackfoot terms and expressions used to illustrate his essential multidimensional changeability (e.g., Naapi's many names).

To address change factors in the written record, this book also examines the ways Blackfoot and other Algonquian/Algonkian languages are described in very early accounts. Journals by missionaries, trappers, commissioners, traders, vacationing tourists, and the like document some of the earliest collections of Naapi stories, beginning with Peter Fidler in 1792 and continuing to the present. Almost a century after these initial collections were accumulated, linguists began to study vocabulary lists and Naapi story compilations, with some of the earliest being several works by the linguist C. C. Uhlenbeck (1866–1951), whose work after 1900 includes several published collections that amassed multiple stories. For the remainder of the past two centuries, there has been, generally speaking, a separation between linguists' work (e.g., structural anthropology)—specializing in diagrams, grammatical breakdowns, and descriptions into classificatory systems and categories, such as works by Donald Frantz (e.g., *Blackfoot Grammar*, 2017)—and writers who focus on Naapi or "Trickster" and their Algonquian/Algonkian–related stories (e.g., Grinnell's "Old Man Stories," in *Blackfeet Indian Stories* [1926]). Uhlenbeck and J.P.B. de Josselin de Jong (1886–1964) excepted, story collections are rarely linked to linguistic analyses, and language studies likewise limit references to the stories to excerpts or separate statements only and do not analyze entire stories, much less multiple stories. As such, attempts to answer questions about who Naapi is rely on generally abstracted linguistic approaches or on interpretations and tellings of individual Naapi Trickster stories, with little cross-conversation. Many of these efforts lack detail or large overviews of how Naapi earned his "Trickster" title, since it takes the body of them together to see how he changed through time, so that is my focus.

As a result of this separation, limited research exists on assumptions made about the ultimate meanings of Trickster and other aspects of the Blackfoot and other Algonquian/Algonkian languages. Separations between discreet linguistic analyses and verbatim stories repeated without any accompanying comments, criticisms, or analysis of Trickster in holistic ways result in a lack information about how overall sociocultural or sociolinguistic priorities are expressed with Naapi stories as their vehicle. Naapi stories are "teaching stories" and are constructed to advance values, but by what applications or rules? Have strategies been overlooked by collectors and commenters because (1) literary critiques interpret them as "myths" and "legends," a somewhat dismissive categorization that discourages the view that they merit analyses as stories that pertain to the real world; and (2) linguistic studies have been predominantly concerned with grammatical organization and systematic classification and with assessing, assigning, and comparing these stories to their linguistic family counterparts. These studies have, respectively, contributed greatly to the understanding of Algonquian/Algonkian relatives.

My approach in this book is to integrate these studies and to interpret Naapi's character as primarily an expression of the environment, which is universal, although its local development is context-dependent. Naapi stories use language to alternate Naapi's constantly fluctuating Trickster persona; from one moment to another he changes, a characteristic he shares with other Indigenous Peoples'

Tricksters. His recognizable trademark is his many energetic forms, and the count-less variations on his name struggle to keep up with his identities. Trickster story language and its multiple manifestations of Naapi can be used as a *method* for ana-lyzing Naapi stories. This poses the question about whose language to use to speak about the reality Naapi describes. Whose reality is being prioritized when language doesn't want to "behave," either because for centuries the Trickster genre itself has been neglected as a source of truth, as an accurate descriptor of ultimate reality, or because in Indigenous languages Tricksters do not adhere to or fit neatly into easily identifiable conceptual linguistic categories?

This book began as I prepared Naapi stories for a presentation that required an introduction to concepts of space and time, including the notably identifiable space known as the Blackfoot homeland. Naapi's creator energies are involved in the cycles of the planets and seasons—the largest orders of things—and yet supersede time as we know it because he lived before it and will continue after it. Many per-tinent questions arose. How, or does, the language account for these features? One thing Algonquian/Algonkian languages, including Blackfoot, do is *constantly adjust descriptions of action* (which are often classed as nouns). A feature of Naapi's name, the final syllable, which usually connotes animate gender grammatically, has also changed status over the centuries. Why? The term *Trickster* is English, so what is the meaning of Naapi and his Algonquian/Algonkian counterparts *before* translations? How are references to Naapi and his Algonquian/Algonkian relatives distinct from or similar to those to other Algonquian/Algonkian or Plains Peoples' Tricksters? To other Indigenous Peoples' Tricksters? What can we learn about the implica-tions for grammatical meaning and participation from the ways Naapi language is used regarding Trickster specifically? Do Blackfoot, Algonquian/Algonkian, and Plains Peoples' grammars reflect any priorities, ethics, or sociocultural or human-istic concerns, for instance, of their speakers by the ways they use language (maybe only) to describe Trickster energy, in story and more generally? What are some meta-linguistic understandings about Trickster energy *not* captured by studies that continue to cover Plains Peoples' and Algonquian/Algonkian Trickster stories and that do *not* investigate whether speakers adjust expressions (i.e., language) to more clearly show intent? How are speakers' intentions influenced by language (e.g., grammatical) choices made to accommodate/approximate meaning?

A key consideration and motivation behind these research questions is a focus on non-verbal signs as a form of communication used by all living Beings that humans can interpret and imitate. Sign are the basis of *non-human* forms of communica-tion systems that Indigenous Peoples expanded upon and developed as Plains Sign Language (PSL). This study also asks how PSL understands and informs Plains Peoples about Trickster and how it contributes to the analysis of Naapi stories as a source for understanding meaning and context of spoken forms of Indigenous languages, especially the early Naapi stories; for Indigenous Peoples, collections of all Trickster stories collected among Algonquian/Algonkian and Plains Peoples were translated directly from sign, not speech. PSL has its own idiomatic expressions, shorthand, variations in lexicon, and other features that are comparable to spoken modes of communication, even including specific expressions.[4] Most notably, PSL accounts for and attaches meaning to direction and placement. Speakers represent utterances that occupy a spot or locations in a spatial relationship vis-à-vis the cardinal directions. These types of physical, non-verbal orientations are functionally significant pointers, aimed toward intended meaning in this communication system, so they deserve consideration in any treatment that aims to discover the intentions behind the language of stories originally told in this medium. Language and literature studies can contribute mutual sharing of insights and interconnected analyses, since signed interactions use the "language" that speakers of Algonquian/Algonkian and Plains Peoples' languages claim was "given" to them by nature. PSL was a lingua franca when the misinterpretations about Naapi and other Indigenous Peoples' Tricksters began.

This book is a result of several years of considering options for methods of analyses of early Trickster stories because at their core they are about place, and they belong to increasingly displaced Indigenous Peoples the world over, who traditionally retain a connection to place through story. These place- and space-specific storytelling traditions are stories/story personas who detail specifics of the natural surroundings as Trickster stories do, and also describe how (various) Peoples have inherited them. Amid academic and cultural traditions that exclude or excise the import of these stories, how do we scholars, describers of the places that birth unique Peoples in them, account for these stories? Indigenous Peoples' ties to land involve myriad collaborators and creators, all of whom contribute to the sense of *who* the People are, which is defined in great part by *where* they are. The Blackfoot connection to Naapi is reaffirmed in part through telling Naapi stories, which are invariably tied to the places in which they occurred and recur. As long as Trickster stories are told, they affirm entire Peoples' long-standing orientations vis-à-vis the landscape and thus of knowing what it is to be Blackfoot. This is also true for the other Algonquian/Algonkian languages' legacies, as well as for other Plains Peoples' Trickster stories. These Trickster-land-Peoples ties supersede linguistic family groupings because while they encompass them, unique geographic placements by neighbors with dissimilar language families but who share similar ecosystems and environmental conditions, for instance, allow additional data/experiences to inform story forms and values. Since these are accounted for in the universal energies expressed in Naapi and other Trickster oral traditions, emphasis on location in space is an appropriate place to begin a study of Trickster language.

Other factors contributed to the difficulty of this study. Many Naapi stories have been edited out of the traditional series because they were deemed offensive and subsequently banned. Of those that remain, some have been published repeatedly, whereas others have been deleted from collections with such vigor that they have become obsolete in oral accounts and are nearly nonexistent in written documents. This situation has resulted in a dearth of details, which severely diminishes potential for analyses. To compensate for this, I include explanatory material gathered from multidisciplinary sources to complement stories that are available to conduct analyses of the Blackfoot language and interpretations of the character(s) who interact with Naapi. Some of these sources include artists' memoirs; police, agent, commissioner, and army reports; journals of fur trappers, mountaineers, missionaries, and explorers; meteorological and land surveys; and interviews with or records of Blackfoot elders' stories over the past two centuries. I have also consulted with fluent Blackfoot speakers and ceremonialists on this topic.

I was teaching and conducting research for my doctoral dissertation on Blackfoot star stories in Canada when I was invited by Harry Stabs Down of the Kainaa (Many Chiefs) Band (i.e., Blood) of the Blackfoot to share my ideas about the future of place-based research, a project the Blackfoot People see as relevant because of its ties to Blackfoot language and cultural maintenance. The different communities of Indigenous language speakers mentioned in this study conduct these types of studies in their own ways, and my goal is to contribute to these efforts. The Naapi stories in the appendix of this book represent a small sampling of the possible stories that could be used as examples of how the People identify with a place. Apart from a few conference presentations, however, I have not published any work on Naapi stories. I have nonetheless taught about these stories as a professor of Native American studies at the University of California, Berkeley, and at Blackfeet Community College back home on the Blackfeet Reservation in Montana. Sharing this research with the community has been a joy. I have expanded the topic over several years, so this book draws from a large body of research.

Many people have supported this work and helped my thinking. I want to thank Robert A. LeVine and Marcelo Suárez-Orozco for supporting me through the dissertation phase of my graduate studies on Blackfoot star stories, which is when the inspiration for this work began. Through the many phases of this manuscript, the following people have been immensely helpful: Omi (Naomi) Crawford, Kevin Crawford, James Hatley, Narcisse Blood, Frank Weasel Head, Martin Heavy Head, Pam Heavy Head, Lorna Crowshoe, Reggie Crowshoe, Rose Crowshoe, Peter Weasel Moccasin, Frederick ("Rick") Tailfeathers, Mike Swims Under, Alice B. Kehoe, Darryl Kipp, Rod D. Bullshoe, Allan Pard, Irene Diamond, Joe Eagle Child, Martin Frey, Tracy Newkirk, Robert W. Traver, Alfred Arteaga, Mae

Tallow, Edward Kennedy, Martin Frey, Dwight Jennings, Neil Eisenberg, Leon Rattler, Arthur Westwolf, David Kaufman, Jeffrey E. Davis, Lakhota Hasie Frasier, Conrad Knudsen, Mae Tallow, Earl Old Person, Alberto Pimentel, Alfred Arteaga, Molly Kicking Woman, George Kicking Woman, Michael Brooks, Chevi Baby, Valiant Norman, and Ovide W. Mercredi. I thank Eleanor Bernal, Dody Riggs, Manuel Hernández, Joan Kocsis, Joyce H. Hernández, and A. Tau Hernández for editorial assistance, and Darrin Pratt and all the staff at the University Press of Colorado. The interpretations presented in this book are mine, as are any mistakes or misinterpretations.

I am also grateful for the opportunity to conduct much of the fieldwork and research that was made possible by grants and fellowships that supported this work, especially from Harvard University Women's Studies in Religion Program, the Fulbright Scholar Program, Harvard University Center for the Study of World Religions, Rockefeller Foundation "Ecological Conversations: Gender, the Sacred, and Geography," the Smithsonian Institution Native American Awards Program, a Mellon Foundation Grant, and a University of California Committee on Research Enabling Grant. The archivists and staff at each of the locations where I carried out the fellowships and conducted research provided invaluable and much-appreciated assistance. The same is true of the assistance I received during my research at Yale University Beinecke Library and Archives and at Yale University Sterling Memorial Library Manuscript and Archives, the Smithsonian Institution's National Anthropological Archives in the National Museum of Natural History, the Glenbow Museum Archives, the Southwest Museum of the American Indian, Montana State University Library Special Collections and Archives, and Ball State University Archives and Special Collections. Finally, teaching my seminar on Naapi stories at Blackfeet Community College, Browning, Montana, offered yet another opportunity to reflect on Naapi's language.

RETELLING TRICKSTER
IN NAAPI'S LANGUAGE

Chapter 1

Who Is Naapi?

Sign as First Language

Retelling Trickster in Naapi's Language is an in-depth study of the language of the story cycle of Naapi, who has many names and is most commonly known as "Old Man," a Trickster in Blackfoot oral literature.[1] This study expands on a land-based genre of stories to discuss how they use the land and environment as a teacher, with Naapi interpreted as myriad expressions of nature's forces. This chapter introduces some of the ways Naapi stories effect language use by the many ways his energy is expressed and stems from the acknowledgment that particular aspects of Naapi's identity are not restricted to his story activities but extend beyond the storied context to describe their source in his actions/personality, breath, expressions, songs, and signs. Naapi's power is partially attributed to the ways the Blackfoot language *refers to* him and *speaks to or with* him. Traditional Indigenous Trickster literatures throughout the world are built around characters fundamental to the creation of a particular People, and entire story sequences are built around the creative activity of this entity. Not all Tricksters are the same, nor is the term itself Indigenous. In common with other Algonquian/Algonkian language traditions, Naapi's is a creator of the Blackfoot, and he thus lays the groundwork for other Blackfoot story genres, all of which constitute the body of oral literature that makes the Blackfoot a distinctive People. Trickster stories share in common with other Indigenous communities the universal energy that manifests differently across linguistic similarities and geological or geographical differences.

DOI: 10.5876/9781607329794.c001

Translated directly from the Blackfoot language, sometimes from Plains Sign Language, and drawing additional data from Algonquin studies, this book is a critical collection of Blackfoot language studies analyses complemented with multidisciplinary contributions focused on Blackfoot and Algonquian/Algonkian language and translations. It includes published and unpublished works in an effort to conduct research within a richer context than has previously been attempted for a focused study of how the Blackfoot use language to represent Indigenous understandings of Naapi's role as an energy source and creator. The combination of sources and research questions may provide a model for viable comparisons across Algonquian/Algonkian and Plains Peoples' oral literature traditions.

COMMONALITIES WITH OTHER TRICKSTERS

Naapi stories outline Blackfoot ecology, cosmology, and philosophy, or what Indigenous Peoples call a "way of life." Blackfoot language use conveys critical information about Blackfoot views on all life forms and about how People can live properly with them. This is evident when comparing Naapi's characteristics, adventures, and escapades to those of other Tricksters: Nanabozho (Ojibwa), Wisakedjak (Cree, Algonquin), Iktomi (Lakota), Kokopelli (Hopi and Ancestral Pueblo), Manitou (Dene), and Glooskap (Wabanaki) comprise a sampling from a diverse group that includes Raven (Kwakiutl, Haida, Athabaska, Bella Bella), Crane, Rabbit, and Coyote. Many more are found throughout other Indigenous Peoples' oral traditions. Much of the research approach regarding Naapi is summed up with the statement "Old Man was also known to other plains-tribes and by different names. Some of these myths are fragmentary and incomplete, but all bear an unmistakable stamp of the primitive and childhood period of Blackfeet history. Others are samples of Indian humour, told as we tell fairy tales and using Old Man for their central figure."[2]

This study is a seminal work on Indigenous language that introduces and develops a unique paradigm based on analyses of the *ways* these stories are told and the *places* they mention that highlight landscape features and patterns of the flora and fauna and that focus on the incorporation of all these aspects expressed in Naapi stories. It models a way to understand other Trickster traditions and to connect them to the natural world from which they emerge. Tricksters share similarities in that their origins are mysterious, the stories of which have been told since long ago, and there is a sense that they arose out of or manifested into form, seemingly from air or speech. Often, when they depart, they go in the direction from whence the weather comes. As a result of the unique circumstances that contribute to the different homelands of every Indigenous People considered here, where the weather "comes from" for them has varying implications for interpretations of Tricksters; it is the universal life-giving energy that creates life on earth, in whatever form that takes depending on the many options of land and skyscapes. Trickster stories, because their essence is to capture these essential descriptions, have the lead to change constantly and occupy a niche within their Peoples' traditional story paradigms that is similar to Naapi's.

This project began as an assignment to identify key locales to map Naapi stories in a geographic and ideographic sense. Naapi stories occur at the beginning of the Blackfoot creation story order and are among those first told to young children as a way to introduce them to the Blackfoot homeland, their new home. The stories explicitly identify and explain the landscape and those who live on or from it, as well as the several Blackfoot story genres, and each respectively identifies with a series of specific locations and seasons. Hence, when discussing these stories in the Blackfoot language, correct interpretations depend on a story's location and time in the seasonal calendar. Seasonal movement of People and animals is more significant than static references to particular places, and it is time, not a geographic point, that centers stories' meanings. Naapi's language, speech forms, and acts in stories acknowledge the participation of others with whom he interacts, and thus we know him and ultimately ourselves through his experiences because they are all part of the homeland matrix.

"OPPOSITE-SPEAK" AS TRICKSTER ARTFORM

One of the most prominent and pervasive features of Naapi's speech style in stories is that he frequently counters others, in intent and action and through the use of words or songs. Among a host of other speech-related acts, he implores, begs, demands, threatens, mocks, mimics, and orders others. He also utilizes a mode of interaction that is meant to highlight the *opposite* of what he says or does, which occurs in Blackfoot sociocultural practices not directly in reference to Naapi. When he is out of control and being blown about by wind, grasping for life at anything that can help him stop and be still, for instance, he catches a lucky break when he gets "caught" by a tree, and this ultimately rescues him from peril. Instead of thanking the tree, however, he decides to punish it while admonishing it for interrupting "his fun." On another occasion, he is dancing wildly and showing off when he accidentally sets the grass plains ablaze and ruins the fancy dance outfit he was showing off to everyone. When he has to take recourse in water to save himself and he ruins his clothing, he pretends that everything is as he planned it, as in he "meant to do that." A key aspect of many of these incidents is that Naapi creates, calls forth, or performs in ways that initiate the calamities he later has to get others' help to "solve" or from which he needs to be rescued. Such pointed self-referential orientation is designed to encourage self-analysis and reflection and to highlight communities' role in healing or resolving all those affected by his self-induced mishaps.

The spirit of knowing one's limits and yet balancing them against public pride, ego, or arrogance is always a part of these stories. It is also revealed in other aspects of Blackfoot life, such as when you are expected to say the opposite of what you want to happen: if you want the leader of a sweat not to make it very hot, then you must say you want it hot; if you want the piercings for dancing in the summer ceremonies to not be too deep, you have to ask for a deep cut. You even have to think about how you want to be known, since many names are the reverse of the meaning they intend the listener to understand about the person in question. One of Naapi's many names is Fooled-a-Little, which means just the opposite. Other examples include ways the forces of contrariness and balance override and work out in the end in ceremonial roles, in the use of certain items, and even in directions.[3] This basic paradigmatic stance of Blackfoot language use can obviously wreak havoc with ideas about having "gotten the message" when listening to stories. This is especially true for translations that interpret the original quite literally, as they will render the exact opposite of what Blackfoot speakers intend.

For the Blackfoot, salient topics, themes, and subjects of language use in refer- ence *to* or *by* Naapi include the significance of the Blackfoot language in inter- preting elements of stories, kinship between People and other Beings in nature, reciprocity, limitations on excess and rules against abuse, the comedy to be found in mistakes, self-actualization through assisting others, gratitude and generosity, and *using language to turn situations inside out*, thus inverting or reversing the recipient- giver, abused-abuser, or living-dead relationship for analysis and reflection. Naapi's would-be victims turn out to be much like him and vice versa—the "self" turned "other." Expressions, turns of phrase, salient syllables, and some grammar all play a part in how the Blackfoot use language to create a unique framing of appropriate interaction with the world. Naapi stories demonstrate how to live well by using Naapi's mishaps and misadventures as negative examples and by providing language and images that enable listeners to observe themselves in his misbehavior. Naapi epitomizes chaos and order in a fluctuating, frustratingly unpredictable bundle, and his oppositional stances, in word or deed, are mirrors for everyone else.

There are now diminishing numbers of fluent Blackfoot speakers and even fewer who are familiar with Naapi stories, which once were common knowledge. In addition, like other Indigenous languages, Blackfoot has changed over the past two centuries, so it is imperative to access the earliest forms and stories to inves- tigate lessons in human-animal coexistence and examine how they promote eco- logical, physical, and spiritual sustainability and resilience simultaneously. This is found in Naapi's various names and speech patterns, especially his name calling, self-justifications, excuses, explanations, nicknames, and insults and his back talk in general, which inverts situations and increases the possibility to interpret them with ironic humor and to be involved in his activities—which often turn into full-fledged debacles—that show how Naapi *is* life itself. Defining Naapi involves understanding how oppositional, interactive, and counterbalancing energies work.

Naapi stories are frequently compared to Aesop's Fables, and many authors assert that every story has a motto. Unfortunately, such views emphasize a view of Naapi as a human-like entity, like that of the other Beings he interacts with, including People. When understood through the ways the Blackfoot use language, in turns of phrase, naming practices, and Naapi's multiple names found across his many stories, it is clear that Naapi is not human and neither are his companions. Rather, they represent energies and entities that create circumstances and moments within which humans can pause to observe their actions, not only with each other but with all of nature. Blackfoot language use beyond Naapi stories reflects this reality of interconnectedness. In common with other Tricksters, Naapi stories perpetuate knowledge and awareness of proper dealings and the nature of human nature in light of what works or what doesn't for all life. The language emphasizes an ecological (i.e., social) context within which to interpret Trickster stories and language.

OF NAAPI'S NATIVE NATURE

This study is the most extensive and meticulous investigation of traditional Naapi identity through language paradigms thus far conducted. To the uninitiated, Naapi stories seem simple because they focus undue attention on Naapi's actions alone and thus are presented in a fashion that belies their deeper environmental, social, and cosmic lessons. This complex, encompassing, and nuanced analysis of Indigenous language and land-based identity identifies Naapi as a creator of Blackfoot consciousness. Naapi's counterparts in other Algonquian/Algonkian languages and oral traditions function similarly. The Blackfoot have occupied the People's traditional homeland in the northwestern United States and southwestern Canada since unknown times.[4] Like other Indigenous Peoples in their respective homelands, Blackfoot interactions with the local landscape, climate, seasons, winds, rivers, mountains, plains, flora and fauna, and all the animals who share the homeland are recorded in storied anecdotes. These are collective recollections about the Peoples' origins and about the interrelatedness between People and these other Beings, full Persons, through which the People's relationship with nature is expressed: "The Blackfoot creator is known as *Napi, Napiu, or Napioa*, according to the dialect spoken by the different tribes of the Blackfoot confederation. Quite extended stories are told of how he made the world, and of his adventures . . . a time before the creation of the earth as we know it to-day, and treats of an incident in the boyhood of Napi."[5] This discussion of Trickster reviews definitions and analyses of Naapi's name and nature and relevant comparative work on Algonquian/Algonkian or Plains Peoples' studies on these topics. Unfortunately, the literature on Naapi is rife with misnomers, mistakes, and repeated misinterpretations. A study of Naapi's name and its meaning could fill volumes; therefore, the aim here is to review the literature to track what has been lost, first in interpretation and then in comprehension, to discover and reconnect essential elements and to discuss Naapi and Naapi stories to reflect Blackfoot traditions and values as expressed in Naapi stories. The identification of key points about Blackfoot language use helps us reinterpret these stories to discover Naapi's essential nature.

NAAPI'S ANCESTRY AND FUTURITY: EPITOME OF OPPOSITIONAL FORCES

Naapi stories collected over the past two centuries were recollected by elders who had learned the stories from earlier generations of elders, so that by the time they were written down, their versions of these stories were centuries old. The antiquity of Naapi in the Blackfoot consciousness is long-standing, for example:

> The story was related to me by an old Blood chief named *Men-es-to-kos*, which means "all are his children," though the word is commonly translated "father of many children." Men-es-to-kos is not less than seventy years old, and perhaps much older. He told me that he first heard this tale when he was a small boy, from his great-grandmother, who at that time was a very old woman—so old that her face was all seamed with wrinkles, and . . . her eyelids hung down over her eyes so that she could not see. I have not the slightest doubt that the tale was told to me in good faith, and it is so remarkable that I consider it worth putting on record. It was told one night when a number of other old men had been relating stories of early times, many of which referred to the doings of Napi.[6]

One of the most ubiquitous interpretations of Naapi is through Christian tenets, thus the insistence that his actions be divided into "good" versus "bad," as in the following: "Napioa is the Secondary Creator of the Indians. There are two kinds of stories told concerning him. One class reveals him in the character of a good man, and the other class as a bad man. He is not, however, a man, but a supernatural being, able to perform deeds which no human could perform."[7] Since the Blackfoot, however, refer to other-than-human energies when speaking of Naapi, particularly regarding the creative forces of the landscape, it is said that the "Indians do not know the manner of his birth, nor the place from whence he came. He is still living in a great sea away to the south."[8] This means the stories tell that he was created *by* the elements rather mysteriously, like all creation, and that he returned to them in one form or another, generally traveling by way of some form of water. His "good" or "bad" effects are thus balanced out over time as the Blackfoot review his creative work. One extensive exposé on the topic of this balance of energy is as follows:

> Thus, in this one [story], the good and bad brothers stand for Light and Darkness; Light overcomes Darkness; God triumphs over the Devil. Whether the original meaning was such is still a mystery . . . Together the two groups of stories form an engaging pair, both for points of similarity and for contrast . . . They explained the World's wonders to the Indians, and, as there was no written literature, they served as a history book for them. As we remember these quaint old tales told here in our own Province, it makes it easy for us to understand something about the people who inhabited Alberta so long ago.[9]

Rather than reinforce the "good versus bad" binary invented and advanced by non-Indigenous beliefs, Naapi's "quaint old tales" require reevaluation in light of the environment that gave birth to them and that still informs them if there is to be any chance of understanding them at all. Naapi stories are refined and comprehensive contemplations and redefinitions of the environment writ large, including the atmosphere, climate, and astronomy, and of how People came to live in it—in short, the wonder of creation. Naapi's power is not uncontrolled, nor is it wanton or without reason, as often portrayed in Trickster literature. The presumably malevolent aspects of his personality are interpreted incorrectly, since they *should* be interpreted as part of a creative matrix of universal energy. Naapi stories also do not offer a discrete or distinct description of People because Naapi frequently inhabits or represents himself through other identities. Analyses of Blackfoot creation stories, including those of Naapi, too often perceive "the rich imagination and high quality of the story teller"[10] while dismissing the actions described as exaggeration or fantasy and unreal, but Naapi's antics, antagonized participants, and end results are actual. For all Naapi's heroic moments or dastardly deeds—and there are plenty of both throughout the Naapi story cycle—a new definition of him and the energy he represents is essential. Redefinitions that reiterate the idea that Naapi is some sort of mythical god are not really innovative, descriptive, or accurate. They simply continue his misinterpreted character, not as the Blackfoot know him.

Interpreted through the lens of nature's elemental forces of creation, for instance, Naapi, like his Trickster companions, is constantly reborn, transformed, and reshaped into new and ever-evolving identities. He undergoes forms of immortality, reincarnation, and rebirth, which is why he represents a process of continual renewal that epitomizes the spirit of earth's new growth every day, year, and season. Indigenous Peoples understand such cycles to be part of Peoples' spirit and the foundation of human—and the universe's—nature. In common with other Tricksters, Naapi's regenerative powers are ever-developing and universal among the hemisphere's Indigenous Peoples:

> There are countless Napi stories still in circulation. These vary greatly among themselves from the didactic to the "pornographic." Generally, they deal with the nitty-gritty side of life, not the lyric nor the romantic. Thus they reflect the many-faceted nature of Napi himself. He is the old Algonquin god, and appears as creator, trickster, thief, scoundrel, libertine, wise man, judge, nit-wit and the brunt of jokes. He is a culture-hero and messianic figure of the Algonquin peoples. His Blackfeet name Napi means both "old" and "white," and usually with the suffix -*koan* (person) the word is applied to the white man. Thus he reminds [us] of the Mexican Quetzalcoatl and may have the same origin. Such a figure crops up in myths from all over the Americas. Curiously enough, modern Blackfeet frequently call him redundantly "Old Napi" as if they had forgotten the true meaning of his Algonquin name.[11]

STORY GATHERING

A corollary to Naapi's free-flowing energy is that his stories have been recorded loosely and in mixed order, which was in accordance with traditional Indigenous storytelling norms; context either did or did not determine the appropriateness of a story. This means that for this study the story collection is very uneven because storytellers did not divulge everything they knew to every collector. Rather than assume that this is necessarily a feature of Naapi stories, it is worth considering the role of data collection, as people often share what they believe data collectors want to hear, what they believe they can handle, or what they have time to listen to or record. This is particularly true when stories are requested on demand and lack an interpreter. It is worth considering how this scattered style of story groupings could affect the order in which stories exist, either at the societal level of Indigenous Peoples' understanding for backgrounding and contextualization or in the experiences of individual storytellers, or both.

It is often argued that Indigenous Peoples could not have done better than to have scattered story collections, as "there was no strong priesthood to carefully preserve the stories and they were changed slightly with every telling. However, their framework remained the same, and the descendants of one group can sometimes be traced [to] the similarity of their folk lore [*sic*]."[12] This argument is only partially correct and generally excuses the ignorance of collectors; the Blackfoot have very strong, organized, and highly private associations in which initiated members learn stories about Blackfoot traditions. In addition, certain story versions were passed down through several generations of families. All Blackfoot ceremonial traditions are rooted in a story matrix, and Naapi stories are only one genre among many: "Indian legends are divided into two groups: the old tales and the new ones. The first group consists of all the 'golden age' stories in which animals can change into men and many supernatural events can happen. These are usually 'how' stories: how did the World begin? How did the Kingfisher get his lovely feathers? How were the Rocky Mountains made? These things could be explained only as works of wonder."[13] Naapi stories answer these great mysteries. This is why the Blackfoot say they have been around since the beginning of time. It is also why the Trickster is referred to as a "lesser deity": "They were never attributed to one Supreme Being but to animals and lesser deities. The most popular of these gods was the Trickster, who performed miraculous feats purely for his own amusement. He has no counterpart in our mythology; he is one-quarter god, three-quarter devil. Here is a typical Blackfoot legend, telling of the creation of the world by the Old Man, or Trickster."[14] This is, unfortunately, the best non-Indigenous interpreters could make of this confusing non-human, non-animal, non-God entity.

To clarify, stories do not always change at every telling, although some details have dropped out over the generations because of the outside religious and political pressure placed on the People to stop telling these stories. In addition, in many cases stories or details were left out because they were untranslatable. Some editing was done by storytellers to protect the stories; some would purposely leave out crucial sections or references. Other missing details were erased, including entire stories that were expunged from the record by non-Indigenous recorders who felt they were too problematic or even heretical. As such, commentary that is typical of the reductionist and simplistic views dominating generations of Naapi interpretations shows that Naapi stories are basically too advanced in concept, form, and epistemology to be handled by amateurs who claim expertise in them. Even Naapi's "Trickster" status is an oversimplified concept used to examine his escapades, apparent comedic tendencies, and exaggerated personality. For this reason, Trickster literature should be considered in any serious study of Naapi, as he appears as comparable personages in many Indigenous oral traditions, which justifies this book's consideration of a multitude of stories (see the appendix for a sampling) and perceptions of Naapi and entities like him, drawn from the stories as a body.

SIGNS IN SPACE

Another factor that influences interpretations of Naapi is that many analyses conducted in English, French, and other Indo-European languages are problematic in their efforts to understand the Blackfoot way of seeing and expressing the Blackfoot world. English, for instance, is commonly regarded by Blackfoot speakers as intensely limited in its ability to express or otherwise convey the relationship between place and person, especially compared to Blackfoot. As an Algonquian/Algonkian language, Blackfoot is concerned with clarifying action, process, character, and quality, or the knowable personality of each Person/Being discussed. For example, the manner of a river's character reveals the personality of the landscape in relation to People. Status is accounted for by forms, sources, and energies, not by isolation or static representations. Spatial dimensions and other specifics about conditions are required in a Blackfoot world, where *beings are known by the way they move*. Questions such as what is it like, how does it go, where does it stay, and where does it happen are central concerns that emphasize spatial relations and movement as signals of vitality and life-giving forces.

Struggles, conflicts, or challenges are central protagonists in Naapi and other creation stories, and those who undergo them rarely involve humans but instead recall opposite-speak conditions. Those challenges that in translations appear to refer to humans actually do not. To the contrary, they typically refer to elemental or universe-level matches of energy (e.g., thunderstorms, tornados), but they are ascribed human-like attributes upon and as a result of their translation. Furthermore, these Naapi stories often describe something or someone who speaks or turns into human form, which reflects a world where Beings (e.g., rocks) have the power and will to make themselves known to humans, to be recognized *by* rather than *as* humans. This does not, however, "turn them into" humans in the Blackfoot experience. People can communicate and be understood by other Beings without meaning that Being *is* human-like. Other living Beings—elements, plants, animals—do not so much "turn into" humans as make themselves *comprehensible* to humans. This means they are intelligible because they are perceived, felt, and sensed with an intent to be understood, to make an effort to communicate. They are able to communicate as intelligible and intelligent Beings that have a soul and are worthy of respect and reciprocity.

In Blackfoot, as experienced through Naapi stories, being and becoming human means learning to be intelligible and intelligent with regard to other Beings and to be understood by others who share in the gift of spirit or can understand it. A fully realized human Person can understand and relate to other non-human Persons or Beings, providing the participants in the exchange are noticed and noticing—that is, communicating successfully. In the Blackfoot world, "animacy" refers to Beings who deliver messages to People because they want to communicate and want the People to comprehend. Such transformations or patterns of change and exchange, such as those the earth goes through, are evidence that People *do* pay attention.

Land-based homeland formations—such as riverbeds, mountains, plains, valleys, forests, caves, and glaciers—create their own weather patterns, have unique terrains, and interact with flora and fauna in unique ways. Together they form the episodic and rhythmic rhyme and reason of the natural cycles on which traditional Blackfoot life has been, and in many ways continues to be, based. For example, whirlpool shapes are created in both air and water. Throughout the homeland, several sites created by the forces of that place at a particular time show their strength and unpredictability and reveal how these natural forces give them shape and power that defines their character. This is another expression of the respect the People accord them.

Similarly, the various shapes in and around mountains—such as basins created by avalanches—show the movement of snow and ice on a massive scale, caves' unique air conduction, the erosion of hillsides and riverbeds, and the kinds of rock that predominate in the area, as they all have Trickster stories that relate their ancestral and current activities. Earthquakes, caves, coulees, hoodoos, and sand hills are parts of the story of the People who live among them; thus they appear in Naapi's stories to teach People how to live completely. *Spirits* is simply a term used to describe the creative energies that reside in these places throughout the homeland, Naapi's energy in particular. The Blackfoot identify with each Naapi story; animals, plants, and places are traditionally appreciated for their valued traits, medicines, and the sustenance they give to the People, the subject of Naapi stories. Naapi shows People the highly esteemed species, climates, areas, times, or other Beings that have the power to transform themselves and adapt to the larger environment; all are co-creators.

Naapi, creator and main protagonist, shapes the homeland landscape and consciousness concurrently. Some of the notable strengths the Blackfoot absorb by observing natural cycles include adaptability, transferability, changeability, flexibility, transformability, generosity, foresight, honesty, attention to detail, respect for limitations and rules, persistence or perseverance, and gratitude, which are referred to in Blackfoot as "staying power." This expression refers to psychological, mental, and spiritual aspects of persistence and enduring challenges and hardship, physical and otherwise. The Blackfoot expression *Mokakit ki akakimaat*, meaning to be strong and persevere, is an expression learned from Wolf; it is a teaching about having staying power or stamina for life that differentiates between just getting by and thriving. The expressions "what goes around, comes around" and "we are all relatives" connect the People to the natural word, to the sky and cosmic realm, and to all living Beings sharing space, time, matter, energy, and the like. The Peoples' obervations and the stories that relate them connect weather patterns, animals' behavior, growth cycles, and forms of plants to ground Naapi stories in physical reality and identify ideal models of social and ethical behavior for the People.

Naapi's energy manifests as the architect of the space that others occupy. Naapi gives each meteorological, animal, plant, and human family its place in the homeland by opening up spaces to grow plants, medicines, and animals that provide for and offer protection to the People. His nature sets the pace and context. Life forces exist within the setting and land and within the Beings in it, life is presented to and interacted with by everyone, and ceremonies have concomitant spirit-locating processes, which are initially outlined in Naapi's transgressions and gifts and bind the People to the places where Naapi's episodes occur. Discrete site mapping and naming, however, fails to capture the extent of their intended meaning, as it is limited to specific land sites and to a noun-based space- and place-oriented project. It misses out on the dynamic, unpredictable, and encompassing aspects of Naapi's activity, which eventually omits all sorts of unmappable material (e.g., climatologic and meteorological phenomena such as winds and lightning) from analyses that focus too much on nouns or place determinants. Naapi stories combine distinct yet connected phenomena and descriptive and discursive patterns, which is how they are "speaking" to People. These are the many signs in space that communicate to the People. Even these signs are described in terms that focus on aspects of the movement of energy in ways that English, for instance, does not; wind is described as "going to" a direction as opposed to "coming from it."

These communications or signs require a response through ceremonial and spiritual involvement and commitment of the People, and this is what is meant by saying the People develop their consciousness along with the landscape. Naapi stories initiate the People into a similar consciousness and awareness of the potential unhelpful or hurtful effect that the mere act of living has on others. Practicing traditional Indigenous Peoples' ceremonial life based on such stories is itself an exercise in ethical and moral consideration. Through the reflexive meditation taught by Naapi's examples, other Beings become ourselves and vice versa. Naapi stories highlight moral principles that shape and restrain human behavior, but not as the human struggle against the confinement felt by being bound to place or even as strategies that demonstrate ways to transcend or disregard morality. To the contrary, Algonquian/Algonkian and Blackfoot "morality" is derived from and therefore defined by its contextualization within ecologically sustainable realities as wellsprings from which rules are born. These traditions assert and affirm the ecological limits placed on human excess, much of which originates with Naapi's examples, which model the sustainable limits of our own physical and spiritual health—albeit through the negative example of his outright denial of this imperative to refrain from living in the margins of excess.

PARADIGMATIC OPPOSITION AS KEY TO BALANCE

In Algonquian/Algonkian and Blackoot traditions, the best teachers of eco-logical, physical, and spiritual balance are the environment and its myriad inhabitants—the animals, birds, winds, geographic features, weather patterns, and landscapes. Naapi experiences the entirety of creation as the foundation on which social rules and customs are built, exemplified as those whose lives super-sede the ecological, physical, and spiritual breaking point. He takes the maximum that life can offer him and is still unsatisfied and restless. He takes all that the earth and everyone who resides on it can provide, is at the forefront in any act of consumption, and shows how taking more than is needed is a true source of death. The Naapi imperative is revealed through reflection on his devastating acts and by observing him and his actions in a turned-around form. To listeners of the stories, lessons are revealed in the complete opposite of his actions, attitudes, comments, and desires, as Naapi's detrimental activities demonstrate and encour-age more conservative consumption and synchronism in relating to the energy of place. Naapi epitomizes the potential power for human destruction. He reveals that the preservation and sustainability of the earth's resources is beyond human debate or contests concerning social rules or customs, moral or ethical laws, or principles established by nature and that things already in balance can be altered by Peoples' maneuvering or manipulation. Naapi demonstrates that such med-dling with the rules threatens ecological disaster, population demise, extinction, and other horrors. Naapi's escapades remind People that flaunting the rules of the natural world ensures our unnecessary daily struggles, such as being cold, hungry, or dying. These become protracted and extensive in their potential to affect the grand scheme of things.

In Algonquian/Algonkian and Blackfoot traditions, destroying, usurping, or otherwise manipulating food sources, for example, constitutes a first-degree crime. Naapi and his Algonquian/Algonkian equivalents teach that People may take from and use nature to help ourselves. We must, however, retain a level of humanity, awareness of the needs of all other Beings, and understanding that People will need those resources far into the future. The world is not created by humans; we are born into and sustained by it. Viewed through Naapi's adventures, regard for the entirety of creation is the basis on which societal rules and customs are built. The People are children of it; creation is our "relative"—a grandparent or parent or other kin. Excesses such as killing beyond one's need or inhibiting potential life in true Naapi style push beyond the tipping point of the ultimate provider, causing death. These matters are laws established by nature, over which human maneuvering has little and a mostly detrimental effect unless handled with great care.

Algonquian/Algonkian and Blackfoot inclusivity functions in consideration of who belongs to the multiple families that are all intertwined in creation. It concerns itself with the stages of development of plants, birds, and animals and in all of these seeks parallels, comparisons, and contrasts with People. These details are how the human element of the People is revealed and defined; identifying People cannot be done without reference to these other dimensions of our shared world, so Algonquian/Algonkian social and cultural mores are based on exigencies set by nature's limits. Ceremonial life is modeled on ecological boundaries that simultaneously constrain and nurture while maintaining a connection to the vitals that replenish People. The misuse, abuse, and excesses of others are ultimately suicidal acts, since it is on such others that the People depend.

The land's spirit is not an object of imagination and ritual that Indigenous Peoples manipulate to guide votive offerings and ceremonials. To the contrary, the universe's obvious animateness informs Peoples' ethical, moral, religious, and philosophical tie-downs by offering its truths of the natural world. This Indigenous metaphysics forms the core of countless ceremonial traditions that recall Peoples' interactions, observations, and experiences with nature. It is taught and recollected through Naapi's experiences that become the Peoples' mapping of the world passed down and codified in their linguistic, artistic, and cultural shorthand in story forms that shape interpretations of events and processes that may occur with more frequency or, more recently, with more intensity than is customary. The stories re-create a homeland specificity through precise toponyms that place Naapi virtually all over the land. These areas accentuate points of reference that all the People recognize, so Naapi, the land, and self-identity are all intertwined.

These observations and interactions encompass millennia and are encoded and told through story and other, accompanying artforms. These media traditionally recorded changes (e.g., in oral, material, and visual arts), from those that are instantaneous to those of longer duration—devoting particular attention to elements, shared space, or other Beings affected by changes. Naapi's transformations partner with co-creator powers' patterns founded by his parents Naato'si (Sun/Old Man) and Ko'komiki'somm (Moon/Old Woman), along with Naato'si's second wife, Ksaahkomm (Earth). Working together, they establish Naapi's archetype of his countless manifestations and myriad shapes and forms. They create the spaces that plants, medicines, and animals occupy, which establish the beginning of human residence in the land. These creations reveal the wisdom of the homeland, communicating wide knowledge of the mechanisms that make the earth's ecological, solar, and spiritual system work—all captured in Naapi's constant changeability, disruption of order, and changeability.

SIGN AS FIRST LANGUAGE

The Blackfoot word "*ksaahkomm*, earth (personified),"[15] is an animate noun, meaning it has the life energy that gives it "personhood" status and thus membership in the "we are all relatives" class, or part of the group with whom People have a Person-to-Person or Being-to-Being relationship and communication. As a shaper and communicator of the world, Naapi is based on the first speech known to the People: that which is left in the land as markers and communications and constitutes the Peoples' and other Beings' tracks. Ernest Thompson Seton reminded those hiking to "never forget the trail, look ever for the track in the snow; it is the priceless, unimpeachable record of the creature's life and thought, in the oldest writing known on earth."[16] This is the oldest "writing" or system of communication, which both Coyote and Wolf used to convey messages to the People; they were read and understood by the ancient Plains Peoples and became incorporated into their way of life and thought.

For the Blackfoot, philosophy, literature, and environmental consciousness and conscientiousness are based in frequent interaction and very close proximity with nature and human character. The environment is a source of philosophy and a way of life. Having a focus on non-linguistic communication systems, such as trails and scent markings, enables People, animals, plants, and stars to be equal interlocutors/communicators/speakers. This enables these other Beings to "speak" to humans and opens us to our relationships with them, making them our "relations." Indigenous Peoples interpret our lives as intertwined and intersecting with all our relatives. When we make time to listen and respond to all sorts of non-linguistic messages, we "speak" to the universe and know that we are heard, not just seen. When singing the early songs and telling about the early People, scholars should not limit themselves to the linguistic, since doing so emphasizes the awkward and unrealistic position of regarding human speech as more important than other forms of communicating—which, of course, it is not. If it were, we would never understand the universe; we would be inarticulate translators of the wisdom that resides in all our relatives who share the universe with us. Like Indigenous Peoples all over the world, the Blackfoot must be "multilingual" and know how to function in different modalities and contexts, which means understanding and integrating the nonverbal into our knowledge systems. These are not theorized, abstract commandments because the signs are real reflections based on the physical realities in the Plains Peoples' homeland. Plains Sign Language is

> the method of communicating thought by means of signs [which] has been brought to such a degree of perfection among the plains Indians that any idea can be expressed as readily as if words were employed. Every want can be made known,

questions asked, and stories or traditions told. The signs employed are very expressive, and usually convey an idea so clearly that no explanation is needed, even by one who has never seen them before. They are often so forcible that they give an insight into the Indian imagination which could never be conveyed by words. An instance of this is related by Captain W. Clark, of the United States [A]rmy, who made a long and thorough study of the sign language. He noticed that the Indians, in referring to the Milky-Way, made the sign of death and another sign for trail, and after much inquiry he learned that the Indian superstition was that the Milky-Way was "the direct and easy trail to the happy hunting-grounds made by those who had been killed in battle." In the sign language different races and tribes are designated by movements of the hands, referring to some real or imaginary characteristic.[17]

To the Plains Peoples, Plains Sign Language was inspired (i.e., "taught" = demonstrated) by the sky realm Beings (e.g., Sun, Moon, Stars), and it represents the strategies offered by nature, such as a star's "twinkle" as a demonstration of an intention to communicate. For example, Plains Peoples notice the "sign language" communicated by the twinkling stars of the Big Dipper and learn to read these signs as meaningful. Flashes of light are messages, sent with intent. They are signs: "TWINKLE. Make the sign for STAR, and while holding [your] hand in that position snap index and thumb as in LITTLE TALK."[18] The movements of the stars and other sky realm Beings also "speak" using the first "sign language" in contrasts of light and dark. Sun and Moon, Naato'si and Ko'komiki'somm, establish this contrast between Sun's daylight rays and Moon's nocturnal light. To the Blackfoot, the stars are this pair's children, so it is fitting that they speak the same sign language. Blackfoot stars are named for their aspects, including whether they are flashy or have a tinge of color, are cloudy, or give the appearance of a scintillating or shimmering Being. To the Blackfoot, signs of light given off by the universe are a primary language, and the stars first taught the People that this is the original sign language. The essence of Plains Sign Language practiced by Plains Peoples is that it attends to nuances in shades of color, levels of opacity, and blinks or shimmers of light, however brief or faint. Stars and other flashing lights help People and send messages by blinking, so that we learn to interpret the communication system already extant and happening in the world, to send messages, to read, and to interpret the cosmos, animals, plants, waters, and their messages—none of it linguistic. This is how to hear and experience the spirits, the cosmic consciousness.

Plains Peoples' use of light information, such as flashes, as a method of communication is a long-standing tradition, especially applicable for situations requiring communication across great distances, such as during war or hunting party movement. Examples of alternating, blinking, or shimmering light and the absence of it in the form of shadow appear in Naapi stories as a principal technique employed by hunters to gain and retain animals' attention. Contrasting light/dark thus became an ancient first-order tool in Plains Peoples' communication systems, with many instruments. Some of these are based in naked-eye astronomy and observations of the astros using calendrical methods. Others are more immediately implemented with tools on the ground, such as rocks or shells, and in later times with mirrors, ribbons, and bright cloth.

On another level, interpreting tracks' meanings is analyzing information based on angles, shades, and subtle nuances in contrasts of light. Hand and other physical signs and gestures used for communication between People were perfected and widely practiced in Plains Peoples' lives. According to Blackfoot tradition, the People learned signs from the Sky People, particularly stars, as hand signs were developed and employed simultaneously in a context in which contrasts of light, coupled with sounds across vast distances, were recognized as signals to which birds and animals are attuned to respond. This system is based on the observation that if these Beings attended to the movements and lights of stars, this is communication, albeit non-verbal. Naapi stories also frequently reveal how using spoken words can destroy hunters' potential catches by scaring off game, thus the preeminence of sign usage. Songs, meanwhile, are noted as less disruptive than speech and sometimes even as helping to attract animals. Songs are thus used in hunting as a signaling system, often integrated with methods involving lights and intermittent flashes of color, depending on the animal whose attention was sought.

The Plains Peoples' experience, told in Naapi stories, is rife with interpretations and observations that are a result of the lived landscape shared among all the other Beings who were here before humans. One reason Naapi, as Trickster-traveler-creator, occupies this position in many Indigenous Peoples' traditional creation stories is because of the non-verbal "language" he conveys through the signs he leaves in his wake. These long-since identified patterns are presented below with some possible interpretations:

"Coyote Trails and Possible Interpretations"

Understep walk. Extreme rest: I have found this pattern around dens, especially when a coyote shifts from one bedding spot to another. *Extreme attention/fear*: This is also the gait used when stalking prey very slowly—like a cat. It could also be used to sneak away if the coyote felt at great risk and wanted to avoid detection. *Exhaustion.*

Direct register walk. This gait is more often a reflection of substrate or grade rather than mood or behavior. In deep substrates, coyotes direct register walk when traveling. However, Jon Young points out that in specific locales, coyotes use this gait to travel about. He explains that the potential dangers in an environment, such as a high density of cougars, influence when, where, and how coyotes move.

Overstep walk. This is the typical walking gait for canines. *Exploration*: Often coyotes shift from a trot to a walk when investigating and pinpointing any odor they cross in the woods. They'll walk around scenting out apples buried in early snow, investigating squirrel activity, and checking another coyote's scent post. *Ease*: Coyotes walk when they feel relatively safe, often in the company of others or in areas with good visibility or where scents carry far and well. They feel most at ease in the heart of their own territory. *Scenting and communication*: Coyotes may shift to a walk in order to scent, before moving on. A great deal of social exchange is done while walking, but many gaits are used. Movement in the immediate area of dens is usually done in a walk. *Well fed*: A coyote who is not actively hunting may walk. *Caution*: A cautious coyote walks.

Understep trot. This is a rare gait. I have seen this pattern as a result of playing with others—like a slow prance.

Direct register trot. This is the natural rhythm of the coyote. *Hunting and patrolling*: Coyotes move through their range in a trot. *Awareness*: Coyotes are actively investigating their surroundings in this gait. *Comfort*: . . . Although the animal is keenly aware, this gait shows little stress or discomfort. This is the usual gait for moving about the home range.

Overstep trot. This is an uncommon gait for coyotes. *Dominance*: I have seen this gait used in pack communication on several occasions. I believe that the vertical "hop" of this gait may be involved in a visual communication of dominance. *Stress*: Dan Gardogui noted this gait and track pattern in females trying to keep up with the insatiable appetites of their maturing pups and in coyotes skirting wolf territories.

Straddle trot. In coyotes, this is a transition gait found only in short sections of trail. However, it shows that the animal is not alarmed or reacting to something in its environment, in which case a transition gait would be skipped altogether.

Side trot. Travel mode: This gait may indicate that a coyote has a destination in mind and has picked up the pace slightly. It is often seen on easier travel routes, such as beaches, roads, and trail systems. *Increased awareness*: This gait is often used when coyotes are exposed and away from cover or between areas of cover but not yet in full alarm. Trespassing coyotes might also pick up their pace when moving through another pack's territory.

Extended direct register trot. Eager/excited: John McCarter reported finding this gait when coyotes had just found a carcass or a moose dying of brain worm or some other bonanza. The extended track pattern looks very much like the standard direct register trot, but the strides are nearly twice as long, often around 40 inches.

Slow lope. Play and communication: The "rocking horse" lope uses tremendous energy and is often found in coyote interactions. Sticks are sometimes picked up and carried for short distances in this gait. Motion is often erratic and circular. *Hunting in tall grass*: Jon Young has watched coyote use this gait while hunting cottontails in high grass. *Safety*: A coyote using the gait is not alarmed.

Lope. Discomfort and fear: The coyote has picked up the pace to move out of the area for some reason. A coyote may lope when it is exposed between areas of cover or when it is trespassing. *Transition*: A coyote that is not in immediate peril but still alarmed may transition from a trot to a lope to a gallop. *Play/excitement*: Often, faster gaits in mammal species show fear, but the same gaits can be interpreted in the opposite way. Playing coyotes lope, as do coyotes that are eager and excited—a similar interpretation to the extended trot. *Hunting*: Coyotes sometimes run prey to exhaustion, although this is more likely done at a gallop.

Bound. Alarm and fear: Frightened coyotes use this gait to move from stationary or a slow gait to full speed. *Chasing*: This coyote has just taken up pursuit of prey, a trespasser, or a playmate. *Deep substrates*: Bounds are also used to increase the speed of travel in deep snow—in this case, all four tracks are made in the same hole.

Gallop. Fear: Coyotes run from what they fear most. *Hunting*: Coyotes run down their prey, twisting and turning in pursuit. There is less time between footfalls than in the stretch gallop, allowing the coyote to react quickly to changes in direction

Stretch gallop. Extreme fear: This coyote has lowered its awareness of the area in exchange for putting distance between itself and a sound, predator, or location as fast as possible. *Hunting*: A coyote stretches fully and invests everything to capture prey, which in turn replenishes its energy supply. Most often, prey twist and turn when closely pursued, so it is difficult to maintain the highest speed through turns; look for regular gallops as the coyote closes in.

Patterns created by rolling, lunging, attacking, holding onto prey, or other specific behaviors, as well as the various interpretations of coyotes in varied habitats and conditions across North America[,] must be learned in the field and with experience.[19]

The complete list of Coyote's trekking patterns is presented here because a sampling does not show the great range of "signs" Coyote conveys. That said, there may be more we do not know about. Those listed here demonstrate Coyote's advanced level of communicative ability, since other mammals' gaits are not perceived to give away as much information. Large game animals, for example, may only leave four or so identifiable "signs" that might be read consistently. People "reading" Coyote's paw prints to determine what the animal feels, knows, or intends receive a basic lesson of land-based knowledge in how to connect patterns to increase understanding. Beyond the physical messages left in prints, efforts to decipher the meaning of all the multiple types of messages that are out there to be discovered and decoded can include studying broken sticks and branches, chewed leaves and grasses, scat and urine markings, and scratchings and tears into trees or dirt that identify occupation or territories. It is important to offer a sample of the types of analyses Indigenous Peoples traditionally undertook all the time as part of everyday understanding. These are just the physical aspects. Hunters occupy a deeper level of understanding of animals' intentions through the practice of getting into another's footsteps by interpreting and following their tracks. Hunters need to know how to occupy the heart, mind, or spirit of the animals sought, and they use their tracks' communications to do so.

Naapi or Coyote or Naapi *as* Coyote means Naapi is a great traveler and a particularly smart hunter because Coyote goes everywhere and is constantly on the move, and he gets his prey. As he moves into new territory, he learns about the as-yet unknown and becomes a pioneer who is forever seeking new knowledge to communicate. This is what the focus on his footsteps is about; he is a fluent, even masterful "speaker" in sign. To the Blackfoot, his pursuit of knowledge and new terrain and its conditions, occupants, and patterns of life includes Indigenous Peoples. From this perspective of Naapi as Coyote, he is a great conveyer of non-verbal information. He is a consistent traveler in the physical sense *and* in the spiritual sense on the journey to learn new metaphysical realities. He is on a perpetual vision quest, always the seeker, as he explores uncharted territory, on land and in the metaphysical. Blackfoot oral tradition is based on these types of messages, and the better one is at capturing their range, the easier it is to understand Naapi.

CONTEXT AND SPACE DETERMINE MEANING IN BLACKFOOT

The Plains, with its wide open spaces on which it can be difficult to hide, is the space, the backdrop against which Plains Peoples and the other Beings in their midst communicated since ancient times, leaving their mark on the Blackfoot language. John MacLean (1898) explains that in the Blackfoot language, nouns are shaped by the elements or quality they consist of or create, and gender—that is, the distinction between animate and inanimate—organizes those things that are considered to be alive in the animate category. These are "trees, plants, and various objects of vegetable nature [and] nearly all names of implements,"[20] so that tools and technology are considered to be alive, to have the force of life within them. Beings related to the life forces in the Indigenous cosmos, such as the astros and rivers, are classed as animate as well: "*Natos* = the sun. *Omuqkatos* = the great sun. *Kukutos* = a star. *Kokumekesim* = the moon. *Neetuqta* = a river. *Natosiks* = suns, also moons and months. Kukutosiks = stars. *Kokumeksimiks* = moons. *Neetuqktaks* = rivers ... The *Animate Nouns* form the plural by adding *ks, iks*, or *sks* to the singular ... *Inanimate Nouns* form the plural by adding *ts* or *sts* to the singular."[21] Things that are considered animate move, make, or give signals or signs, otherwise known as making "talk" or communicating. An interesting element of this list is that all of the beings noted above are from the sky realm except the rivers, at least one of which is understood to flow into the sky by way of the Milky Way. Ultimately then, the river takes its own spot where it is at home in the sky. This is one example of the flexibity of context in terms of determining animate versus inanimate gender; just as there is no neat separation between the sky realm and the underwater realm, there is no neat separation of noun and verb or of animate and inanimate, since these conditions move with (i.e., in relation to) the speaker. People live on the earth, between the underwaters and the sky waters. Animate entities' interactions with People determine their level of animate energy and include some places, rocks, hills—land sites. While knives, axes, bows, arrows, and guns are tools for survival, so are powerful stories. Places affiliated with creation or creators, such as Katoyis (Blood Clot) and Katoyissiksi (Sweet Grass [Pine] Hills), are animate; as tool or person, both are life protecting and life preserving.

Blackfoot also distinguishes between the different actions of humans or other Beings within a given context and the actions inherent in or occurring within certain contexts. This separation acknowledges the Peoples' impact on a place and demonstrates Blackfoot's ability to convey keen awareness of each entity, grammatically identifying it with action and respect. Every living Being has unique perspectives and experiences, if not exactly a separate identity. The difference between human actions and those of other animate and living and active Beings is crucial; it is not so much a *separation* between the human and others as a tally of *interactions* by both that is of interest. Their relationship is explained by identifying their separate contributions to it and by negating binaries between the two by focusing on shared qualities, so it is essential to know who does what. These distinctions are so nuanced in Blackfoot and nonexistent in English that translations in this area often fail.

One way this relationship dynamic is addressed is by considering how all action happens in relation to space and direction, to deixis, and within a particular place. A deictic word refers to "a word, the determination of whose referent is dependent on the context in which it is said or written."[22] For a Blackfoot speaker communicating in Plains Sign Language, for instance, east is implied to be the direction the speaker is facing, which in turn defines left (i.e., northward) and right (i.e., southward) in signing, or that which the expressions or word pictures are doing or describing. This means that the delineation, definition, and use of space defines meaning; it could not function without an acknowledgment of the role space plays in the Blackfoot use of Sign Language, since it depends on it as a foundation on which to make meaning at all. Blackfoot verbal forms follow similar requirements or allowances.

Blackfoot speakers, in telling a Naapi story for instance, can also differentiate space from action, clarifying the difference between terrain and users of terrain. That is, if terrain can be animate, then it has will, intelligence, or intent, which is accounted for in Algonquian/Algonkian languages; they form a dual pattern of semantic categories between the ways they express land and what one does there or what takes place there. This is a crucial point regarding Naapi, since he simultaneously exists outside particular locations and everywhere at any moment. He also has a key role in creating and defining certain spaces by his actions in them. Naapi is thus both a Being and a creator of place, and understanding him requires that one knows this. With such divisions, "these underlying categories define a natural division between terrain, including the waterways themselves, and the life associated with it."[23] Blackfoot speakers can differentiate and separate humans' actions that are taking place within a context from talk of the context itself.

One way this is revealed is in Naapi's travels along waterways. When Naapi encounters People or other Beings, he often does so as he emerges from or takes refuge in a source of water. Following Naapi's singular or numerous encounters with others, he returns to the water element, in the sense of either entering it or becoming it. Throughout numerous Naapi escapes, water is thus the method of transportation as a way of transformation. This use of the water element, with its many forms (e.g., liquid, solid), can become a deictic demonstrative, making it an excellent example of the ways the Blackfoot use Naapi stories to refine a distinction among those Persons or Beings who are from certain areas, the land, and the Blackfoot People. In this context, "areas" can include fluid, transient, inconsistent, highly variable conditions; and this is key to Naapi's characterization as fickle or impulsive because he embodies these changes, as much as is possible for someone who has no body. A sample of some of Naapi's arrivals and departures through this energy source is listed here, with examples of how Naapi's actions shape and make places: "*eno-kimi* 'long lake': *eno-* 'long', *-kimi* 'lake' . . . *awy-kimiska* 'the lake that runs up and down': *awy-* 'running', *-kimi-* 'lake', *-ska* collective suffix . . . *amiskapoʔomakaty* 'big south river': *amiskapo-* 'south', *-omaxk-* 'big', *-axtai* 'river' . . . *aka-oto-tughty* 'many rivers': *akau-* 'many', *-etaxtai* 'river' . . . *ponokaisisaxtai* 'elk creek': *ponokai-* 'elk', *-sisaxtai* 'creek' . . . *mo-ko-un-se-te-ta* 'belly creek': *mokuan* 'belly', *-sisaxtai* 'creek.'"[24] In other instances, names reflect what happens to People or Persons in certain places: "*Oh-ty-nehts-ope-piney* 'where we were drowned' cf. *it-ni-inetsi-ope-otspinan*: *it-* . . . *-ope-* 'where', *-ni-* 'we exclusive', *-inetsi-* 'drown', *-otspinan passive* . . . *mastowisto-ek-oka-pi* 'the lodges with crows painted' . . . *maistoikokaup* 'crow-bird-lodge.'"[25] Throughout Naapi stories, Naapi acquires new names to fit his current condition in that setting and at that time, which it is understood may not have another appropriate occasion to be used.

With these examples, the message is that "by understanding the ways the world is discussed and thought about, it is easier to understand their use of toponyms, and we can learn how languages crystallize the spatial dimensions of experience and imagination."[26] In Blackfoot this is not really a binary contrast between places and persons, since the actions of animals in a place are what form it; hence the expression for "elk creek," noted above as a way to specify that something happened in, resides in, or frequents a specific place. This is one definition of a relationship between Beings and place. This enables speakers to discuss different actions People or other Beings take in, upon, or around a particular context, as well as the already extant actions occurring within the context—a distinction that acknowledges their impact *on* a place and shows respect for each entity *within* that place. Peoples' actions are different from those of other animate and living and active Beings, so while they are acknowledged as integrated with and responsive to one another, they are identified separately. The focus is not on demarcations of opposition between the two, although analyses conducted in any of several Indo-European languages might confuse them. For instance, English has a limited ability to express or make a relationship between place and person, especially compared with Algonquian/Algonkian languages. Blackfoot clarifies the character and quality of each "Person" discussed, of each terrain. In the examples offered above by Eugene Green and Celia M. Millward (1973), the *manner* of the river is key, so that the character of the landscape in relation to humans becomes known or is revealed. Blackfoot terms not only lay out pertinent spatial dimensions, they include specifics that are required in a world where everything is known by the way and where it moves.

Naapi's frequent water travels are yet another area where confused or unclear translations make a world of difference. Many translations describe Naapi as traveling "by" (i.e., "via") water; other translations have him traveling "by" (i.e., "next to/near") water. Muddled interpretations cloud readings and interpretations of Naapi stories, even though both or either reading could be correct depending on the Blackfoot speaker's intended emphasis on deixis, spatial relations, and movement. There is a difference between Naapi traveling by being *in* the water versus his walking along *beside or around* it. Once again, however, a native English, Dutch, or French speaker who knows neither Plains Sign Language nor Blackfoot will be unlikely to determine which of these meanings is correct; considering such nuances is unexpected, hence they remain unexplored.

The context in which Blackfoot speech occurs is such a crucial part of expression and determining meaning that the combination of multiple valencies with some transitive verbs can create confusion when translated into English, which is complicated when compared to corresponding terms in English: "The semantic indetermination of these categories, however, is more pronounced, since each of them covers a much wider semantic spectrum than the English subject . . . [An example is] the existence of transitive verbs with 'atypical' valency frames, such as *receive*, which disrupt the common correlation of the English subject with the semantic roles of agent or experiencer in the transitive clause; for if the verb stem did not provide any information pertaining to the semantic roles of its valency-bound participants, there would be no way of interpreting the subject of *receive* as a benefactive."[27] Because of their flexibility, Blackfoot verb valencies and "to be" status forms produce multiple possible interpretations, which makes the Blackfoot language difficult for non-native speakers to use properly. When it is used properly, this same quality is responsible for the language being pointedly precise when creating referents. Blackfoot speakers have multiple options in the construction of new phrases and meanings, depending on how the features of space, relationship, and context are worked.

In his discussion of the person indexing system, Donald G. Frantz explains yet another way space and relationship are described in the Blackfoot language,[28] which is reminiscent of Christopher C. Uhlenbeck's distinction between centrifugal and centripetal motion.[29] The animate-inanimate distinction is what drives grammatical hierarchy, which is sometimes a comment about relative life-force energy, making speakers powerful and their speech full of life-enhancing or life-deterring forms. Knowing when this is the appropriate interpretation depends on several factors, many of which relate to the context in which the thing is being discussed and on whether that context infuses it with meaning.

As will be discussed in more detail in further chapters, the animate is rather complex in Algonquian/Algonkian languages and not because it is misunderstood by speakers, which is still, unfortunately, a popular academic argument. Rather, this perception is a result of the fact that translating the animate into English or explaining Algonquian/Algonkian grammar in English is difficult because of the limited ability to accurately render meaningful categories in the latter language. European linguistic traditions unintentionally obfuscate attempts to achieve clarity in Algonquian/Algonkian languages because they are radically different in their structure and their ability to produce or render accurate and meaningful translations.

A brief example of the person indexing abilities of Blackfoot versus what the European context provides demonstrates why this is so. In Blackfoot,

> The basis for the person indexing system beyond second person is the classification of all animate and some inanimate participants (other than speaker and addressee) of a discourse as primary, secondary or tertiary. These, all classed as third person in terms of Indo-European semantics, have been called third, fourth, and fifth persons (or proximate, obviative, and subviative by Algonkianists). In this discussion I shall refer to the following persons:
>
> first person = speaker
> second person = addressee
> third person = primary topic
> fourth person = secondary topic, subordinate to third person
> fifth person = topic subordinate to fourth person.[30]

One critical way analyses of Blackfoot linguistics help to comprehend Naapi is that the social structures he helps define throughout the stories are drawn from formations observed in the natural world, whether they are clouds, plants, mountains, herds, or a number of other possibilities. The excerpt above illustrates a great example of this; the leaders of the discussion occupy the first and second persons' roles, and together they are reminiscent of the two leaders of a Wolf pack on a hunt. The principal action involves two chief players who initiate the action, and others take part by following their lead, each in accordance with his or her rank. Blackfoot speech is based on observations of such leadership, and in this instance that dialogue (by signed actions) is initiated or established by the first and second persons whom Blackfoot observers identify as leaders. In the Wolf context it is initiated by the alpha, where "dialogic" action, even if just physical, is taken or begun; dialogue—like sign language—does not require speech and focuses instead on *movement in space*. This example can begin to show how in traditional Indigenous communication systems, bearing witness, participation in storytelling, heraldry, coup counting, and a number of public speech acts including prayer encompass the dialogic and include listeners as participants, albeit sometimes distant ones. The overall structure is similar to that of the Wolves in pack formation. It is interesting to note specifically that many Indigenous traditions credit hunting, coup, courting, and prayers' efficacy to Wolf. The Blackfoot observe and integrate a great deal from nature's Beings, and Wolves are considered great teachers in part because of their communicative practices that Blackfoot and other Indigenous Peoples adopt, which is attributed to their extraordinary acumen.

Naapi stories are microcosms; they are expressions of Blackfoot animate/inanimate forms of grammatical gender distinctions that are fluid categories of spirit, activity, and community action that are graduated or otherwise expressed as degrees on a continuum and are changeable. In this framework, time, too, is nonlinear. All times are present at all times, and our experiential connection with a space and place marks the story of our being here. People's lives, names, and stories are meaningful because they bear witness to our presence and relationship to place. It's a symbiotic relationship, and we are who we are because we are where we are when we are and vice versa. Like Naapi, the Blackfoot mark the earth, leaving footprints, camping sites, remains, and stories in places.

Chapter 2

Naapi's Name

Old Man Naapi is probably more appropriately called something like Long-Ago-Person, as in "has been around a long time," but there are so many variable references to his energy that it is important not to get too invested in any one particular manifestation of it. The requirement for Naapi's loosely attributed and frequently changing affiliation with temporary labels of state originates in the places in the homeland where they are said to have occurred, been noticed, or made. They are based in rules, behaviors, and habits of the animals, weather, rivers, or plants in question and involve universal biological, geological, and physical aspects observed by many Indigenous Peoples. Specific sites associated with Naapi locate Indigenous Peoples' knowledge of dynamics that occur thereabouts—physical, invisible, seasonal, or onetime events. Analyses of Naapi stories cannot possibly encompass the variety of similar stories, Blackfoot or otherwise, or convey all they mean to Indigenous Peoples. This chapter does examine Naapi's many weather-related monikers that refer to rain, snow, hail, frozen fog, wind, and other elements and to water as his preferred mode of travel, used to transition him from story to story. Naapi also travels in winds and through the force or exertion or personality of other elements or geographic features. Naapi essentially becomes whatever form is most pertinent or capable at the moment; as such, he is the epitome of metaphysical transformation, every element at once, none exclusively, and, most concisely, that which expresses itself within a place most forcefully during known times or seasons, locating them simultaneously in space and time. This is a radical redefinition of Trickster energy,

DOI: 10.5876/9781607329794.c002

so it is necessary to revisit some of the first non-Indigenous characterizations of Naapi to investigate the history of his misconstrued identity.

NAAPI: WHITE LIGHT OR WHITE MAN?

To begin with, in addition to confusing, comparing, or conflating Naapi with Naato'si (Sun), several interpretations combine Naapi's arrival with the "white man's" arrival in the homeland: "The white man came from the far east. They call white men 'Napi-akun,' but cannot tell whether this has any reference to Napi the Ancient."[1] Too many similar interpretations dominate the Naapi literature, mostly as a result of unfamiliarity with Blackfoot language and life. The term *Naapiikoan* does not, however, express any equivalence between these terms. Associations between white men and Naapi come more from the imaginations of non-Indigenous observers than from early Blackfoot records as told in Naapi's story, so such statements are less a confirmation of a fact than a question about this relationship, which remains open to speculation, possibility, and doubt. There are, notwithstanding, plenty of associations and expressions to note the craziness of the "white man" and parallels in Naapi's errant and dangerous acts.

Such questions were common in the early days of non-Indigenous Peoples' awareness of Naapi, helped along in no small part by authors who envisioned and elaborated upon details the Blackfoot never mentioned. In one classic example, it was said about Naapi: "He was the same as any of us except that he had yellow hair, blue eyes, and a white skin, and had very powerful medicine which enabled him to do great things."[2] This description matched figments of the author's imagination, since there is no evidence that any Blackfoot ever described Naapi as such. The myth these misinterpretations established was that the Blackfoot description fit a "white man," but no Blackfoot story substantiates this assertion. It is a fairly large creative and conceptual step to translate a description of a white-colored Being into a "white man." It makes sense, though, considering the combination of cultural and human-focused ethnocentrism with constraints of Indo-European languages at work in attempts to describe Naapi. Writers following this standard set by Robert Nathaniel Wilson[3] and James Willard Schultz[4] established over a century ago about the Blackfoot include George Bird Grinnell, Walter McClintock, Clark Wissler, and others in their respective works cited and discussed further in this book, all of which perpetuate this false story.

Blackfoot terms for Naapi and white man both reference "white," and the fact that an animate Being is referenced is about all they have in common. A generation later, these misinterpretations still cloud Naapi studies. In the following examples, Naapi, the color white, Sun, and Caucasian people are all conflated:

I first encountered *Nahpi* as the schizoid old gent who is the central figure in Blackfoot mythology (in the Chief's story, "Why the White Man Will Never Reach the Sun," the *Nahpi* image is composed of two separate characters, one named *Mokahki*: wise, and the other named *Mut-tsahp-tsi*: crazy or stupid; but in the common run of *Nahpi* stories—and there are hundreds of them—*Nahpi* appears as a single character who is alternately clever enough to create the world, and stupid enough to get into all kinds of [D]utch with the very animals he has created). My search for a valid English translation of the word *nahpi* (which most scholars have translated as "old man," but which translation does not satisfy me) turned up "'old man," "old White man," "crazy old White man," and a few others. One informant suggested that the phrase does not mean "old White man" but rather "White old man" (there is a significant difference between these two translations) and I would be inclined to go along with him if only for the reason that sometimes the Blackfoots [*sic*] in their prayers to the sun will refer to the sun not as *Nah-toh-sey* but as *Nah-pi*. "Old White man" would refer to an elderly Caucasian, whereas "White old man" could refer to an elderly (hence, in the Indian belief, wise) man of any race . . . [For] Caucasian, he takes the term *Nahpi* and adds the suffix *quon* to it . . . in its broadest application, *quon* means "man" in the sense of "person" . . . At any rate, I am a *Nahpiquon*, but in regard to whether this means that I am a "Sun-person," "The-son-of-a-foolish-old-white-man," or something in between, your guess is as good as mine.[5]

In another, similar characterization of Naapi's behavior: "There is 'Napiu' of legendary duality—'Old Man' and 'Apistotskiwa.' As 'Old Man' he confuses truth with fiction; is malicious, selfish and weak, and is a contradiction of wisdom and foolishness. He is nature's child, and victim of human frailties. His faculty of talking with animals leads to many interesting episodes. 'Old Man' is portrayed by some as a beneficient [*sic*] power, working for their benefit; but for others, he is the grotesque butt of farcical humor and innocuous witticism."[6]

Another illogical comparison about meanings of Naapi's name follows: "Long before the Jesuits reached the upper Missouri, the Blackfeet shared with them a fundamental belief: religion and daily life were inextricably entwined. But their views diverged when it came to identifying the source of sacredness. Although the Blackfeet knew Napi as their creator, they did not worship him. They regarded Napi as very human. In their mythology, he is alternately depicted as powerful and impotent, cruel and compassionate, wise and foolish, sad and joyful. The Blackfeet worshiped the Sun, where they believed Napi went to live after he left the people."[7]

To explain some aspects of the distinctions found in the literature, there was confusion about Naapi's true nature, as in these examples: Grinnell points out that "there is some reason to suspect, however, that the Sun and Old Man are one, that

Natos is only another name for Napi, for I have been told by two or three old men that 'the Sun is the person whom we call Old Man.'"[8] Wissler and Duvall state, "It is of interest to note that the earlier writers are disposed to treat *Natos*, the Sun, as the home of the Old Man while the later ones make each a character."[9]

Some versions of the stories relate to details of Naapi's "last days" in Glacier and Waterton National Parks, which span the US-Canada border. The Blackfoot refer to Naapi's last refuge when he went in that direction in the end; the manner in which he went is detailed further in the Naapi story sequence. Conveying an Aamsskaapipikani (Southern Peigan/Blackfeet) viewpoint on this question, Chewing Black Bone[10] describes the relationship between Naapi and Glacier National Park:

> In the mythology of the Blackfeet are hundreds of tales about *Napi*, or Old Man. Like Wisakedjak in Cree lore and like Coyote in the lore of many Western tribes, Old Man is an interesting combination of power and weakness, of goodness and maliciousness. Each of these mythological characters might be considered "an allegory of the human race." The serious stories, like "Old Man and the Beginning of the Blackfoot World" and "Old Man and Old Woman," make it easy to understand that, as late as the 1880s, Old Man was still reverenced and still addressed in prayer. In other stories he is selfish, mischievous, even cruel; playing tricks on animals and on people, Old Man got into many difficulties, at which the narrator and his audience used to laugh delightedly. To at least some modern Blackfeet, many of these humorous stories are obscene.[11]

Once again, confused interpretations of Naapi's "obscene" status reflect church representatives' decision to eschew repetition of Naapi stories even while transposing, transcribing, and amassing large collections to use to indoctrinate the Blackfoot to Christian beliefs. Naapi stories that did *not* contribute to this end were outlawed, and records of them were intentionally destroyed (e.g., Scalp Robe, Red Crow, and Big Plume's contributions to Wilson's original papers were burned after his death). All the stories were designated "myths," regardless of whether the People took them seriously. Indeed, these missionaries acknowledged that the threat to conversion was the People's continued belief in "their principal deities . . . the sun, and a supernatural being known as Napi (Old Man) who appears to be an incarnation of the same idea."[12] As a result of such vehement suppression, Naapi became just another member of the unreal to whom the Blackfoot prayed.

An additional element of confusion over the ultimate meaning of Naapi is found in how input from Aamsskaapipikani consultants was used in the process of renaming the mountains in Glacier National Park along part of the western edge of the home of the Blackfoot; this further confounded Naapi's significance by dedicating his name to a mountain in the park and immortalizing him in this way: "Napi Istuki. Old Man Mountain. Mount Cleveland. Our council decided that this, the highest mountain in the Park, should bear the name of the once greatest god of the Blackfeet tribes."[13] This may have been the Blackfoot attempt to make an explicit connection to a specific story about when Naapi retired to the mountains to escape pursuers (see "Person's Face" in the appendix). It may also reveal an interest in using the chance to rename the mountains to reassert Naapi's presence, if not predominance, in a landscape that was rapidly taken over by non-Indigenous Peoples who quickly renamed everything, including the mountaintops, in their honor. In so doing, they displaced all of the land's stories, including Naapi's. The attempt may also not have even been proposed by the Blackfeet, who ultimately worked with James Willard Schultz in the renaming project because he felt the Blackfoot had been cheated out of their cultural inheritance by the loss of their traditional homeland with the advent of the park.

In 1913 Schultz informed the world that Naapi appeared as a "white man," but by 1926 he claimed that Naapi represents first light:

> The actual meaning of the word is light—the light of breaking day. Old Man made the world and all life upon it; he performed miracles; and at the same time was a trickster of no little cruelty. Worship of him largely declined when, several centuries ago, the Blackfeet obtained the Sun religion from more southern tribes, perhaps the Arapahoes. Light personified, the faint white light that gives warning of the coming of the sun, is the supreme god of other tribes of Algonkian stock. The *Miche-Wabun* (The Great White Rabbit) of the Crees, for instance, is, literally, Great White-Light.[14]

By the time this reinterpretation of Naapi was published, the damage was done by previous creative license. Schultz, like other writers on Naapi, had great difficulty discussing him for the aforementioned reasons of censorship and exclusion. The stories he could consider publicly were always circumscribed: "Many of the best legends which explain the different phenomena of nature are related with the doings of the Old Man, but unfortunately they are so indecent that they cannot be translated and printed."[15] Once again, the standards set by Victorian mores, coupled with the goal of indoctrination and religious conversion, took offense at nature's processes, particularly those of the human body. Not of Blackfoot customs or worldviews, such analyses are ill fitting for Naapi.

To begin with, the spelling of Naapi's name, on rare occasions, was written with the article *the* in front of his name, indicating that it is not a proper noun or a Person but a phenomenon, a process, a cycle: "The Napiue" to Napiu (Napie). Wilson, however, was told by the Blackfoot speaker who explained Naapi to him: "Napi.

We never did, or do, pray to the Napi. Whenever we use that word and say 'To Napi' in our prayers, we mean the Sun."[16] This use of Naapi's name is just another way to say that prayers are being sent out to nature, the reigning force of the environment, not "the Sun" in the physical sense but in how Naapi is an extension of Naato'si (Sun); both terms refer to their shared sacred energy, so both comprise parts of the Blackfoot universe. Naapi-Naato'si refers to the inseparable combination of the visible and invisible, physical and metaphysical aspects of these creative energies. This distinction or similarity between the physical bodies and respective energies of Naato'si the father and Naapi his son is key to Blackfoot metaphysics. Naapi specifically creates on the land while Naato'si's place is in the sky realm, but their energies are obviously inextricably connected. Life exists in their dynamic and mutually complementary exchanges. Their bond is the subject of "The Torture Ordeal at the Blackfeet Sun Dance":

> The form of religion of this people is sun worship. Their name of god is Na-pi-en, or the Venerable Old Man; but him they regard as unfriendly to mankind, and bestow their worship upon the especial friend of their people, Na-tush, or the Man-in-the-Sun, whom they regard as a white human form of surpassing grandeur and beauty. He is the bestower of buffalo and other game and good, gives succor in war, cures diseases, and governs in the land of spirits. He it was who bound the rain spirits with the rainbow, and who fights the spirits of evil. To propitiate the Man-in-the-Sun they offer religious sacrifices and proffer votive offerings of cloth, war-like implements, robes, and other Indian valuables, which they hang to trees in such position that the sunbeams may fall upon them.[17]

In this description, Naapi is an animate Being but not human. Many of the earliest references to Naapi reflect claims that "there is one common ancestor for all the Indian tribes. He is not an ancestor in the proper sense, but a secondary creator. He is called Napioa, the Old Man. He is not the creator of the gens, or tribe, but of the whole Indian race."[18] Such confusion between Naato'si and Naapi is rooted in the fact that they share Naato'si's creative energy, which imbues all living things, including Naapi and, by extension, whatever he creates. The Blackfoot are not confused about this subtlety, although confusion dominates the body of scholarship on Naapi and Naato'si; the bright white eastern light is confused with Naato'si's body, since both Naato'si and Naapi refer to their shared sacred energy in their respective ways:

> To this extent, Blackfoot religion was probably pantheism. But if the Sun was actually as important as some would lead us to believe it was not even a pantheism, but a true monotheism. Not enough, however, is known of the details of it to justify any

conclusions on this point. And moreover, it is not an important one; for, with the bias of our own experience, we are looking for a primacy which to the native was of extremely minor importance. So unimportant was it, indeed, that the Blackfoot constantly confused the Sun with Old Man, the culture-hero of the western Algonquian peoples, and the counterpart of Old Man Coyote among the Siouan tribes. Lowie has been at great pains to distinguish between these two deities among the Crow, and concluded that there was no "absolute ascendancy in the Crow universe"[19] ... Now, Natoas was certainly recognized as a powerful deity, revered, and petitioned for all manner of blessings. It seems safe to say that he was a beneficent and exemplary god. Napi, on the contrary, was an impish and often immoral rascal, no better than an average man and often much worse. Yet he was more or less consistently credited with the creation of the world and all that is in it, as the mythology bears out. Obviously, if Napi created the world he created the sun too, which would give him pre-eminence; but the Sun is considered the all-powerful deity beyond a doubt. Did the creator then create a being more powerful than himself, or were the two but the visible manifestations of one and the same being? The anomaly simply did not matter to the Blackfoot; he never even took the trouble to follow either course of reasoning to its logical conclusion. For him, it was sufficient to "acknowledge that there is one great power, always invisible, that is the master of life and to whom everything belongs, that he is kind and beneficent; and pleased to see mankind happy."[20] But how far this god was "pleased to interfere with the concerns of Mankind, they are not agreed; some think that his providence is continually exerted [so] that they can have nothing but what he allows to them."[21] The world was peopled with spirits, just as it was with men and animals; some were naturally stronger and some weaker; the Sun was obviously the most powerful and therefore the one who had to be reckoned with above all others. Which of these, if any, created the world, and was therefore the primate of them all, was of no importance. The culture-hero could be confused with the sun-god without incongruity. The important point was to gain the favour of one of these spirits, to have a supernatural helper by whose aid many difficulties could be overcome. Religions centered about the vision-quest and not about cosmogeny [sic]. And it was not necessary to harmonize the two. Hence probably "nowhere ... is there a clean cut formulation of a definite god-like being with definite powers and functions."[22] Though few of them tried to solve the riddle of the universe, the Blackfeet were much impressed by the manifestations of supernatural forces which they beheld round about them. "The Blackfeet made daily prayers to the Sun and to Old Man"[23]—they also smoked daily to the spirits of departed relatives[24]—"and nothing of importance is undertaken without asking for divine assistance."[25]

Naapi refers to Naato'si's (Sun) energy, since this is his birthplace in the space—the universe, the cosmos created by Sun and Moon, Naapi's father and mother, respectively. They are different, however. Naapi is his own entity, not to be confused with Naato'si, an assertion that debunks the arguments of some previous paragraphs: "The Indians also have believed for ages in the existence of a Supreme Being whom they designate as Napi, but I never remember hearing any of my people praying to this deity. The Indian does not offer his prayers entirely to the Sun. Living creatures of every description are included in his daily devotions, though he doesn't pray to these in the light of a Supreme Being. Far from it."[26] There is a union of physical and metaphysical realities, brought together in the phrase Naapi-Naato'si.

Other Indigenous Peoples of the Plains share a like concept of life processes, whereas to the Blackfoot understanding of Naapi, this "white" is more complex than it has thus far been given credit for in most of the literature treating this "white Being"; as essence and light, it is related to the sacred. In this connection, the Gros Ventre Being known as Above White Man was called upon and his name was always used, according to Takes A Prisoner, "when about to begin their ceremonial performances."[27] This is because "tradition told by the early day Gros Ventre was that this name of Above White Man was taught to the Gros Ventre by the legendary, Old Man, who was called White Man, who was to have taught them all they knew from the beginning in the ways of living, and who taught them to know right and wrong."[28] According to this account, the Gros Ventre do not claim to know Above White Man's origins, since more importance is placed on his character, style, habit, tendencies, and preferences and on his role as a teacher. By knowing his character richly, deeply, intimately, and thoroughly, the Gros Ventres can then continue to relate stories about Above White Man to the People's newest generations.

Many Indigenous Peoples' original characterizations and descriptions of Naapi-like energies refer to the past, present, and future concurrently. Naapi-Naato'si and Naapi stories explain Naato'si's role in Naapi's origin story, which reveals that while Naato'si is the source for Naapi's energy, Naato'si's body is sky-bound while Naapi impacts the atmosphere and landscape filled with Naato'si's power. Their close connection and correlation is found in observations among states, actions, and effects in conditions influenced by the pair in their respective realms. This bond is what many non-Indigenous writers mistakenly call "Sun worship," as exemplified in the following characterization of Naapi: "The native religion of the Blackfeet was a form of Sun worship. 'We believe that the Sun God is all powerful,' said an old man puzzled by the white man's religion. 'We can see that all life comes from him.' They made daily prayers to the Sun and to Napi (Old Man), and they undertook nothing of importance without first praying for divine aid. The Sun sent them dreams to tell them what was going to happen."[29] In direct contradiction to these types of portrayals, Scalp Robe and Red Crow of the Kainaa (Blood) band of the Blackfoot shared stories about Naapi that describe his land-based effects. In these depictions, he more greatly resembles Ice Age conditions and other geological processes and their remains than he does mystical or mythical characters: "This personage came from the South and [traveled] to Southern Alberta and then went Northward. He was wounded and bled as he came. Wherever this blood fell there is found to this day red earth used by Indians as paint. In some places there is found white earth, which was caused by matter flowing from the wounds when in a bad state."[30]

There is a process about the direction Naapi takes through the cycle of stories that assume a connection to the homeland's archaeological and geological history. During the early days of the muskeg country, the ice left red (iron) deposits that later became the lowest layer of dried lakes and riverbeds in what were water deposits all over the country, which in turn left salt and brine deposits connected to the various names attributed to Naapi that range from white (pus) to red (blood) and so on and which capture the dynamic of Naapi's changes. The stories describe his movement as heading northward and his having taken one last rest as he approaches the farthest reaches of the Blackfoot homeland near the Red Deer River in the north, the area of the glacial meltback and the opening of the northland muskeg and tundra. Naapi eventually reaches the southern oceans, when the form of water is explained as his living in the ocean in the south, having left the Plains Peoples' homeland with the river water. Naapi as weather, glaciers, or any of many climatological phenomena corresponds to the landscape's early creation times, which makes Naapi stories' claims climatologically, geologically, and meteorologically accurate, since they all give birth to action associated with Naapi. More of these patterns become clear through the stories, which show that there are several ways of seeing and being Naapi.

In another example, Tail-Feathers-Coming-over-the-Hill, an Aamsskaapipikani (Southern Peigan/Blackfeet), explains that Naapi is not just light because Old Man or Naapi's "light" alone does not have the power Naapi used to create the world, as believed in early times. Beliefs about creation and practices were also transferred with stories about creation and Naapi through his energetic forces, only some of which are light. Naapi "was the god who created the world, and all life upon it, and he was the god of the Blackfeet until, some centuries back, they got from some southern tribe another religion, of which the sun is the principal god."[31] In this version of the evolution of the Blackfoot People, the first creators involved an interplay between the earthbound experiences of the Blackfoot. As these early People learned from Naapi, southern Indigenous Peoples also celebrated Sun, adopting and exchanging with the Blackfoot, whose celebrations of Sun and the myriad expressions of Sun they share.

Schultz paraphrases Tail-Feathers-Coming-over-the-Hill's meanings and contexts, however, and distorts more than clarifies this relationship because of his emphasis on singular entities when he says about Naapi: "However, they still pray to Old Man, as well as to the gods of the later religion, although in time a great many stories have grown up about Old Man that make him appear to be more of a buffoon than a god."[32] Extrapolating from what he was taught about Sun and Naapi, he states: "An interesting point about the word *nap'-i* is that, while it is the term for an old man, its real meaning is dawn, or the first faint, white light that gives birth to the day. And so, in common with the ancient Mexicans, various tribes of the plains, the Aryans and other ancient races of the Old World, the original religion of the Blackfeet was the worship of light personified."[33] This opinion appears often in the literature on Naapi.

Language studies sometimes interpret similarities in the sound of the language to mean that entire ceremonies are borrowed elements from other Indigenous Peoples, which is another aspect of investigating Naapi's name. For instance, similarities between Algonquian/Algonkian linguistic terms correlate with like ceremonies across Peoples and prove common ceremonial origins: "We find, accordingly, that the word for 'sun,' which in the Blackfoot language is totally different from the corresponding word in all other Algonkin tongues, bears an evident resemblance to the Kootenai name of that luminary. In Blackfoot the word is *natos* or *natusi*; in Kootenai it is *natanik*. The words differ merely in their terminations. There can hardly be a doubt that, when the Blackfeet borrowed from their former neighbours their most peculiar and remarkable religious ceremony, they borrowed also the name of the sun-deity to whose worship it was devoted."[34] Indigenous Peoples share terms and sometimes the origins of ceremonies, hence linguistic and ceremonial commonalities. The shared environmental and astronomical insights, however, are less emphasized in these studies. Like other Indigenous Peoples who recognize Sun as the life source, the distinctiveness yet simultaneous inextricability in the unit of Naapi-Naato'si's identity makes sense. This apparent duality often makes it more difficult to sort out any distinctive naming attributed to Naapi. It is to this and the aspects of the Blackfoot language that continue to be misinterpreted on this question that the next section turns.

THE PEOPLE'S STORIES

Chewing Black Bone nonetheless conveyed Naapi stories as stories of the People,[35] as did "Spotted Eagle . . . a noted medicine man, who made a specialty of the Sun-dance ceremonial."[36] Many traditional storytellers were also ceremonialists, and this remains true today. Blackfoot stories about the origins of the Sun ceremonials comprise a different genre of storytelling and differ in their telling from Naapi stories, although they sometimes overlap and many storytellers therefore often know both.

Even so, Peoples' individual proclivities and personalities play into the type of storytelling they prefer, as does their relationship with the interviewer, so that "in the following myths about Old Man, related by Spotted Eagle, the reader will observe the striking contrast between their crude character, and the beauty of conception, dignity of imagery and vividness of description characterizing the star-legends as told by Brings-down-the-Sun."[37] Both Spotted Eagle and Brings-Down-the-Sun were Sun ceremonialists and thus familiar with the stories about Naato'si in such ceremonies. The meaning of a Naapi story is conveyed in the experience of listening to a gifted storyteller who is enjoying relating Naapi's adventures. Spotted Eagle's humor and style, for example, add to the content: "Spotted Eagle had quite a reputation as a wit, and was widely known as a joker. When startled by a sudden noise, such as the barking of a dog, or the whinn[y] of a horse, he had a comical way of giving an odd cry, made more ridiculous by the peculiar intonation of his voice and the expression of his face. After each of his jokes, he would turn towards me, winking vigorously, and was greatly pleased if I laughed at them, which I did at every opportunity."[38] The expressions and antics of some storytellers were part of their unique flourishes and specialties, which characterized their renditions, enlivened by their transformation *into* Naapi-like dramatics. Quirks and voice changes were part of this rich repertoire that exists for the sake of laughter.

Spotted Eagle's stylistic and personal peculiarities were applied when playing the role of Naapi, which made him a great storyteller. Despite these efforts, story analyses nonetheless succumbed to the Victorian values that hindered attempts to understand Naapi and declared that Spotted Eagle's stories were the "obscene" renderings of a childish man of a childlike People: "He was specially fond of telling stories about the marvellous adventures of Old Man (Napi), a mythical character of the Blackfeet, whose contradictory qualities are difficult to understand, or reconcile."[39] Indeed, especially to those unfamiliar with the social context to say nothing of the ecological or cosmological one, "many of them were vulgar and even obscene, which have an ethnological value, but cannot appear in a book for general circulation. Spotted Eagle had a fondness for them because they had been handed down from the ancients, and he also had that common trait, which finds enjoyment in hearing and telling such stories, because of a keen sense of the humour in them."[40] This ribald sense of the ridiculous is one source of the difficulty involved in deciphering what appears as a messy cluster of situations caused by a rather vulgar and shameless character. Even when Naapi slights or offends the well-mannered, he is the extreme of ridiculousness, and this is what makes him so amusing to the Blackfoot sensibility. The more serious lessons he brings forth are based in his unique energetic dynamic, which is explained in more detail throughout the remainder of this book but which essentially shows that interpretations of his actions require consideration in light of sociocultural and environmental contexts; his is a complex, multidimensional, seemingly contradictory dynamism:

> The character of Old Man as revealed, even in the most serious of these myths, is a strange composite of opposing attributes, of power and weakness, of wisdom and passion, of benevolence and malevolence. He associated intimately with the birds and animals. He conversed with them and understood their thoughts and language, and they understood him. Although believed to be the creator of all things, and as having omnipotent power, he was often helpless and in trouble, and compelled to seek the aid of his animal friends. He was, in fact, like an animal in his instincts and desires, which, strange to say, were exercised in conjunction with his supernatural power. Old Man, like Hercules of Greek and Roman legend and Thor of the ancient Scandinavians, was the personification, in human form, of strength and supernatural power. But it was a power uncontrolled by reason, and wanton in its exercise. He was a deceiver and a trickster and his name was a synonym among the Blackfeet, at least in later years, for mischievous and immoral adventure. Spotted Eagle said of him: "Old Man first came to the Blackfeet from the south. The last we heard of him, he was among the Crees, and disappeared toward the east, whence he is not likely to ever return."[41]

When he moves on from his world-creating adventures among the Blackfoot, it is said he continues on his way, moving north and in either a northwesterly or northeasterly direction (depending on the story version), to transform the lives of whoever lives in the place where he is going.

NAAPI'S WHITE ENERGY

Maintaining a relationship with Naapi depends on understanding who he is: a sacred Being or Person infused with Naato'si's—Sun's—energy, the life-force energy that infuses all living things, including Naapi. When the Blackfoot created a word to signify an individual who works with the most powerful creative energy in the universe, they combined the terms for Sun's energy with that of a man/person to make missionary: "*Nato* = Holy . . . *Natoapekwan* = the holy man, a missionary . . . *Natoapikwan* is composed of *natos*, the sun, *api*, the contracted form in word formation of *matupi*, a person, and *kwan*, the singular personal ending."[42] These first impressions were important, and it seems that the initial understanding non-Indigenous missionaries had of the meanings associated with Sun energy is that Naapi could be thought of as half-man and half-spirit energy. "Person" here, however, is understood to refer to a Being but not necessarily a human or "pre-human" Being: "Back in the days before man, the only ones on the prairies were animals and a deity called Napi. Like man, he was a mixture of wisdom and stupidity, good and evil, stinginess and generosity."[43] Alika Podolinsky Webber's analysis of Naapi's name is based on Marguerite Mackenzie's report on Algonquian/Algonkian terms, which states: "I have heard of the network charm from the Cree—it is used to capture evil influences or spirits. The word is the diminutive form of the word for net *ahipii* = ahipiish. The *h* makes it an eastern James Bay pronunciation; Davis Inlet would be *aNapii* or *ayapii*, and Montagnais *aNapii* or *alapii*, depending on the dialect; the initial *a* is usually dropped at normal speech speed . . . I wonder if *aNapii* pronounced *Napii* could be etymologically linked to *napeao*, meaning 'man.'"[44]

In discussing the nature of nature and of Persons who reside in the environment (e.g., Naato'si [Sun] and Ko'komiki'somm [Moon]), Naapi's name links to Sun, which confused their association in non-Indigenous Peoples' comprehension of Naapi's identity:

> Under the name *Na'pi*, Old Man, have been confused two wholly different persons talked of by the Blackfeet. The Sun, the creator of the universe, giver of light, heat, and life, and reverenced by every one, is often called Old Man, but there is another personality who bears the same name, but who is very different in its character. This last *Na'pi* is a mixture of wisdom and foolishness; he is malicious, selfish, childish, and weak. He delights in tormenting people. Yet the mean things he does are so foolish that he is constantly getting himself into scrapes, and is often obliged to ask the animals to help him out of his troubles. His bad deeds almost always bring their own punishment. Interpreters commonly translate this word Na'pi as Old Man, but it is also the term for white man; and the Cheyenne and Arapahoe tribes tell just such stories about a similar person whom they also call "white man." Tribes of Dakota stock tell of a similar person whom they call "the spider."[45]

There are many grammatical concerns regarding an accurate interpretation of Naapi's name. One of these centers on whether his referent is to be considered a verb-ish or a noun-ish word: "In reference to his name, which Mr. Wilson and others write *Napi*, and Father Lacombe *Napiw*, and which Mr. Grinnell renders 'Old Man,' it may be mentioned that *Napi* is an adjective, signifying 'old.' Used as a name, it might be rendered 'The Old One' (in French, Le Vieux; in German, Der Alte). *Napiw* is a verbal form, used also as a name, and signifying, properly, 'He who is old.'"[46] Depending on the record, Naapi is not exactly a noun, verb, or adjective; he defies the classificatory rigidity these terms impose on his ability to transfer energy, which has its source in an animate universe.

Stories of Naapi and Blackfoot collections began with the first record of Blackfoot stories made by Peter Fidler in 1792,[47] followed by "Alexander Henry, in 1808 and continuing on down to modern times. Among the recorders of myths whose material has been published we find the names of Petitot, McLean, Grinnell, Schultz, Knox, McClintock, Wilson, Michelson, Linderman, and Wissler . . . In scope the contributions range from the single magic flight tale of Knox to the large and comprehensive collection of Wissler, R. N. Wilson, whose published Blackfoot mythology heretofore consisted of a few star myths."[48] More could be added to the list, such as Christopher C. Uhlenbeck, Truman Michelson,[49] and others, including some members of the Blackfoot community. Divisions of the stories may not make sense in terms of the original Blackfoot story order. Fidler jotted down stories associated with land sites in the homeland that the Blackfoot and other Indigenous Peoples showed him, and he included brief summaries of how they related to Naapi. Despite being among the first of several observers to point out these coincidences, Fidler did not know exactly what they meant. Notwithstanding his ignorance of their meaning, his mention of the stories "Lone Pine" and "Plays Wheel Game" (see appendix) clearly ties Fidler's description to Blackfoot interpretations of Naapi's image composed of rocks—as he is stretched out, lying on the ground—and to the various effect he had all over the land.

A similar cross-shaped referent is found in another description of Naapi: "The Blackfeet have the same god of wisdom, Nepo or Nebo [Naapi], as the ancient Assyrians and the Swastika Cross is sacred to them as it is to the T[i]betans."[50] Rather than ascribe sacred attributes to Naapi, however, "*Napi* is associated with mischievous-making activities rather than any supreme being,"[51] even though he is acknowledged as a creator. To the Blackfoot, this is an important but subtle distinction; Naapi's troublemaking tendencies are highlighted in many retellings of the stories about him and his activities. In many ways, this is what the non-Indigenous Peoples who visited the Blackfoot focused on all along because he was interpreted too literally and simultaneously grossly misunderstood. Much of what is currently known about Naapi and his jaunts stems from just such interest, making it difficult to reconcile certain details that should be considered to achieve a holistic interpretation of him.

NAAPI'S ALIASES AND ALTER EGOS

Naapi is also known by several different names, which adds to the confusion about their meaning. Claude E. Schaeffer asks: "*Me-ko-ki-a* as name for *Napi?*" "*Napi's* blood becomes red paint? Pus white earth?"[52] James Willard Schultz's novel *The Danger Trail*[53] contains "Red Old Man was the first man made by Old Man."[54] Uhlenbeck offers another description of his name: "The name *Mekyapi* has been translated . . . by 'Red-man', as that ancient chief is often called in English, but the literal translation is 'Red-old-man', *api-* being the form which *Napi* takes, when used as second member of a compound."[55] In another expansion: "'*Napi*,'ˣ the old Man, was called by the Blood. Sometimes called by the Pegans [Piegans] *Ke-nue-a-cah-atsis*; by the Blackfeet *Me-ki-kia*; by Nez Perces 'Cayute' [Coyote]; by the Sarcees 'Big Head'; by the Crows, 'The Big Old Camp-Ground'; and over the Mountains, [or] 'Left Hand'";[56] "*anna* (animate), *anni* (animate and inanimate) that . . . *ap-* white";[57] nd "*matapi(ua), -tapi- person . . . mik- (mek-)* red,"[58] meaning Red Man.

Many other stories in Blackfoot oral tradition introduce a distinction between two brothers created by Sun and Moon, of which Naapi is one. In describing the relationship between these two, they seem to parallel the directions of North and South, and they also have connections among Left Hand, the Hand Story, Naapi, and the Milky Way. Left Hand refers to Naapi (re Plains Sign Language) and to his being the younger brother, since the "good" brother went back up to the sky and joined his parents, Naato'si and Ko'komiki'somm. "Left" is the simple (i.e., imperfect) brother who created the People of the North, while his brother created People in the South. Red Old Man/Other Old Man = "Very smart." When People die, they are said to "leave a red mark," like Naapi does against the rock at his sliding place and as did Katoyis (Blood Clot, another early Blackfoot creator) did in the riverbed where he last lay. This is all part of the traditions that dictate that chiefs and other significant individuals are wrapped in a red blanket when they die, which the People say has left its stain where the person lay.

All of these names show that these entities are merely *representatives* of certain energies that have their origins in the creative forces that bring life to all things in a universe that is infused with transmutable energies that *act upon* and *interact with* other Beings and thereby transfer energy to another mode or agent. The Indigenous world and languages accept the appropriateness of the myriad forms this flow takes, at times in static forms and other times in ways that show that the demarcations between things belie the unity of the metaphysical backdrop they share. Naapi carries this energy from the original creation and transfers it to others through his actions and their reactions. From such a context, it is possible to see how Naapi's name can change to fit the setting, the time, place, and occurrence of his effects, and this is one way the Blackfoot accept his ever-changing monikers; one minute he is a rainbow, at another he is a blizzard, and in another, a berry. This is the key to the metaphysical aspects of these stories' teachings, to acknowledge the flow of energy flowing through Sun all the way to the berry and then into whoever eats the berry.

If sociocultural saliency is what drives certain words to appear to contain more animacy, then Naapi's actions might explain another level of this connection because in so many of his actions on the land, he creates confluences full of life. Even though rivers, for instance, are grammatically "inanimate" in Blackfoot, they are nonetheless also shaped by Naapi. The many rivers and creeks associated with

Naapi, including "Old Man River" and "Old Man's Butte," are translations from the Blackfoot expressions for "Old Man Lies There" and "Old Man Sleeps There." Combining this with multiple levels of intertextuality that abound in Blackfoot life and Naapi's links to all forms of water (e.g., ice, moisture, mist, rain, hail, rainbows, snow, snowstorms/blizzards, and glacial activities), he therefore also contributes to avalanches, crevasses, rivers, valleys, lakes, coulees, alluvial plains, and flats and the shaping of hills, outcrops, and mountains. He gifted the foothills' bountiful plants, flowers, and medicines and created the natural boundaries that protected all the families of plants and animals of the Blackfoot world and kept out all others, People included. Naapi is a forceful, powerful creator at times, such as when he's pushing mountains and moraines and sliding down mountains at his favorite "sliding place," at his "jumping-off place." All these areas relate Naapi to glacial and tectonic activity, to sedimentary situations, as well as to floods, relocated rivers, and such—in essence, the growth and reconstruction of the earth through all its inherent processes. The wide variety and combination of Naapi's forms, actions, and monikers refers to these processes.[59] Indigenous Plains Peoples accept that these changes occur as a result of great energy. This is why the Blackfoot could adjust the term to accommodate spiritual white men (i.e., missionaries), although it never meant half-human half-god, as "*Natoapekwan/Natoapikwan*."[60]

Similarly, *náápiikoan* means "member of the Causasian race, white person."[61] Much confusion surrounds Naapi's name where it appears with assumptions that it is referring to and subsumed under multiple definitions related to men and human Beings, such as when "napikwan [*sic*] is proposed as the name for the second Plains cultural tradition which includes the Besant and Old Women's phases,"[62] as well as where it is understood that "napikwan [*sic*] is the Blackfoot word for Old Man Person. It was commonly used to refer to white men but may also refer to *Napi* the Blackfoot creator. The word as used herein refers to Old Man Person."[63]

The connection between Naapi and an old white animate Being, as in a long-ago time, is the translation of what was originally likely something loosely translated as having to do with a "white Person," meaning a "light-colored Being" in reference to his color. Since "Being" can potentially describe any number of living Persons and other animate and inanimate matter in the Blackfoot world, it does not solely tie this origin to humans. It could also refer to climatological forces affecting the earth or atmosphere, and its prefix *áápi-* does in fact mean white or light colored, but it can be widely applied. Because of difficulties translating Blackfoot into English and other Western European languages, however, collectors' propensity to turn everyone of interest into a male by default, unless specified otherwise, converts this animate Being into a man in most translations. This tendency is further exacerbated by grammatical limitations of these languages in terms of encoding and explaining animate and inanimate—the nature, degree, condition, or state of something or someone converts an animate Being to a "man." This seemingly minor technicality is the source of two centuries of confusion about Naapi, whose name in the traditional Blackfoot language was never meant to be limited to, nor does it now only link to, a white "man" in this sense. The Blackfoot expression *matapi*, "person," does not equal man, even though this is a common mistranslation of the term. *Matapi*, like Naapi, refers to an animate Being, a living Being who *may* be a Person; however, in Blackfoot there are many different types of Persons, only some of which are humans, so the term really refers to some living thing that has the status of personhood. This class comprises a very large group of Beings, including animals, birds, planets, stars, winds, mountains, and spirits. All of this requires a breakdown before even tackling the animate-inanimate or gender situation of Blackfoot.

Another related topic on the question of Naapi's animacy concerns articulated silent vowels in spoken Blackfoot, discussed more fully later in the book. For now, it is important to note that Blackfoot connects air with *animateness*, as in having or displaying the quality of life (just as "spirit" does in English). Some expressions that express this bond are "air, *a-mik-puk*";[64] "alive, *e-te-pi*";[65] and "to live, *e-ta'-pi*; I live, *nit-se-ta'-ta-pi*; you live, *kit-se-ta'-ta-pi*."[66] Taking these in combination with the final unarticulated syllables *-oas* and *-wa* to reflect the air expressed and expelled in exhalation, a proper rendering of the term *Naapi* necessitates the expression of both age and animate status in a person, thus "*Naapii (-wa)* 'Old Man; whiteman'"[67] and "*aapi-* 'white'"[68] do not equal a "white man" so much as they refer to elderly Persons, that is Beings, Blackfoot ancestors writ large, who are not necessarily humans but who may be, depending on the context: "old, *na'-pe*; a white man, *na-pe'-ku-un*, literally old people; applied to a female, *ki-pi'-ta*; an old woman, *ki-pi'-ta-a-ki'-wa*."[69] The basis for assigning any association between the color white and age is a factor added on to the basic status of personhood. Old people's white hair is an accurate aspect of their appearance, and such features in Blackfoot tradition are the basis for much naming, except perhaps for names earned by the selection of a particularly noticeable characteristic feature or outstanding behavior. Blackfoot terms related to old people/people/person refer to so much more and are expansive and inclusive, far beyond just humans. "Ancestors," who are included in this reference, include rocks and stars.

Misnomers associated with Naapi are the persistent repetition of an initial blunder in comprehension still touted as a correct interpretation of Naapi. Much of this is a result of the separation of the terminological aspects of his name from investigations into his intentions, motives, aspirations, and speech patterns, as these are revealed in Naapi stories. In other words, from everything we know about Algonquian/Algonkian languages, the *emotive context* of Naapi's actions determines how we should interpret them. A thorough review of the historical, ethnographic, linguistic, and philosophical precepts concerning interpretations of Naapi (and likely his fellow Algonquian/Algonkian and Plains Peoples' Tricksters as well) shows that many are founded on multiple errors of observation, notation, judgment, comprehension, and interpretation and are often flatly incorrect.

THE SOCIAL NETWORK OF TRICKSTER NAMES

In Algonquian/Algonkian traditions, though, there is no "there" there, no "being" without an explanation of place, a description of where, when, and with whom, as in which community that state of being happens. Selecting discreet items or classes and focusing on them to the exclusion of the context does an injustice to wholistic worldviews where energy flows from state to state, object to object, emotion to emotion, and so on, so that Naapi truly represents a manner or mode of agency rather than a strict or permanent condition. Rules for transitioning something from inanimate to animate form in Ojibwa, for example, show that the form used to effect animate/inanimate status can be used on similar terms by just changing this aspect of their identity.[70] Determining which category something belongs to also depends to a great extent on the point the speaker is making vis-à-vis the topic at hand. This is also true for Blackfoot. Once again, the meaning is in the method; it is not possible to separate *the ways* meaning is communicated without also changing the meaning of *what is being transmitted*. Language is never just language.

The following lengthy excerpt exemplifies the foregoing argument; it demonstrates how aloneness or Lone Wolf status, as discussed previously, does not work in Blackfoot or in Chippewa:

> It would afford us pleasure to pursue the consideration of the verb, in its various modifications and involutions, where it [is] compatible with the limits assigned to us; but we feel that such a course could not be adopted consistently with the notice we wish to bestow on some other points of the language. One further trait in the verb, we deem it, however, important not to pass over, in this place. We refer to the use of the substantive verb, To Be. The idea of its absence from a stock of languages, whose whole syntax is based on a classification of the creation into beings and substances, vital or inert, appears to have originated in total misapprehension. And whatever doubts there may be as to the capacity of the Indian languages *to affirm or declare*, independently of the operation of the *affirmation* or *declaration* on mind or matter, a simple consideration of the facts adduced by philologists shows that there

can be none, respecting the power of most of the languages to denote simple *existence* or *being*. The data brought forward in relation to this topic, so far as relates to the Chippewa, [show] . . . the generic words *Iah* and *Atta*, indicating respectively, To Be, in animate and inanimate nature, run, like two principal arteries, through the whole language, and although they are not used as declarative auxiliaries like our term "I am," yet they enter respectively, as component particles, into the entire classes of the active, passive, and neuter verbs, and admit *themselves* of independent conjugation. The Indian does not habitually, and by the rules of his language say, "I am sick," "I am well," "I am hungry," "I am cold," contenting himself with a simple indication of his condition. Yet when the occasion requires it,—when impelled by passion, or inspired by superstition,—he can exclaim, *Nindow iah w'iahn!* "My existence is," "The body that it is!" An opinion has been expressed by persons versed from infancy in the languages, with whom we have conferred, on this point, that the word *Iah* is a part of the name of the Everliving, or Supreme Being; that there is connected with its utterance, in the separate form, a high degree of awe; that this particle is used in the sacred and mystic songs of the Indians, in which it excites a strong feeling of fear and dread. It is also asserted that Monedo, the modern name for the Supreme Being or Great Spirit, is a personal form of the verb, To Take, derived from the supposed abstraction of the food, placed as an offering to the Supreme Spirit, upon the rude altar-stone . . . The practical operation of the verb *Iah* is shown in the subjoined colloquial terms. "It is!–It is!" *Iah!-Iah!* [are] exclamations used by the Indians when endeavoring to recollect the name of a person, or a forgotten circumstance.

"He is there"; *Iah-e-mau.*

"He is a spirit"; *Monedow'iah.*

"And Enoch walked with God, and was not." *Enoch Ogiwejiwan. Geezha Monedo, Kaween ah'weah.*

"I live," "I exist," "I am here." *Nin Diah-Neen.*

As the full conjugation of this verb has been communicated in the observations of one of our former numbers before alluded to, its parallel, in the *inanimate kingdom*, may here be given. *Atta*; "To be," or "exist," as inert matter. (As no personal pronouns can be employed, the conjugation is of course restricted to the neuter "it" and its plurals.)[71]

According to this 1823 discussion of Chippewa, the element of the sacred is inherent in the ability to express the concept "To Be," for without it, the relative animate energy of the Being in question is not fully expressed. This is similar to the Blackfoot patterns of use concerning the infusion of animate life energy into concepts related to existing at all, as in "to be."

NUMBERS, SETS, AND PAIRS

To further emphasize complements and paired social status as the basis of life and to in turn contrast this with the aloneness of the Lone Wolf, Blackfoot keeps things paired or whole whenever possible. When split, some numbers are complicated, as seen the following examples: "*Nisoo, niso, niso* four . . . *nitukska, nit- (-it-)* one, has been compared to different Algonquian numerals for 'one.' Of course it is not permissible to start from the independent form *nitukska!* . . . *niuokska, niuoka, ni-(-i)* three. As in the preceding case it would be incorrect to start from the independent form . . . The Algonquian numerals offer a great many difficulties, which I am unable to solve . . . *oma* (animate), *ami* (inanimate and obviative animate) 'that.'"[72] Blackfoot speakers corroborate this information and explain that as a reflection of the *context* in which numbers have meanings, speakers consider multiple options for the expression of the singular; $4 = 2 \times 2$ or two halves of one, or $4 =$ whole $= 1$, and so forth. Numerals 1, 3, and so on cannot stand alone but are considered parts of a larger whole. In this sense, grammar matches or maybe even dictates and reinforces the Algonquian/Algonkian idea that "everything comes in twos"; expressed another way, this means that numbers have to be paired in order to be discussed. The assumption is that everything has its balance, its match, a counterpart, a partner, and these must be acknowledged in utterances.

A few obvious examples of this type of understanding come from observations of nature. Sun and Moon, for example, are considered a pair and thus form a creative unit, so they are two but one at the same time. Male and female work similarly, in that they are two but together make a unit of at least one but maybe three, and so on. As Sun transits across the sky, counting dawn, midday, sunset, and night equals a four-part "day" cycle, which is also a single cycle, so one. Moon has four stages: new, waxing, waning, and full; so again "one" cycle is made up of four parts. Then again, the Indigenous calendrical systems count the nights, even when Moon is not visible, and they are also worked into the lunar calendar year, which is broken down in the same way. Seasons work similarly, with stellar charts and rotations counted, and animal and plant cycles are included as well. Astral movements and cycles, rivers' flow, flowers' growth, and the alternating winds and constantly changing weather patterns are all are predicted and explained, since all existence, visible or not, is integrated into Naapi's everyday universe. The movements of the constellations, seasons, activities, elements, structures, crucial relationships, and interconnections that balance and continue life are expressed as Naapi's insatiable appetites, rebelliousness, creativity, impatience, persistence despite adversity, humor, presence, and longevity; they are eternal transformations of constantly changing conditions. Algonquian/Algonkian languages express an interpretation of a constant balancing of energies in the universe; Naapi's behavior and character *epitomizes* imbalance, which in turn highlights the comparatively harmonious system at work most of the time in the homeland space.

On the question of individuation in Blackfoot, "A great wealth of forms is exhibited by the numerals. By the side of the primary forms which the Indians use when counting without special reference to persons or things, animate or inanimate, there are also two different sets, respectively, for the animate and the inanimate gender."[73] This and other studies conducted over the past century and more document cumulative changes in the language, some stemming from inconsistent use or knowledge of Blackfoot as a result of the influence of other languages. Many word forms that are classed as either animate or inanimate signal nothing particularly significant in a linguistic sense, even if the Blackfoot numerology systems that become apparent in studies of the stories reveal that some numbers are more relevant to life and thus more socially salient. This, however, has not been investigated in Blackfoot language studies.

Blackfoot Naapi story language emphasizes specific interactions between animals and birds that customarily function in pairs (e.g., Dove, Raven, Beaver), often including their offspring in discussions of families and taxonomies. Due attention is paid to species that appear to prefer a more solitary existence (e.g., Wolverine, Badger, Porcupine). These Beings, animals and birds, are distinguished markedly from those that maneuver in the world as members of herds, flocks, or similar groups. The Blackfoot think very highly of birds and animals that prefer to be paired and grant them a great deal of esteem and respect; they also admire their teammate status, especially if they mate for life. Animals living in groups with leaders (e.g., Elk, Buffalo, Wolf) do not have just one leader; their entire band resembles a hierarchy that has varying degrees of familiarity with and formality toward the leader. These distinctions between animal types and their preferences were traditionally considered significant enough to mark with story, and their interactions with People and with other Beings are noted in verbal and non-verbal communications and social circles. They are examples of how even numerical systems are thought to have potential for a social life. These exchanges are the source of many Blackfoot oral traditions, including Naapi stories, showing that these animals and plants *are* our relatives.

These brief examples show how social context plus space is the way speakers of Algonquian/Algonkian languages make sense of the world and speak in forms that express their observations of the way energies move within it. Sun and Moon move across space, or they change shape to occupy space differently (e.g., a full Moon *appears* to fill more space) as part of their transitions. Sun moves up and down the eastern horizon, more north or south depending on when and where one is talking about in the seasonal shifts. The variability in Algonquian/Algonkian expressions does not belie some misunderstanding or confusion about the way energies constantly adapt of transform. Rather, the expressions are almost too accurate to fit into the linguistic categorizations that would have them, be they verb-ish, noun-ish, adjective, or whatever, outside of the context in which they were originally conceived or perceived and which speakers' descriptions match.

DEFINING ANIMATE ENERGY, WHISPERED
VOWELS, AND DIALOGIC PRAYERS

A number of aspects of Naapi's nature offer insight into the way the Blackfoot language explains who he is. Some of these aspects concern the grammatical and syntactical dimensions surrounding Naapi and the world he inhabits. Blackfoot conditions in and expectations of life are premised on the acknowledgment of an animate universe, a fact that influences the formation of Blackfoot linguistic expression such that nouns are shaped by the elements or a quality they consist of or create or engender, a distinction made broadly in English by a rough animate/inanimate delineation. Blackfoot nouns sometimes distinguish between animate and inanimate based on a determination of things considered to have a certain type of life (i.e., Sun) energy. Beyond this is an additional consideration about whether said energy is transferrable. Then, too, there are terms and expressions that seem to have no relationship to this assertion, so this assessment is strictly in reference to some animate nouns. It is understandable that from outside the culture and language it could be difficult to see this, so many studies view the animate/inanimate distinction merely as a grammatical rule bearing no additional significance. This grammatical distinction describes only some of the things the Blackfoot consider to be infused with invisible life forces; there are groupings of expressions that for the most part are animate.

What Naapi and other Blackfoot stories show, however, is that the determination about whether a particular noun, for instance, is in this category has to do with sociocultural aspects or contextual aspects related to the item's connection to the creation cycle. Whether this means that the context of the item's use and integration into Blackfoot life determines its grammatical gender is difficult to say with certainty. The fact is that only some terms of a given grammatical gender are considered "animate" while others are not, and this depends on speakers' intent and context. Simultaneously, other terms are considered grammatically "inanimate" even if they are from the same "animate" category as many others and vice versa, with the ultimate determination often dependent on the *context* in which these terms are used. The seemingly indiscriminate or random distribution of these expressions is not arbitrary, although a focus on the grammatical classification systems alone does not reveal why. Their use in story reveals why they acquire certain grammatical options. There is much mystery in the history of the development of the Blackfoot language about many linguistic elements *not* connected to the animate/inanimate distinction. Ancient stories explain the classification of some of these terms as either animate/inanimate. Some examples are offered here, but not the exhaustive list that arises from all the Naapi stories considered in this study.

VOICELESS SYLLABLES ON ANIMATE NAAPI

The Blackfoot language has, unsurprisingly, been losing features for over two-and-a-half centuries, during which time interpretations of Naapi's character have simultaneously become increasingly misunderstood, maligned, misnotated, and misquoted. Inconsistencies appear throughout linguists' and other collectors' records of the language who perceived that some groups of Blackfoot speakers using the language also refer to it as dialectical. For instance, by the time linguist Donald Frantz published his research in the late 1980s and early 1990s, many linguistic distinctions had already been declared lost in modern Blackfoot studies, despite the fact that they can still be perceived in Blackfoot speech, although not necessarily in morphological or phonological differences. Rather, close studies of Naapi stories show that categories of meaning are what has been most misunderstood in written comparison of terms and expressions lacking a contextual reference, but it is almost impossible to assess how much of this reflects the degree to which the Blackfoot linguistic tradition was already lost in some places or even how much was a factor of linguists' or translators' unfamiliarity with Blackfoot.

Evidence showing that the use of Blackfoot silent final vowels on Naapi's name was gradually diminishing is confirmed in a 1992 letter from Hugh A. Dempsey to John Ewers regarding the work of some early linguists, such as Uhlenbeck. Dempsey observed that while he was able to study the language at the syntactical or grammatical level, such as recalling discrete item analysis or correlation of sounds, Uhlenbeck's analyses do not entail great enough comprehension of the way the language functions to use it to render narratives effectively: "In Uhlenbeck's *Blackfoot Texts* is an article 'How the Ancient Peigans Lived,' [which] consists of an interview with a Peigan named The Blood. Most of the events take place in southern Alberta . . . most of the translation is correct but it is so pedestrian that it's almost impossible to read. It's a language study more than a narrative. I was thinking of re-translating it into more readable English, much as I would do if I was interviewing someone. It's a fascinating account of an annual cycle, probably in the 1860s."[74] Many native Blackfoot speakers agree with Dempsey's assessment of the value of Uhlenbeck's translations. Its detailed language study is why it is nonetheless able to render important information about the classes of words that are on either side of the animate/inanimate distinction.

Unfortunately, this still seems to be a problem for the field, as exemplified by relatively recent Blackfoot linguistic studies (e.g., see note 77), which account for many aspects of the language but are still perplexed by Blackfoot's silent vowels, including Naapi's name. Meanwhile, research shows that older speakers use the form more than younger generations, which indicates that it is not simply a remnant of insignificant breath patterns or dialect alone. Rather, grammatical constraints of foreign languages affect younger generations of Blackfoot speakers, and sounds and meanings are lost. Sheena Van Der Mark, like other linguists before her, also documents the degeneration and demise of meaningful Blackfoot inflections in the section of her work "Appendix A: Blackfoot Syntax and Morphology"; her footnotes are excerpted below in their entirety to illustrate how clearly linguistic changes are felt by native Blackfoot speakers, including a distinction between Old Blackfoot and Modern Blackfoot:

> Old Blackfoot[75] distinguished between animate and inanimate nouns, but this distinction seems to be being lost in Modern Blackfoot. For example, Frantz . . . notes, "A singular animate gender noun has -wa,[76] and plural animate gender has -iksi" This quotation shows that omitting -wa as a gender marker was already in process during Frantz' work. This is likely a result of a phonological phenomenon that is occurring in Blackfoot. Often the last syllable of the Blackfoot lexeme is devoiced, and sometimes deleted completely . . . Sometimes the same lexical item would be spoken both with a devoiced final syllable and again with the same syllable deleted completely. In fact, speaker B sometimes used the suffix -wa, although she indicated that it made no difference to the meaning when it was used. This may indicate that there are still some traces of gender distinction within Modern Blackfoot. *In fact, when eliciting the form for "What is it?" speaker B said that there was a difference dependent upon whether or not the object was animate or inanimate.* In this case, the gender is within an object agreement marker on the verb and is not the final syllable of the lexeme. This demonstrates how a phonological phenomenon is affecting the morphology and ultimately word classes within the language. Modern Blackfoot has a basic SVO [Subject-Verb-Object] word order; however, there are some exceptions. The transitivity of the main verb within the Blackfoot sequence has a large effect on the morphology and syntax of a Blackfoot phrase. In some instances the word or morpheme order is changed as a result.[77]

As noted above, the changes in word order structures are influences from foreign languages. These, as well as phonemic differences in sounds on individual words, combine with the recurring problem of the final vowels to reflect changes not simply in pronunciation but also in meaning, based on whether the object was animate or inanimate.

Richard Lancaster also finds fault with the help in comprehending Blackfoot that he is able to draw from Uhlenbeck and Van Gulik,[78] referring to their work as "vocabulary lists" and noting that for further inquiry into Blackfoot language and structure, one has to look elsewhere.[79] In the following excerpt, he explains why his approach to learning Blackfoot focuses on ceremony and name traditions; in his discussion of the practice of making kin, he centers on the *connotative* or *emotionally* related contexts and speech acts: "Blackfoot . . . is a language which lends itself in the spoken form to the most intricately precise and most colorfully imaginative of employments. Aside from its marvelous store of metaphors . . . my special interest at the moment revolves around the existence in the Blackfoot language of personal forms. Broadly expressed, I am interested in the connotative implications—implied variations in meaning and/or emotional expression—which derive either from the use of ordinary expressions in special situations (with notable difference in pronunciation or stress) or from the use of extraordinary words in ordinary situations."[80] Once the resources had been gathered in anticipation of a Beaver ceremonial, Lancaster believed he sensed a change in his friendship with White Calf "Chief" refers to Running Wolf, James White Calf of the Aamsskaapipikani (Southern Peigan/Blackfeet), son of White Calf, "the 'true chief' of the Piegan":[81] "The Chief chanted prayers all night, and . . . was praying for me. The Chief did not get up until 8:30, and separately and out of hearing of each other, both Jim and the Chief said good morning to me in an entirely new way. Usually they say '*Ah-siks-kah-noh-toh-nay*'; this morning they both said '*Aht-sahpi-nah-koh.*' '*Ahk-sah-pen-a-koh,*' I know, means 'Good daylight,' and this apparently is a variant of the same word-phrase. Whether this new phrase has any special semantic significance—whether it is a personal form—I have yet to determine."[82]

Blackfoot speakers were still employing ancient Blackfoot final-syllable distinctions on Naapi at that time, a tendency that began to disappear from the records of the Blackfoot language at an early point. This is documented in missionary records about boarding schools over the past 250 years. Their records, like those of others who often misunderstood what they were hearing, show changes for the future of Blackfoot's final-vowel status that gradually disappeared from increasing numbers of Blackfoot speakers' usage in the pronunciation of Naapi's name.

Mountain Chief (Black-Horse-Rider), an Aamsskaapipikani (Southern Peigan/Blackfeet) and the principal informant for Uhlenbeck's work, displays such habits in his speech, which was recorded a century ago: "One of the most striking peculiarities of his pronunciation is his liberality with apparently superfluous *a*'s and *i*'s, which come limping behind, separated from the word proper by a glottal stop."[83] In speech and in story forms, these articulations are intentional and not simply surviving vestiges of old forms. When queried about them, Mountain Chief (Black-Horse-Rider) reassures Uhlenbeck that they should be included: "Now in Prof. Uhlenbeck's texts likewise a few of such forms in -*o* occur. At first hearing he in two or three of these cases recorded forms without an -*o*, but when asking whether these forms should not properly end in -*o* he received an affirmative answer from his interpreter. So, judging by our joint results, we may be pretty sure that in most cases the forms in -*o*, though still lingering on in actual Peigan, are about to disappear."[84]

Indirectly, Uhlenbeck and J.P.B. Josselin De Jong show Naapi's silent syllable status to be in doubt and in jeopardy from the time of the Blackfoot Peoples' initial interactions with non-Indigenous recorders. The animate/inanimate distinction of the world, actually the universe, and of the inference and reference it assumes in the Blackfoot language means something in the context of ancient pronunciations of Naapi. The occasional disappearance of these sounds was recorded and then sometimes not noted, for they began to disappear within a single generation, although they still remain intact in some speakers' pronunciations. Extrapolating from this loss and from that of the guttural discussed earlier, the sacred or animate element of many Naapi stories is diminished as this sound became increasingly altered to delete the final so-called silent syllable "-*wa*" and as the trend of omitting it increased through the following years. The *natoyi* energy referred to here is "Sun energy," the invisible life force that inhabits living things and that is the same energy that in early creation cycle stories was transferred to Naapi, to be forwarded on to the People: "The meaning of the word *natosiu*, mentioned here, is 'has (or: having) supernatural power,' when speaking about a person or an animate thing in general. The inanimate equivalent is *natoyiu*. The supernatural power itself, the orenda of the Iroquois, is expressed by a verbal abstract noun (*otatosini* 'his supernatural power' occurs in this new series of texts . . .). *Natosi(ua)* as an animate noun means 'anybody who (or: anything which) has supernatural power,' and is used especially for the sun, the moon, a medicine-man."[85]

Most of those who collected Trickster stories, as the following excerpt epitomizes, could comment on *either* linguistic aspects *or* the larger story class but did not usually couple any in-depth story study with grammatical analyses, so Uhlenbeck can only suggest comparisons: "I regret that I cannot give references to the mythical tales of other cultural areas. I have read a good deal of them and know that there are many parallels to Blackfoot stories, especially in Ojibway and Cree folklore. In a number of cases I ought to have referred any way to Kroeber's Gros Ventre myths and tales—the Gros Ventre being a Plains tribe—but I did not have that collection at my disposal, while preparing my texts for print. I used this opportunity to correct a less accurate statement in Bear-chief's life-story."[86]

As an animate creator, Naapi's name changed in pronunciation and concept, although importantly, not necessarily through the same processes even if coinciding ones as in some cases the language formerly used to describe him fully lost its overt markers that indicate animate/inanimate status. Reestablishing ancient stories and their relative position vis-à-vis the land and the climate is one way of recovering Naapi's animate status to retrace the Blackfoot experience on the landscape and with the homeland.

Uhlenbeck spent years studying Blackfoot grammar and the acute awareness and significance of inflection, sound, meaning, and voiceless articulations in Blackfoot. He was interested in distinguishing and defining what these signals imply about meaning. Speaking to the importance of refining comprehension of Blackfoot, he asserted that the basic distinction between the animate and inanimate laid the groundwork for many other layers of meaning in Blackfoot, since the distinction has such a comprehensive integration throughout the language: "The distinction of two genders, animate and inanimate, so often met with in aboriginal American languages, is as important in Blackfoot as it is in other dialects of the Algonquian stock. Properly this distinction belongs to the noun and its substitute, the pronoun, but as gender requires congruence in Algonquian, nearly all parts of the Blackfoot grammar are affected by it."[87]

Uhlenbeck's study of Blackfoot concepts of the sacred, including Naapi, centers on how the animate/inanimate genders (i.e., energies) are divided throughout the Blackfoot universe and cosmology. Naato'si (Sun) is male, and Ko'komiki'somm (Moon) is female—again, in a social sense—and both are of the animate gender. Such differences define apparently dichotomized or otherwise easily classified energy categories that in reality merely highlight degrees of difference along a continuum. Importantly, animate and inanimate energy is also part of the Blackfoot understanding of simultaneous complementarity and energetic balance. Often, these terms are marked by the *use* or *type* of specific items in question and are *not* represented as large grammatical categories, such as types of noun classes.

A number of Blackfoot nouns with an animate/inanimate gender classification, with seemingly unsystematic assignments, refer to a collection of things ranging from the very sacred to the mundane, a difference that is often determined by stories about their first creation/arrival. In many cases, these terms are identified by their *life-giving* or *life-sustaining* properties, regardless of the rules that apply to their general class or to the umbrella term or label that identifies the rubric for their entire class. Some examples of this are described in the following: "Animate are the names of persons, supernatural beings, animals, and many other words, e.g., ksaxkum, *earth*, natosi *sun, moon*, kesum *sun, moon*, kokumikesum *moon*, kakatosi *star*, Ipisoaxs *Morning-star*, Myoxpokoiiks *Pleiades*, Ixkitsikamiks *Dipper*, osaki *back-fat*, moxsistsini *hoof*, motskinau *horn*, motokis *hide*, maiai(ua) *robe*, imoiani *robe*, (m)atseks *leggings*, atsetsi *glove*, mamin *feather*, auastam *flag*, auana *rattle*, axkeminaniks *beaver-bundle*, amopistaniks *beaver-bundle*, manistami *lodge-pole*, amakasi *wagon*, isk *bucket*, moksis *awl*, kaksakin *axe*, istoan *knife*, auaksopan *bullet*, pokun *ball* (*to play with*), pun *bracelet*, apis *rope*, mikskim *metal*, mataxkimist *black al[k]ali*."[88] To describe all of the reasons each of these terms is considered animate would require extensive explanations and examples that go beyond the scope of this book. What can be said here, for the purpose of understanding Naapi's animacy despite morphological, dialectical, or other differences, is that every item in this list refers to items that are included in the oldest stories of the People that relate to ceremonies, hunting, and healing or feeding People and other Beings. All—maybe coincidentally—are Beings, activities, or tools that sustain Peoples' existence by attending to and elevating hierarchies of importance for things that strengthen physical, spiritual, emotional, or community dimensions. These life-affirming terms are animate, since Blackfoot understanding of life energy is that it is transferred from original creators, and one has to have it in order to give it. Again, sociocultural value has to signal which "supernatural beings," for instance, could be considered "animate." If saliency influences semantic categories or interests, they could impact grammatical choices over thousands of years.

Blackfoot grammar differentiates between nouns that are more or less life affirming when dealing with large classes, so, for instance, plants are complicated: "One would expect all the names of trees to be animate, and, indeed, some of them belong to the animate class (e.g., paxtoki *pine-tree*), but some others are inanimate (e.g., sekokini *birch*), as [are] most words belonging to the vegetable kingdom. The compounds with -skim *tree*, however, are animate (e.g., asetsiksim cottonwood-tree, omaxksiksim *big log*). Some other botanical terms of the animate gender are masi *turnip*, otuksksiis *bark*, ksisiis *thorn*, kini *roseberry*, kapseks *hard-seed-berries*, miksinitsimi *bulberry*, apinikimi *whiteberry*, but by far the majority of such terms are inanimate (e.g., matuyis *grass*, katseksi *root*, okiu *stem*, suiopok *leaf*, apistsiskitsiu flower, mini *berry*, &cet.)."[89] Once again, if we review these items, specific species that have particular sociocultural relevance, attributed in large part to that species' life-affirming properties, connection with the sacred, or similar history and as told about in story, are grouped with animate forms. Specific species, constellations, or parts of plants are identified as animate nouns, and such selection is often (though not always) based on the sociocultural import or value they hold for the Blackfoot, which is likely why they are animate while others of their same grammatical noun classes are not. Plants' male and female genders are noted. The other botanical terms listed above are all included in ceremonials and are specifically referred to in stories that describe the development of the Blackfoot.

Notice, however, that labels for general categories, such as grass, root, stem, leaf, or berry, do not identify particular species but rather are umbrella terms for groupings. These need not be classed in a similar way to other specific ones with very clear stories about their contributions to the well-being of the People. This is also true for geographic features and locations or certain objects or plants that may be grammatically inanimate: "Inanimate are also geographical terms as mistaki *mountain*, nitummo hill, omaxksikimi *lake*, nietaxtai *river*, asetaxtau *creek*, &cet. To the same class belong axke *water* and other names of liquids."[90] There is a noticeable difference between the general and specifics included in the semantic aspects of the nouns in these categories. Some of these examples compare and contrast levels of animate and inanimate gender energy, considering a range of topics the Blackfoot consider to participate in this noun category.

Attention to the range of concepts and Beings encompassed in this category provides an abundance of information about many levels of existence permeated by Blackfoot "animate" nouns, which could be mixed with the "inanimate"

> The parts of the body are inanimate, except moxpskinau *jaw*, moxpsspi *eye*, mokitsis *finger*, auotanokitsis *finger-nail*, apotstsinau *biceps*, motoksis *knee*, moxkinan *calf of the leg*, mastsiu *vein*, and perhaps a few more. It is to be noticed that mostumi *body* belongs to the inanimate class, whereas makskini *carcase* is animate. The nomina instrumenti in -atsis, and those beginning with ixt- and ending in -opi, are partly animate, partly inanimate. The same suffix -opi is to be found in the local nouns with the syllable it-prefixed to them, but these are all, as far as I know, of the inanimate gender.[91]

Once again and most important, attention to data collection is key, as "some words may be animate or inanimate, according to their meaning."[92] This is another aspect of the determination of animate/inanimate that confuses studies, since it points to one of the central points of this book, which is that the context is what determines how to classify terms.

NAAPI'S FINAL WHISPERED VOWELS

Another aspect of this confusion over noun status is that it complicates understandings of the early pronunciations of Naapi, which differ significantly from current spellings and pronunciations. Naapi is animate, and the oldest written records of his name show a pronounced final syllable, the Blackfoot terminal sign of animate nouns (discussed further on in this chapter). What happened to the signaling of animate power through function, role, and participatory power as the final syllable became less pronounced? A brief analysis of Algonquian/Algonkian grammatical rules is provided here, since Blackfoot shares many of these assumptions. Many turn-of-the-century Algonquian/Algonkian language studies observed and recorded that speakers used vowels that are nearly inaudible, sometimes termed

"whispered vowels." Linguists commented on this Algonquian/Algonkian convention, calling it a lazy habit, chaotic, inconsistent, and similar characterizations that
cause irresolvable problems for interpretation. Truman Michelson, for example,
discusses final whispered vowels in Chippewa in the dialect of the Mississippi band
at White Earth, Minnesota; vowels are observed in speakers' lip movement, but
they appear to be inconsistently sprinkled throughout their speech.[93] Chippewa
and Fox, as Algonquian/Algonkian languages, share this trait with Blackfoot; final
vowels are uttered with an exhalation of breath, with no obstruction of the flow of
energy speakers in articulations. Such customs may emphasize different meanings
at particular times, as the inaudibility factor is emphasized more on some occasions
than on others, depending on the speaker's intention behind what's being expressed
and possibly for a host of other reasons we cannot determine devoid of context.
They all represent speakers' action with words through breath, which has meaning,
even if knowing exactly what that meaning is is not possible outside of the immediate setting in which the utterances were delivered. One example of such specific use
in Blackfoot is observed when describing noun-like Beings, whereas the Chippewa
examples seemed more verb dominant to the researcher. Importantly, silent (non-
vocalized) aspirations or even simply "mouthed" gestures can be interpreted by
Blackfoot speakers as the expression of a "syllable" and therefore possess similar
value as other vocalized syllables. Recall that in Algonquian/Algonkian and Plains
Peoples' language traditions, to put breath to thought is to commit action toward
the intention being expressed. This might be difficult to quantify in language classification studies because it is so pervasive, but it does not lessen the impact of the
belief in the power of words.[94]

Naapi's meaning, past and present, is in the Blackfoot language Niitsí'powahsin
and in other Algonquian/Algonkian and Plains Peoples' languages is linked to "animateness" that refers to a level of life or spirit energy the subject possesses, which
may or may not be present in an object or a place. In 1956 Hugh A. Dempsey wrote
to his colleague John Ewers about some points relevant to the Blackfoot language,
in particular Dempsey's decisions regarding the notation of certain Blackfoot
sounds. There are gutturals in the Blackfoot language that are important to relay,
as they convey syntactical and phonemic distinctions; that is, they signify something. It is not important how Dempsey or anyone else spells these gutturals as
long as the orthography includes them, since the use of breath in the final silent syllable of Naapi's name is acknowledged and included in Blackfoot language studies.
Dempsey wrote: "The H.B.C. [Hudson Bay Company] were known as: *Ahput-oxs-
apekwan Northern White Man* (singular). In all these cases, I have used the X as the
guttural *och*. Then, you ask me how I spell *white man—Napikoon or Napikoan*. Well,
frankly, neither [of these ways]. Literally it is pronounced as follows: *Nah-pee-kwahn*

(nah-pee rhymes with *happy; kwahn* with *dawn*) with the accent being on the first syllable. However, when writing the word, I use this spelling: *Napekwan*. For some time now I have used the *wa* in favor of *oa*."[95] By the mid-1950s, when Dempsey wrote this letter, studies about Naapi orthography had devolved to the point where the final silent syllables on Naapi were no longer included, even though they had been significant points of argument during the previous generation.

Blackfoot orthography and grammar continued to change during this mid-century period. In one example, (Father) Jean Lessard, while teaching anthropology at the University of Ottawa, began working on a French manuscript he was translating into English: "a manuscript grammar and dictionary of the Blackfoot Indian Language."[96] He claimed that the work was the most complete of its kind because of its many contributors who had learned Blackfoot. Lessard's analysis concludes with a review of said manuscript, which contained an admission of the degree of influence French had had on the Blackfoot language, especially among younger generations of Blackfoot-speaking students in boarding schools:

> There exists [*sic*] many small lexicons of this language, but this manuscript is the only complete grammar and dictionary of the language, with all the little variations of the different reservations. It has in addition charted the evolution of the language from the time of the arrival of the first white man among the Bloods, to the present. Owing to the presence of Boarding Schools on the different reservations, the younger generation of Blackfeet have made and are making changes in the syntax and vocabularies of the language. The manuscript was started by the first French missionary to the Blackfeet in Canada, later the Most Reverend E. Legal, Archbishop of Edmonton. It was continued by his successor, the Reverend Scollen, and in 1905 given to the Reverend J. L. Levern, who spent his whole missionary life with these same Indians. Having worked with these Indians myself and learned the language from his manuscript, I think I am in a position to judge its completeness.[97]

Taking into account the changes noted by Lessard and others mentioned in this chapter, it is apparent that the lack of the final vowel in Naapi's pronunciation began as soon as English, French, and other European-based languages were enforced on Blackfoot speakers. The multiple translators are mentioned here also because the effect of the intermediaries in the registers and meaning of the various languages used as go-betweens influenced interpretations of Naapi and other creators as well. Therefore, all of the orthographic errors or inaccuracies in translations are not the only mistakes; young Blackfoot students, forced to speak in these other languages, began integrating grammar and linguistic forms derived from the languages foisted upon them and began to know the other languages better than their own Indigenous languages. Understanding this trajectory of these changes to the Blackfoot language may prove central to mapping how Naapi's silent syllable began to disappear in Blackfoot language forms. Missionaries recorded changes in their collections of Blackfoot stories, including those of Naapi, along with changes in syntax and vocabulary, which in many cases meant the exclusion of Naapi references or of entire Naapi stories in the prioritizing and final selection of collections. Additional changes in Blackfoot were introduced by those who recorded the Naapi stories who could not distinguish between animate and inanimate forms of the word *Naapi*. Furthermore, sorting Naapi stories for content put further restrictions on their documenting or writing and even on relating them orally. The same is true for other expressions and their corresponding translations, but these cases need to be studied individually.

FIRST-PERSON PRECEDENCE, PARTICIPANTS, AND WITNESSES

Because of the complexity of and possibilities for word creation in Blackfoot, its grammar gives speakers the ability to be simultaneously precise and complex, in particular when describing something but even when just talking, since so many word forms are descriptions. One key feature of Blackfoot grammar is its ability to be widely inclusive, obliging participation by members through concepts of contribution that vary in levels of involvement during conversation and allowing and even inviting non-human Persons to participate, if not as actual speakers, then in auditory or witness roles. This feature of Blackfoot refers to "valency-bound participants: Participants coded by verbal person affixes in Blackfoot are valency-bound and thus, in contrast to oblique participants, grammatically indispensable."[98] This means that all Blackfoot speakers participate in a conversation regardless of whether they speak, merely because they are *present and thus involved*. Being present means being part of the conversation by hearing it, but listeners are not necessarily obliged to speak in order to "count" in dialogic sharing. The word *participants* thus refers to those who may simply be listening, witnessing, or otherwise present for whatever speech acts occur, such as making utterances. These roles are not necessarily acknowledged in grammar as much as they are in sociocultural value, but potential participants could include, for instance, winds, rocks, plants, and a host of other Beings.

In Blackfoot's multipart conversation structure, some auditory absorbers—in earlier times, observers of the Plains Sign Language—account for members who may not contribute to the interaction verbally or by signage; their role as merely an auditory spectator or bystander includes them in the dialogic frame. Listening alone counts as partaking because of the use of the obviation system and valency-bound participant structure:

Therefore, any two participants of an event which are coded by inverse inflexion of transitive verbs and its concomitant obviation system do not merely cover agent-patient or experiencer-patient relations . . . but rather all sorts of events in which at least two participants are involved, such as agent and directional in *go to*, agent and instrumental in *cut with*, agent and source in *come from*, agent and benefactive [*sic*] in *work for* etc. Since, however, neither inverse inflection of the verb or obviation inflection of the noun *per se* provides any indication of semantic roles, the latter must be specified by some other grammatical means: semantic role ascription in Blackfoot is accomplished by the verb stem. Thus, for example, the root *apiks-* "throw" is equipped with different stem forms for expressing the involvement of an agent and a patient or an agent and a benefactive, respectively . . . All stem variants of any transitive verb in Blackfoot share the common feature [that] the one of their two valency-bound arguments is the agent (or the experiencer, if a low-transitivity firm, such as *ino-* "see" is involved).[99]

With this option available to conversational participants, multiple, innovative, entirely new, and as-yet-unheard of phrases in Blackfoot can be invented by speakers on the spot; grammar need not hold back creativity. The fusional form allows for ongoing newness of interpretation and does not interfere with the making of relationships as yet unknown. Furthermore, the multiple valency of the participant group in Blackfoot may be a development that came about after (or even concurrent with) Plains Sign Language included the non-speaker position in "conversation." These grammatical possibilities mean that speakers of Blackfoot and Algonquian/Algonkian languages assume great responsibility, for they oblige speakers to assume the description of the state or reality of a Being, of imbuing it with life or not in the act of verbalizing it, which can be actually naming it. They use language to ascribe, assign, recognize, and capture it as a living Being, formally acknowledging and addressing the power of whatever the subject is. Naming it, talking about it, describing it is one way to be in relationship to it, to make relationship, and thereby to re-create and reaffirm the life of the Being or Person described and that of the speaker vis-à-vis each other. Often during storytelling, similar to the conversations held in Plains Sign Language, terse or crisp suggestions for images could be presented to help listeners envision and "see" action in pictures. Many Naapi stories are done this way, emphasizing imagery and shorthand expressions and often including items or episodes that recall specific ideographic elements or events, that link stories to each other through a shared contextual background.

Because of this unique feature, Blackfoot and other Algonquian/Algonkian language speakers are sometimes viewed by those uneducated about their languages as "egotistical" for having so much power over the statement of affairs. Many of the earliest recorders, for instance, refer to the apparent self-importance of the speaker. Such judgments about ego are not only woefully weak, but they demonstrate the great ignorance about Indigenous languages in general that leads to such views. In Naapi's world, the efforts speakers put forward to effectively breathe life into the acts of naming, observing, and describing go to good ends in that they reify life by focusing on the animate force within the subject, which then creates a bond between it/they and the speaker(s). Even in the case of intended harm, obstruction, hindrance, or death, the speaker's intent and objective toward the subject demands specificity, and the grammatical rules of the language reinforce it. In sum, the degree to which something is considered alive and the degree of animate energy it may have are reflected in the speech and the speaker's grammar in terms of *expressed intent*. Naapi's interactions with others throughout the stories recognize these others as living beings, even when he aims to or succeeds in hurting them.

Granted, this is not the animate/inanimate in the grammatical sense discussed earlier but rather the sense of infusing life within the act of expressing (with breath) that is significant. It is this unstoppable, indefatigable energy that is the source of Naapi's repeated resurrections. He will die accidentally or be killed in one episode, only to reappear as if nothing happened in the next one. As Goddard explains, features of the Blackfoot language have changed over time, another factor that makes it difficult to comprehend Naapi's basic energy. One way to account for this, even if the entire process is not understood, is to acknowledge that subtle elements of Blackfoot may have changed, which affects its current structure and pronunciation, and some features that are readily apparent may impact interpretations of Naapi. One of these elements, derived from evidence provided by early records of Naapi stories, includes detailed descriptions of the pronunciation of Naapi's name. A review of the orthography of some of the oldest recorded versions of Naapi stories shows that older versions often contain signs of additional silent vowels that are absent from more recent versions. These may be helpful or relevant in understanding Naapi's energetic makeup, since the loss of the terminal animate "-wa" ending may indicate alternative interpretations as the termination indicates life within the thought or name being expressed and is a key to correct interpretation and translation of -wa, the Blackfoot indicator of a single animate being.

It is likely that -wa was already being dropped from Blackfoot speech even before Uhlenbeck tried to capture some of the language. As a result of their Dutch background, Uhlenbeck and his colleague Josselin De Jong are unique among their cadre of contemporaries who collected Blackfoot stories; other collectors relied on sign language or oral interpretation and subsequent translation into English, French, and similar languages and were usually anthropologists, missionaries, government agents and surveyors, explorers, fur trappers, military men, or simply self-described historians. Because of these collectors' varied backgrounds and education, their compilations often show little concern for linguistic (rather than semantic) correlations and conversions regarding their respective texts. Collectors often focused more on categorizing by subject or story title than by structure. In addition, they were fully dependent on obligatory translations. Both of these conditions have extremely detrimental effects on the clarity of the stories' meaning in general and of Naapi's stories specifically, which often complicated comprehension even more; Naapi's essence as a vibrant element within a dynamic and living context continues to be replaced in the course of rough and approximate translations and by the near obsession with assigning a name that directly corresponds to an entity rather than simply describing its energy. This propensity to need nouns led to several names being assigned to the same story or Blackfoot term and to a static and staid correlation with fixed meaning, ostensibly to help place the stories by subject. All of these factors contribute to the harm done to Naapi's authentic expression because such stasis is the opposite of his typical free-flowing fluidity.

Concerning the fading out of the final syllable signaling animate status, Uhlenbeck likely heard and recorded correctly the Blackfoot speakers who assisted him by telling stories and explaining the history and language to him. However, as happens when a language is changing, some speakers show more evidence of alterations than others. Individual speaker styles and habits abound as well. Given that language changes are never universal in timing or style, the tendency may have shown itself unevenly even within a single speaker's speech patterns, not to mention across a range of speakers, and was further complicated by regional or dialectical tendencies and emphases. Uhlenbeck's data may simply express dialectical differences that he heard correctly but that other recorders of contemporary Blackfoot speakers failed to note or even hear. For instance, "NAPIW" [sic] (Naapi) (like many other ancient terms) is notable for being one of the terms at the core of this problem, as evidenced in Michelson's discussion of Uhlenbeck's deliberations on how to resolve this issue: "'There are many vacillations in the sounding of the language—and I have thought it better to express these vacillations in my way of spelling, than to efface them by an arbitrary uniform orthography.' I strongly suspect this 'vacillation' is one of hearing rather than of the language. Another point is that it seems to me that Professor Uhlenbeck has done the reverse of leaving these 'vacillations' graphically expressed."[100]

Duration has a phonemic effect in Blackfoot; it gives importance to lengthened syllables by underscoring the intention articulated in shorter syllables. This supports the view that Uhlenbeck detected subtle details correctly; he recorded varying degrees of emphasis in the spoken forms of Blackfoot, which manifest as longer expressions or extensions of the same ideas: the longer the sound is held, the more emphatic the speaker, the more pronounced the meaning. This careful recording accurately describes the way Blackfoot is spoken, thus Uhlenbeck's observations and descriptions match patterns of spoken Blackfoot; hence, his auditory perception is fine. Much criticism of Uhlenbeck's work stems from linguists' attempts to tie Blackfoot to grammatical rules and corresponding orthographies on which all linguists can agree. One problem with this is that the auditory/oral effect of the Blackfoot language that Uhlenbeck detects is not as neat orthographically speaking as his critics insist it should be. Michelson, for example, is not a Blackfoot speaker, so his criticisms should be read with this caveat. The following excerpt reveals the difficulty in Michelson's criticism:

> The most serious defect in Professor Uhlenbeck's phonetics is the non-recording of final whispered vowels. Occasionally he has heard them as full sounding; or possibly they were rhetorically lengthened in the cases in which he has heard them: if Professor Uhlenbeck had consistently used the makron this point could be determined. Examples of these are: *amoma*, this; *Napiwa* old man; *matapiua* people; *kanaitsitapiua* all Indians; *mata'keua* another woman; *ake'ua* woman; *kipitakeua* old woman; *kanaitapiua* all the people; *aka'itapiua* the ancient people; *na'tsitapiua* two persons; *einiua* buffaloes. But we find variants of most of these without the final a̱, and even on the same pages as the forms with *a: Napiu, amom, matapiu, akeu, kipitakeu*. In the recording of personal names and the names of peoples Professor Uhlenbeck is nearly consistent in writing [the] final *a* when the word ends in ua. There are other scattered instances in which the final whispered vowels are recorded as full sounding; but there are dozens of cases where final whispered vowels are not recorded in any way. It is difficult to understand how Professor Uhlenbeck failed to hear them as Wissler-Duvall in their works on the Blackfoot have properly indicated them.[101]

The annoyance Michelson experiences with the inconsistencies Uhlenbeck records targets examples that, according to Uhlenbeck, are noted as he heard them, and he further clarifies this point by commenting on its apparent unreliability. Furthermore, it can be difficult to mark every emphatic detail offered by speakers because duration in Blackfoot varies by individual, thus the meaning of one particular phrase or even of the same phrase used in different circumstances or uttered by another can change. Sentiment and communicative intent vary with length, so they, too, are not easily marked. As Uhlenbeck admitted, the same utterance by the same speaker was not necessarily the same every time.

As an Aamsskaapipikani (Southern Peigan/Blackfeet) and native Blackfoot speaker, David C. Duvall clearly has an advantage in notating accents or "silent" syllables. Duvall's records show that he may be a better transcriber or interpreter than some non-Blackfoot speakers since he was raised bilingual but not necessarily a better translator, since these are not the same skills. In short, there are many explanations for how differences in data occurred. On the subject of marking with diacritics, Michelson explains the comparison of silent vowels in Chippewa, contrasting it with Blackfoot, as pertinent to this discussion:

> Baraga does not record final whispered vowels in Chippewa; he does record some as full sounding; but whispered vowels exist, at least in the dialect of the Mississippi band at White Earth, Minn. For example *kiwabamag* really is *kiwa'bamagi* THOU SEEST THEM (an). The case is more serious when the word ends in *o*; here in verbs the pronominal ending *-wa* is left out. An example is *sta'mitoto* he then went to which I would write *sta'mmitotowa* (the first *o* is slightly shorter than the second). *Sta'mistapo* then he went, *iX'tapo'* he went that way *itsito'to* he came to, *sta'mitapo* he went, are other examples. Final *-wa* after *o* is far more difficult to hear than when after *i*; at times it is nearly inaudible, the movements of the lips alone betraying its existence. Very fortunately final whispered vowels are not as common as in Fox,—at least I have not recorded so many.[102]

Chippewa and Fox, like Blackfoot, sometimes need silent vowels at the end of these terms, and this may be the case for any number of reasons. It is also possible that the inaudibility factor is emphasized more on some occasions and is used to emphasize some specific meanings or is attached to dialectical custom. The articulations, whether verbal or made with lip motions or exhalations of air, are equivalent in meaning, but again, is this always true, independent of context? Lip movement is the only indicator perceived to convey the inaudible syllable in Chippewa; similar action relays the same pronunciation in Blackfoot. Despite his criticisms, Michelson nevertheless commends Uhlenbeck's attention to detail: "From my remarks on the phonetics, it will be seen that these texts do not come up to the standard set by [Franz] Boaz, [Edward] Sapir, [William] Jones, [Pliny Earle] Goddard, and others. Yet considering his brief stay with the Piegans (three months), and that this was his first experience with any spoken American Indian language, Professor Uhlenbeck has accomplished much,—more than could have been expected under the circumstances."[103]

Alas, the search for morphological and orthographic perfection or consistency in English phonological studies complicates Blackfoot language studies, particularly translations of Naapi. Michelson, who never heard the Blackfoot language himself, used written forms as the sole basis for his interpretations. Meanwhile, Uhlenbeck struggled to make sense of sounds he heard, despite unreliable production, to capture them entirely or to fit them into his limited knowledge of the Blackfoot language (a few months of limited field exposure). Not a Blackfoot speaker, Uhlenbeck was unable to fully account for the occurrences of these sounds, despite his best efforts to record them.

Markers distinguishing final-syllable sounds' loss from the linguistic and orthographic data collections of Naapi appeared as soon as they began to be made; his animate dynamic is of social importance or value, if not strictly in the grammatical sense of "animate" versus "inanimate." This may be attributed to the overreliance on linguistic questions arising from a Western tradition that seeks answers to questions more relevant to non-Indigenous languages. The prioritization of certain types of interpretations or classifications of terms, for example, might be vastly different when viewed from inside an Indigenous language or in consideration of sociocultural salience, as I have done in this discussion. Either the last few centuries' collections of Naapi stories have documented changing pronunciations of the term *Naapi* by contemporary Blackfoot speakers or the recorders progressively heard less and less, since earlier forms more often include the final vowel markers. Some Aamsskaapipikani (Southern Peigan/Blackfeet) maintain that such differences in pronunciation are dialectical, but it is a form that was also used by the northern bands (in Canada) two centuries ago. Historically, it may be a dialectical difference conflated with a reflection of changes linguists noted as the language started to transform, as it was dropped increasingly frequently. Its earliest disappearance might have been among some Aamsskaapipikani—the southernmost of the Blackfoot bands—who experienced earlier and more intense interactions with English, but records show some speakers still using it in this century, so the written records are contradictory on this question.

As Uhlenbeck explains it, his seemingly sporadic and inconsistent marking of the final word-ending almost or occasionally inaudible Blackfoot sounds was justified in that it reflected almost too exactly the variation in the speakers' utterances. Once he noticed the lack of any pattern he could make sense of, he chose not to mark the sound at all. He was too unsure to leave the markings as he thought he heard them. It is also possible that the Aamsskaapipikani, as determined by other members of the Blackfoot-speaking community, used an older style of speech or that just some did. This is consistent with the idea that the extra syllable was a remnant that still functioned in Aamsskaapipikani speech forms but was dying out in Kainaa (Blood), Siksiká (Blackfoot), and Aapatohsipikani/Skiniipiikani (North Peigan) speech. Or, alternatively, it remained as a particularity of the southern style while other bands' language never had it. Many Blackfoot speakers today say it was the old form that is no longer used.

Despite inconsistencies in sound production, it seems that a study of Blackfoot—particularly an oral literature study—could have prevented these sounds from being deleted from the text record, thus also from future studies of the language and texts therein. Accordingly, Uhlenbeck's response to Michelson's evaluations of his work is based on his reconsiderations in this vein, resulting in his producing a revised and refined explanation of his position on Blackfoot silent versus vocalized syllables: "Besides collecting new materials I availed myself of the opportunity of verifying the texts I had written down the summer before. The result of this certification is the following supplement to the list of corrigenda, published in 'Original Blackfoot texts' . . . By this new list the small piece of paper with some additional 'Errata,' accompanying those texts, has become superfluous."[104]

Uhlenbeck explains the logic behind the orthography he used in his 1911 study and presents his arguments for maintaining certain features of this method, as well as his reasons for changing other elements to include the sometimes silent animate vowel: "In this new series I have used in general the same method of spelling as in the texts published in 1911. A slight difference is that I have now preferred to write the ending of the inclusive first person plural of -*a* stems without an o̲, because in most cases it is nearly inaudible."[105] This new spelling convention removed the o̲ in between consonants as well.[106] Despite these spelling changes to more closely match what was heard, Uhlenbeck insisted that the emphasis on pronouncing the final vowel, -ua or -a, remained strong:

> I am well aware that my system is capable of refinement and improvement, though I hardly believe that some of the observations made by my reviewer in the "American Anthropologist" (N.S. Vol. XIII, pp. 326 sqq.) are absolutely correct. I admit that a sharper line might be drawn between *a* and *a*, *æ*, e and *i, o (a)* and *u* than has been done in my texts. But where I write -*ua* at the end of a word, the -*a* is a full-sounded vowel, and everybody, who knows something of Blackfoot as a spoken language, who has watched the Indians while talking among themselves, will confirm this statement.[107]

Ultimately, the placement of the stress on the forms of Naapi included in Uhlenbeck's studies, as well as the resolution he presents for how to deal with silent or vocally unarticulated vowels, is understood in light of the fact that Blackfoot speakers, according to Uhlenbeck, view more than one form of the word that represents Naapi as correct: "So *Napiu* and *Napiua* stand as equivalents by the side of each other (the shortest form Napi has a different syntactical value). Nevertheless there may be hidden vowels in some other cases, which escaped my hearing. It is a well-known fact, every moment to be observed, that often only part of a word is pronounced clearly, while the rest of it is not even whispered, but only indicated by articulation."[108]

Indeed, had Uhlenbeck acquired additional linguistic input from a wider range of traditional Blackfoot speakers, he may have had an opportunity to affirm his position—which is expressed more in his recordkeeping and data-jotting style than as an intellectual argument—that, fully articulated or not, the Blackfoot *-oa* or *-wa* final endings merit linguistic and morphological study as syntactically significant phonemes, however brief or inconsistent their appearance. In addition, Uhlenbeck highlights the fact that Michelson was ill-equipped to complete a description of Blackfoot morphology, since relying on written text of Algonquian/Algonkian languages with their unique expressions—whether vocalized or not—is insufficient to make authoritative statements about them. Along similar lines, Uhlenbeck justifiably questions Michelson's legitimacy as a critic, based on his inexperience and the fact that he never heard the language. He states, "I shall be glad if my reviewer will be able some day to give us an accurate description of the Blackfoot phonetics."[109] Uhlenbeck reminds that even though he was not fully aware of the orthographic significance in his reports about Blackfoot, there nonetheless was value in them at the time of publication: "The publication of these texts may cause some delay in studying out and publishing my morphological materials. Nevertheless I thought it advisable to have the texts printed first, because these are not only of interest to philologists, but may also claim the attention of students of ethnology and folklore."[110] These are the best texts he could produce at the time under the circumstances; they provide a glimpse into Blackfoot thought, oratory, and diction. Retracing the process of the loss of the inaudible vowel is central to unraveling the history of how or if Naapi's identity is transformed by its absence.

The old-style Blackfoot who relayed traditional stories to researchers, as well as Naapi stories, often spoke in older forms of the Blackfoot tongue. Their age or dialect may have played into the differential vocalizations captured in the data. Another issue was the choice of whom to select for interviews. Uhlenbeck presents the very real predicament many collectors and researchers found themselves in with Blackfoot speakers, especially while collecting ancient creation stories such as those about Naapi; keepers of some of the People's most valuable traditional information comprising these stories were less likely to speak about it to researchers, including Uhlenbeck. This made the job of translation and interpretation even more difficult, since the purveyors of such knowledge were also its best interpreters and translators. Uhlenbeck is grateful yet regretful: "I conclude this preface with the sincere expression of my gratitude to the Indians, who have furthered my scientific purposes. Still it is a pity that some well-informed and experienced men among the tribe were not disposed to impart their valuable knowledge, and that some others, who were willing to help me along, could not spend so many hours with me, as I should have liked and needed."[111]

The upshot of Michelson's and Uhlenbeck's arguments about Blackfoot pronunciation, orthography, diacritics, and translation is the decision to eliminate the dilemma of -oa and -wa by deleting it from future studies. Together, these two researchers' opinions have had a tremendous impact on the study of the Blackfoot language and hence on studies about Naapi. This debate confused the record of the ultimate fadeout of this final, sometimes vocalized vowel in further discussions of Blackfoot, at least those relying on Michelson's stance. For future generations of linguists, the world of Indigenous Peoples, and scholars of traditional knowledge, this standpoint exemplifies at least these linguists' power to complicate future studies based on arguments as to whether they can hear it, describe it, or comprehend it.

This situation should obligate a reconsideration of how Naapi and other Trickster figures like him exist in the literature, based on academic arguments that obscure the fact that the meanings behind the silent or not silent expressions go unanalyzed. If nothing else, it was noted that Naapi's silent or not silent final vocalization creates syntactical, if not semantic, differences. Then again, as I have pointed out, it is difficult to know whether there are semantic differences if researchers are unfamiliar with the contexts. Final, silent syllables are common across Algonquian/Algonkian languages, where breath is a key feature: "Learning to speak an Algonkian language like Blackfoot, Gros Ventres, Saulteaux or Cree is like learning to sing. The soft sounds of these most smoothly flowing of all Indian languages seem to hang gently on the breath like a lulling whisper, luxuriant in sighing vowels, and avoiding harsh consonants."[112] Naapi's animateness is expressed in the semantic aspects of his *energy* that animates living entities, and this gift of life was transferred to him from even more ancient precursors, his parents, Sun and Moon. One way "spirit" (i.e., "life") energy travels or transfers itself is by wind, air, and silent vocalizations that convey energy in silent or maybe just merely mouthed (physically articulated) air exhalations, all of which concern silent syllables. In this context, dropping syllables and failing to understand the way animate energy, not grammar, is articulated, either orally or by signs or gestures, means losing the trail that would lead us back to a knowledge of how to breathe and sing in Blackfoot—for if we cannot even hear it, how likely will we be to sing it? How do we know Naapi is real if we can't even say his name?

Our ability to interpret Naapi appropriately, to explore the ultimate meaning of Naapi, and to understand the energetic consequences of his name is key to understanding how the Blackfoot interpret his role and participation, not just what grouping of classificatory statements he belongs to in linguistic attempts to systematize his flux. The conditions or qualities of Naapi, as well as several possible referents to him, are considered here to query his identity as a referent of ancient Plains Peoples' environmental and cosmological knowledge. Blackfoot notions of personhood, agency, and participation shed light on old-timers' expressions of the term *Naapi* and its final syllable. The art of Naapi stories conveys functional and purposeful teachings to every generation *along with* the knowledge of local ecologies, cosmologies, and epistemologies because Naapi/Trickster's meanings come from nature, the original "Trickster." In these stories the Blackfoot language specifies locations, spatial dimensions, and experiences identified with locations that are often named for events that occurred in that space, sometimes multiple times. Places are renamed yet again after another remarkable or memorable occurrence there. Naapi's fluctuations play a role in this process. This is why it is essential to see that these stories are true.

Chapter 3

Myth, Legend, and Naapi

The Naapi stories studied for this book are not exhaustive and cannot possibly represent all of the stories that once existed or that still exist but were not considered in this discussion. There are literally hundreds of them, and theoretically, there could be more. Ideally, many other Naapi stories, including alternative versions of those analyzed here, will be given equal consideration in future studies. The selection and collection of the stories studied for this volume has been a lengthy and arduous process, and it was completed in the hope that it may serve as an introduction to the role of traditional Blackfoot stories that goes beyond discussing them simply as objects of imagination and ritual that guide votive offerings and ceremonials. Rather, these types of creation stories, including Naapi stories, are foundational, ethical, moral, spiritual, and philosophical tie-downs for Indigenous Peoples that are based in "truths" that are not necessarily "gods" of the natural world. Analysis of these Naapi stories necessarily begins as observations of and experiences with the natural world and as a shorthand for knowledge that takes several lifetimes to accumulate, organize, and translate into story form. That knowledge is codified in the linguistic, artistic, and cultural shorthand of the People; and the stories, in turn, shape interpretations of events and processes that may occur with more frequency or intensity than is customary. These, in turn, give rise to a cultural specificity that is accentuated by certain points of reference that Indigenous Peoples'—in this case, Blackfoot and other Plains Peoples' and Algonquian/Algonkian—stories hold as uniquely pertinent: the Peoples' homeland cosmology.

DOI: 10.5876/9781607329794.c003

Another feature of Naapi stories is the part whole, general-specific relationship between the macro- and the micro-levels of existence and matter and being in the Blackfoot universe. This is where planetary influences on seasonal weather patterns, adaptations by animals and plants, and the individual changes the Blackfoot make as a community all tie together. The stories connect items or topics from the ancient Blackfoot world that have a meaningful link but show no apparent relationship to the schemata and mapping of Western scientific (or sometimes pseudo-scientific) perspectives. The basic Blackfoot precept captured in the expression "We are all related," for instance, is examined through the actions and relationships expressed in traditional oral traditions, which include Naapi stories. Specifically, the minutia of the Blackfoot ecosystem with its flora and fauna is put into relationship with the cosmology of the People, and they are explored, even if unwillingly or even forcibly, in accordance with Naapi's whims. Larger ontological and philosophical connections link actions of individual plant and animal species, which are revealed through close inspection of the plants' appearance, habitat, growth patterns, structures, seasons, uses, and interactions with other plants, animals, and general surroundings. The animal species' activities, migrations, reproductive seasons, and many recorded interactions with each other—including their feeding, lounging, resting, and running spots and paths—are marked and noted for whatever significance they hold in the stories. Naapi stories include all of these elements and consider the range of information from each of them not only viable but equally elementary and pertinent. The significance of telling Naapi stories that name the land and the People and of focusing on events, processes, and changes the earth undergoes is one of the benefits the Blackfoot, self-acknowledged "Sky People," possess, as reminders of the Peoples' sky realm origins. Naapi stories relate the constant interchanges and exchanges between the sky and earth that gave birth to the Blackfoot.

Many works on the Blackfoot and on Naapi begin in the time of occupation—that is, after Western colonization began—and attempt to explain Blackfoot life-ways, experiences, philosophies, and stories from that perspective. This book begins with the time and place in which the Blackfoot came to know the traditional homeland through story and oral traditions about firsthand experiences that occurred long before that time. Indigenous Peoples' stories are nevertheless undoubtedly also influenced by the effects newcomers had on the homeland; the changes their arrival made to the land and environment brought immediate changes in the oral traditions, and their effect is still felt centuries later. Notwithstanding the impact these factors had on the Naapi stories included in this study, this work concerns the creation of the landscape that gave rise to a particular creation cycle specific to the Plains Peoples, from the earliest times recorded in Blackfoot stories. By maintaining this focus, central or foundational epistemes remain the core topics, despite drastic changes and adaptations in the stories.

My starting point for interpretations in this review of Naapi stories is the stance that *each Naapi story is fundamentally true*. Supplementing this interpretation are the stories and accounts the early non-Indigenous visitors to the homeland recorded. It is understandable that those newcomers and visitors knew little about the homeland and what the place means to the Plains Peoples. It is a given that the Blackfoot and other Indigenous Peoples have inhabited the space that is the basis of original understanding of the Peoples' homeland and that it has remained part of the traditional homeland since longer than we know. This is evident in these traditional stories that reflect some of the earliest geological and atmospheric processes known to the Plains Peoples, which are also recorded in Algonquian/Algonkian stories. These climate-based cycles have their own occurrences and respective placement in time and space and are recorded in respective landscapes. These are the energies captured in Naapi stories, and they are still generating life in the homeland regions.

WHY MYTH?

Ignorance of the landscape and its events and characteristics made non-Indigenous Peoples hear traditional Indigenous Peoples' stories as fantastical or mythical and imaginary constructions. Initially, this problem was not widely influential, but the long-term effect is that now, almost 300 years later, these stories are still mostly misunderstood. The legacy of these misinterpretations is continually misconstrued ideals and repeated assertions about what Algonquian/Algonkian patterns revealed or what Plains Peoples traditionally believed, knew, or practiced. Other evidence—outside of story—of early or long occupation of the homeland is difficult to discern if research is based only on physical evidence, although more recent studies have increased the estimate of how many millennia Plains Peoples have occupied or lived near their present and respective homelands. Nonetheless, such studies are difficult and awkward,[1] and locating the protohistoric or prehistoric evidence for a People's existence involves a combination of cultural and material relationships. Complicating this foci for this type of research is the fact that—apart from oral traditions and the Indigenous languages that tell them—early tools were made of biodegradable materials, which goes back into the earth, dust to dust, so the expectation that physical evidence could or should solely be used as "proof" of residence is ridiculous.

CO-EVOLUTION OF THE LAND AND PEOPLES

Justification for using traditional stories to understand Plains Peoples' life, in contrast, is revealed in life stories about what existed long before humans, Blackfoot or otherwise. The stories, while not physical entities as "evidence" themselves, nevertheless divulge a multitude of details of the first occupation of the land, of when it became habitable for humans, or of having been created in the shape Plains Peoples have long documented in history—with some stories discussing dinosaurs, ice ages, and prehistoric flora and fauna, climate, and geology. Glacial, wind, flood, and animal activities all created the paths, the cirques, cliffs, and bluffs; avalanches and icebergs cleared away and shaped mountain valleys and coulees; and now the snow and Chinook winds blast down these same routes. Animals traced paths to water and provided protection in the form of food, clothing, and shelter; their feeding grounds created soil that produced the rich flora Plains Peoples could eat—the berries, tubers, roots, bulbs, and herbs they gathered. These same plants sustained the animals, who in turn fed the People. The animals showed, through Naapi, how to capture them: what their weak points were, where they were most vulnerable, what their strengths were, and the many ways they were more powerful than humans. The astros gave guidance; the mountains vistas and the forces that make up the weather, environment, and climate became known as a powerful provider and contender that the Blackfoot called Naapi and other Algonquian/Algonkian languages documented similarly. All Plains Peoples relate these processes.

Robert Nathaniel Wilson collected stories during the time he spent among the Kainaa (Blood) band of the Blackfoot, beginning in the mid-1880s to almost 1900, in Alberta, Canada. During this period, he interviewed and wrote about some of the People's leaders. Wilson's manuscript includes a category called "Blood Indian Myths," which breaks down into "Star Myths and Origin Legends" and further into "Napi Stories," about whom he states, "Napi is the Blood Indian version of the creator and trickster."[2] Other recorders of Blackfoot story use similar subject-dominant separations by emphasizing the names of entities, for example, rather than focusing on the processes described with a Blackfoot expression. Some of this habit is shaped by culturally prioritized emphases or story collection. Much of this tendency is caused by the reliance on English, as opposed to being able to explain the stories' meanings in Blackfoot terms. Algonquian/Algonkian languages, like other Indigenous languages, express active processes with verb-centered grammar rather than with static states or names, which is characteristic of English with its propensity to prefer nouns. Separation of earth activity from the sky realm is problematic because Naapi comes from (i.e., is born of sky/atmospheric energy/wind) stories about nature, and if "nature" is tricky or creative, the same is true of Naapi because he *is* nature. Earthbound happenings are constantly interacting with and understood to be the result of sky realm phenomena, so such a separation is completely unrealistic. Other stories are referred to as myths, a useless designation because they pertain directly to reality.

The Blackfoot phrase "telling stories" does not translate to "telling tall tales," although many who record these stories do not distinguish between the two meanings. Blackfoot stories and storytellers refer to known phenomena; some are a physical and present reality, others not. All Naapi stories condense patterns and relationships that can be experienced, which in this case must be understood in the Blackfoot sense; this includes having heard about it, since Blackfoot grammar allows listeners to be participants in stories' action. Naapi is inclusive of nature, although as more than environmental or human nature but the whole of the connection between the many dimensions of Beings in the universe. Naapi stories are homeland-grown and are therefore the best models for our interaction with and within the Plains homeland. They encompass the dimension that refers to ourselves as our deepest spiritual and essential Beings and our most banal physical necessities.

Naapi stories teach that place existed before story, that space and place existed before we the People came into it, and that together they make us who we are. Naapi stories tell the story of the place and of the things that happened in this place, thus we have stories about it and about who we are as a People. Naapi is place *and* time: its condition and character; its history, present, and future; the lessons the place offers humans; and even the place's response when we fail to heed warnings about how to treat it. It is also the foundation of our work, worldview, and personality, our frailties and strengths, attentions and distractions. Naapi weaves together all the energies that make up our lives; he is the matrix, the most energetic, the highest point, the most forceful and active life form in a given scenario; he is the expression of the most virile dimension at work in any situation. The basic grounding of Blackfoot personhood is exemplified in the all-encompassing nature of nature itself, and much of this is told through Naapi, the original expression of Indigenous metaphysics.

The Blackfoot creation involves many beings and many phases, among them Naato'si (Sun/Old Man), Ko'komiki'somm (Moon/Old Woman), Naapi, and Naato'si's second wife, Ksaahkomm (Earth), all of whom were mentioned earlier. Roughly translating from Blackfoot, Naapi is a "Brother/Friend" to the Blackfoot People, meaning he is a recognized and unique personage or Being who created the world. He shares it with us People because we are a part of him (i.e., nature itself) and he of us. This is the origin of "opposite-speak." Naapi creation tells that at some point in the past, Naapi completed a major work in creating the world as we know it, although he did not do this alone. While shaping the world was a big job in Naapi's initial stages, he has not deserted the People because he is still all around; he

continues to demonstrate how to maintain life within the cycles and processes man-
dated by the universe's larger forces. Everything he did and does shows its mark in
the earth, to all Beings. He completed one phase of creation in recognizable phases
of work—first, the foundational stories, then those that are increasingly detailed
and contain very specific instructions so People may continue to live well. All of the
stories involve changes that are the result of processes, so they encompass phases of
growth, alterations, and the recurrence of even small actions that eventually produce big changes.

The deeper ontological questions of the Blackfoot worldview begin with the constant balancing going on in the natural world, the inherent alternation that is at
the heart of traditional Indigenous Peoples' concepts about what are understood
to represent the will or intent of the invisible energies called spirits or Beings, such
as those that live in the cosmos, and their powers more than human rights per se.
The Blackfoot paradigm incorporates a deep and intimate knowledge of nature in
which all Beings deserve the conditions and considerations necessary for everyone
to live richly and People are merely part of a network. The physical and philosophical life of the traditional Blackfoot is founded on such observations, which teach
that the survival of one species is the survival of all. Such lessons are still "the point"
of Blackfoot ceremonial life, and reducing Peoples' impact on the environment, our
"carbon footprint," is a key part of such work. For the Blackfoot, lessening the impact
of the physical and spiritual contamination by humans is paramount. The natural
world is a first-order teacher, and People can be first-order learners and teachers if
we attend to our influence. These perspectives are accepted aspects of the discipline
of Blackfoot life, especially for those who actively pursue deeper understanding
and reflection through active practice in the spiritual and philosophical traditions
passed down for generations.

This study's focus on Naapi stories and story language use addresses the question
of the creation of ethical boundaries. Central questions concern how these boundaries are constructed and reinterpreted as meaningful and necessary for People to
know and how they are defined, primarily in the interactions of natural phenomena
and universal forces at work. Trickster literature abounds with arguments about
Naapi introduced by non-Indigenous Peoples, who, for instance, had to rely on
children for translations. Not surprisingly, the forced fit of language *and* worldview
that permeates these renditions renders them difficult to make use of, particularly
for studies of language and concepts of the cosmos. To move Trickster discussions
and literature beyond skewed views, misinterpretations, and glaring omissions of
the story sequence necessitates a focus on minutia, the details of nature Indigenous
naturalists consulted daily. Traditional ceremonialists, the Blackfoot language, and
the People's own vows, visions, and dreams help us further our ability to know the

sources of the People's philosophical and intellectual life. The Blackfoot still retain a vital oral tradition capable of teaching People how Blackfoot intelligence and creativity link to the nature of spirit or the animate in nature.

LAND-BASED KNOWLEDGE

Here, in the land, is where all the explanations and interpretations of the stories reside; but for many displaced Indigenous Peoples, including the Blackfoot, learning from it is complicated, since much of the landscape has been dramatically altered or otherwise changed or destroyed. Similarly, Naapi stories are appropriately considered in reference to site locators and maps, but they are subject to destruction and desecration as it is, so I hesitate to pinpoint them here. Naapi's "playground" was drowned with the building of a dam, and his "bowling green" has also been altered. The mountains associated with him still hold their place, although his boulders have been removed or destroyed, his animals (e.g., buffalo) greatly diminished, and some birds (e.g., whooping cranes) exterminated, so they no longer have the same impact on the landscape. Nevertheless, as noted earlier, the sum of these locales alone cannot explain Naapi, Trickster-Creator-Destroyer, as place-based analyses alone are limited to land and sites and (once translated into English) to a noun-based space- and place-oriented project that loses the dynamic, unpredictable, "all-over" aspects of Naapi's activity.

To begin with, after mapping some specific sites, all sorts of unmappable material remains: climatologically and meteorologically based phenomena, Naapi's association with winds, stories about Naapi's sisters, stories that include his female partner/co-creator—all of which combine to form descriptive and discursive patterns not tied to a specific place. Finally, there are Naapi's maleness, recurring behavior, unpredictability, regenerative powers, playfulness, and perched-at-the-danger-point positions. Myriad references to Naapi include clues to his "home"—"where he likes to play," his "sliding place," his "perch," how he "floats," where he "sleeps," his "jumping-off point"—and several of his escapades result in his being responsible for the headwaters of trickles, creeks, rivulets, rivers, and similar bodies of water that "give shape" to the homeland and put all people where they belong, also referred to as where they would thrive.[3] Waterways map out boundaries. In each of these areas Naapi left his mark or some condition of the land that would be retold in story to recollect the formation and origin of all the coming generations would benefit from because its bounty was so rich and filled every bit of natural space.

Charles M. Russell, a western artist, spent a good deal of time among Indigenous Peoples in and around Montana, including the Blackfoot. Russell's friend Frank Bird Linderman collected Cree, Chippewa, and Blackfoot creation stories, especially

MYTH, LEGEND, AND NAAPI **79**

those about Naapi and his equivalents among other Indigenous Peoples. Russell and Linderman witnessed storytelling sessions that Linderman published and that gave Russell background on the Blackfoot worldview, which he used in depictions of Blackfoot in his paintings and sculptures. Russell reflected on Naapi—and his equivalents in Cree and Chippewa—and their creative roles, in particular how an authentic understanding of Naapi would prevent what he saw as virtual sacrilege in apparent war against nature, an attitude of non-Indigenous Peoples:

> Nature in Montana, Russell complained, had been disrupted when "nature's enimy the white man" arrived. The whites were inimical to nature, Russell believed, because they could not leave well enough alone and felt compelled to put their marks on things. He expressed his idea allegorically in a letter to Frank Bird Linderman, in which Russell responded to a Linderman story about Napi, the Cree and Chippewa god of creation, and Linderman's comment about a gem pin he had sent to Russell. Linderman had noted that the Old-Man, or Napi, had hidden many beautiful things, and Russell agreed. He added that unlike the whites the Indians—the meat-eating men that Napi had made—were satisfied with nature and used "what laid on the surface." Since their jewels were made of shells, elk teeth, and claws, Napi's "caches would have lane till the end of time Had not another man come. one he did not make—It was natures enemy the white man This man took from under ... He was never satisfide It was he who raised the Old mans caches an still hunts the fiew that are left When Napi saw the new thief he hid his fase in his robe and left this world and I don't blame him."[4] [original spelling]

Russell and Linderman share a respect for and understanding of the power of Naapi as an earth protector and provider, not as a myth or Sun but as an allegory about nature and how it provides us with all the gems, all the beauty we need in its raw state and offered with our barely trying. There is no need to dig or mine for riches because all of earth's bounty and blessings are already here.

Naapi goes into the exact spots where valleys opened up through the "Backbone of the World" (the Rocky Mountains) as a result of his moving things around and pushing himself through when he got stuck between two mountains. Naapi pushes and pulls everyone around, "playing" as he shapes the world. He is often "perched" in a position to have contests with his archrival, who is often some type of rock. Naapi can "lasso" rain near the mountains with his rainbows, which appear near the mountains just as storms and rain subside. Naapi's forceful actions on the land are like avalanches, and they often result in unpredictable consequences that "trick" others, at least for a while—and they trip him up, too. Naapi is powerful, white, and stringy haired; although artistic depictions are lacking outside of story, linguistic, geological, and geographical clues exist. Naapi stories describe a geological world when the present Blackfoot homeland is covered by water and Naapi creates life from a floating position. Naapi is there in the foothills when black clouds go to war with white ones; their conflict is told in a story that includes the birds that accompany their struggles. There are the fierce winds, the morning sunshine reflecting pink off the glaciers, the dark red sunset of a summer night lying on the cirrus clouds, and the blizzards and Chinooks—all somehow attributed to him.

The old-time Blackfoot had amazing abilities of prediction and worked with observations of past patterns in order to see the future; to determine the arrival of the "unpredictable" Cold Maker or Old Man of the Mountains, "Wolf Cap [was] a name given to a blizzard which usually comes in February and that was very much feared."[5] "Wolf" in the traditional stories is a reference to the action of the wind and weather, as well as to the literal wolf, as the wolves came with and acted like the wind and weather that shapes the homeland. The "unpredictable" Cold Maker, also known as the Old Man of the Mountains, is also the rain that arrives every spring as booming electrical storms said to be "reined in" by Naapi's power. Wolves' association with the weather patterns is what makes this connection so important. Too often even today, scholarship on Indigenous story and language forms does not consider the natural world relevant and instead attributes Naapi's antics to questions of a solitary imagination or worse, to a communal hallucination or fantasy.

Linear interpretations of historical time place Indigenous Peoples' arrival after the ice sheets retreated. Naapi stories seriously challenge such theories and establish Naapi as simultaneously a creator and a destroyer, so creations and re-creations, migrations and populations are all affected by his reiterative patterns and their effect on the world. Time, like his cycles around the earth, recurs. For instance, according to Blackfoot stories, one of Naapi's many "resting places" was on a hill that was 300 feet above the highest point ice sheets reached. They describe time(s) when the Blackfoot witnessed life *above* the ice line; stories tell of the big ice times when the camps moved to the tops of these hills where the ancient camp circles are still visible, something that has only recently been confirmed by research on the early climate of the Northwest Plains. Naapi's actions created a beautiful life in a very harsh climate, where life can be gone in an instant and weather's or animals' ferocity can kill a person in a flash.

Much knowledge is lost when the People are no longer in the homeland and thus are not able to observe the loud "crack" of the glaciers melting, the waters roaring, the thunder rolling, the birds singing, and all the sounds of life coming back to the prairie each spring. The Blackfoot, like all of the People's kin, live the landscape. The story of the People is the story of how among all the Beings in our world, Naapi is one of the biggest characters, shaping story forms, thinking patterns, and explanations of the world. He is at the heart of Indigenous Peoples' thought and expression of philosophy or worldview. To know him, though, requires paying attention to the close observation each Indigenous community has devoted to its unique surroundings and ecosystems. Each particular place offers inimitable opportunities to witness and participate in the rhythms and cycles that have been ongoing for eons. Indigenous People tell about them in oral traditions of stories and songs. In the eastern Rockies, home to the Blackfoot Creation, archaeological evidence shows that sacred homeland sites used today by the Blackfoot have been in continuous use for thousands of years. Naapi's activities also show that present-day rivers shifted southward into what is presently Montana from their original routes further north as a result of ice ages, since stories do not necessarily align with modern maps. Knowing this is key when following Naapi's trajectory through the Plains Peoples' homeland. The land developed at the same time as the People, which is what the stories say.

Numerous blessings and bounties are associated with Naapi and other Tricksters' insights; these stories offer admonitions and warnings so People know not only to be thankful but to be careful, too, for the abundance of today can easily be gone tomorrow. Nothing is guaranteed but the unpredictable, and having resiliency and patience means survival. The Blackfoot expression "*Mokakit ki akakimaat*" (Be strong and persevere. Naapi stories show how the Blackfoot learned and taught this. This is a motto to live by from the area's long-term inhabitants who for generations have become familiar with the local vicissitudes that are difficult for newcomers to understand: "It is utterly impossible for a person who is merely travelling thro. or even residing one or two years in the Rocky Mountains to give an accurate description of the Country or its Inhabitants."[6] This work's exploration of Naapi story language is truly about the landscape, environment, and ecology. The Blackfoot have long maintained that as long as the People keep the language, traditions can be transmitted as they were meant to be by the Ancient Ones. This book is based on the idea that the stories are easier to understand in Blackfoot because they need the distinctions Blackfoot syntax requires to validate an utterance.

REVIEWING THE ANCIENT FORMS OF BLACKFOOT
WITH A RETURN TO THE STORIES

Blackfoot's original inflections, lingering half-silent syllables as sounds or merely aspirated lip movements, include philologists researching proto-linguistics who consider Blackfoot one of the earliest forms of Algonquian/Algonkian linguistics, a prototype of sorts and possibly the earliest form of the modern language family. A study of the relationships across the languages in this family reveals the progression of changes over time and, by suggestion, the family's non-linguistic history:

"In general the pattern that emerges is that the greatest time-depth in the family is found in the west, with a series of successively shallower time-depths further east. A number of dialectical groupings can be identified, but except for Eastern Algonquian there are no major genetic subgroups descending from intermediate languages of any great depth . . . The most divergent Algonquian language is clearly Blackfoot. The difficulty in working with Blackfoot materials has been that the innovations are so great that any putative archaisms are difficult to identify."[7] Overall, these changes across the linguistic history make changes difficult to trace: "One index of the difficulties encountered is the fact that, to a much greater extent than any other language, Blackfoot has phonological sequences with no known Algonquian source . . . The search for phonological archaisms has not yet turned up any convincing examples; putative examples, as is typical for Blackfoot, are beset with difficulties . . . There are some apparent lexical archaisms in Blackfoot that seem promising."[8] This argument proposes that Blackfoot is the oldest of the language family "since it underlies the more widespread formative element found everywhere else. It seems probable that among the unique morphology and lexicon of Blackfoot enough archaic precursors of more widespread Algonquian features will eventually be identified to support the at present reasonable hypothesis that Blackfoot represents the oldest layer of Algonquian."[9]

Such stories offer specific opportunities to witness and participate in rhythms and cycles that have always informed Indigenous Peoples' lives. Storytelling, through story, song, prayer, or other oratorical or hand-signed or gestured versions, accounts for "crux characters"—the specific niches or ecosystems of a setting, micro and macro—who emerge. It then presents them as foundational sources from which Indigenous Peoples are invited to interpret lessons based on how much humans resemble Naapi. These crux characters and their reactions to and interactions with Naapi do not always refer to a particular animal, person, so-called anthropomorphic being, or even a plant. Rather, they can indicate a process, a cycle, a living entity that cannot be depicted but is represented by an animal (e.g., Coyote) or, alternatively, as wind, star, atmospheric condition, or cardinal direction, where context means everything.

Changes in meaning depend on directional sensibilities and location when speaking Blackfoot, precisely because relating Naapi's myriad forms in a brief synopsis is extremely difficult and of questionable value, especially to those unfamiliar with the context—that wonderful dynamic that changes entire meanings when speaking Blackfoot. Naapi stories traditionally capture the constellation of seasons, activities, elements, and forms that that world is centered around, the crucial relationships and interconnections that help balance and continue life. Using opposite-speak, Naapi stories invite reflection and connections more than do analyses and explanation. Blackfoot living in the world Naapi creates coexist in a condition of constant recognition of, indebtedness, and gratitude to his creations; Naapi's ongoing creation, as well as the Peoples' indebtedness and gratitude to him, are evidence of the overlap detailed explanations of him provide. Naapi stories' order is based mainly on seasonal and weather considerations but bear the mark of the specific locations. All Beings, including Sky Beings, those running on and under the ground, are also included; they all share the same space, so their interactions create a matrix within which all of Naapi's stories happen. Many themes thus recur and return to be presented again at a different time and place or context. In the Blackfoot language, Naapi's expressed and awesome far-reaching powers are evident to the Plains Peoples raised in the homeland, who experience Naapi's forces on a daily basis. For those unfamiliar with the climate or terrain of the Northern Hemisphere or the High Plains, it is difficult to picture the features that are highlighted in the Naapi stories. The Indigenous Peoples' unique surroundings and each place's particular latitude and longitude are opportunities to witness and participate in rhythms and cycles reflected in story. That is the uniqueness of these stories; based on the actions of Beings in the homeland as they are, mean comparisons can be made to other Algonquian/Algonkian and Plains Peoples' relatives such as the Cree, Ojibwa, and Iroquois Trickster-Creators and others who start in the Rocky Mountain corridor, extending eastward along the 49th Parallel all the way east to Nova Scotia, Canada.

These Trickster stories incorporate information from nature's cyclical redundancies, inconsistencies, and contradictions as they are borne out in specific geographic settings and times. The Plains and other Indigenous Peoples of the Algonquian/Algonkian linguistic family use Trickster stories and creativity and imagination to incorporate information from place-specific natural phenomena, entities, and energies that capture basic, locally available, yet universal relationships—laws of reciprocity, connection, kinship, reincarnation, and the importance of transfer and offerings—that mirror similar universal laws of energy in nature.

NAAPI PHILOSOPHY AND HUMAN/ETHNOCENTRIC ANALYSES

Plains Peoples' traditional ceremonial obligations are not about struggling to differentiate human People from the other Beings in the world but rather are oral traditions that reveal that the existing struggles are concerned with how People reconcile the need to eat, reproduce, and have shelter and friends in relation to other Beings' right to do the same. Central concerns are about how to integrate oneself into extant life-affirming systems. People are already differentiated, and with that difference they overpower and kill animals, plants, and even each other. There is no quandary as to how or if People differ from other living Beings. It is not a question of whether to struggle; it is a full acknowledgment that Peoples' use of their skills and abilities to end the lives of others is at issue. Naapi helps in this acknowledgment by crudely baring it all, with no shame.

Naapi stories offer People opportunities to reflect as a supreme act of self-awareness that forces a rethinking of our frailties and desperate attempts to make up for or otherwise address them. Naapi is at the crux of ceremonial traditions as stories about his parents, Sun and Moon, are at the foundation of the ceremonies and Beings recognized as the creators of everything, including him. Plains Peoples are not focused on the "progression toward humanity" that so vexes the Western mind. This progression is a sense of moving away from an animal awareness or state into something perceived as a higher-order Being. Naapi exposes the opposite; stories are dialogues—occasionally internal—in which Blackfoot are transformed and become, as closely as they can in sensibility, awareness, attitude, and capacity, the animal. He shows us how to become the animal for a time and then how to return to ourselves with a sharper perception and keener sensitivity for empathy. The stories succeed in reversing the world temporarily so that we may see, feel, and experience another Being's life, which compels us to perceive and understand it in relation to ourselves—a process that teaches us about ourselves and about other Beings who interact with Naapi.

The transition in thinking and in the physicality of Beings is an extension of understanding the Blackfoot. The transformations Naapi undergoes allow communication to flow so People can speak from the perspective of animal and plant Beings or be in dialogue with them. In reciting Naapi stories, storytellers switch from speaking in the first person as a plant, animal, or bird back to speaking in the first person as Naapi in a multifaceted first-person presentation from everyone involved. In return, we People—like the animals and plants, winds, rivers, rocks, hills, or other manifestations of nature—respond. This technique of switching perspective in relating a story shows that Naapi successfully turns things inside out, making us switch places and exchange identities with those we presume or plan to kill. We see ourselves in reverse, inverted, as the pursued rather than the pursuer, and we have compassion for them and their families and appreciate their gift of life to us, the People. This traditional dialogic form in which Naapi stories were told, as opposed to a narrator reciting the story, is the linguistic foundation of communication among animal, plant, place, planet, and People in the Niitsíitapii universe. The old-style stories include dialogues between participants and examples of them engaged in prayers, songs, dances, dreams, and different types of movement, depending on the players in question in a particular story. Narrators' voice is an advent of translations. Such distancing was not a part of the old-style telling in the Plains Peoples' and Algonquian/Algonkian languages' storytelling.

Linguistic structures used in story forms are not created only so animals or plants understand why People must take their lives, although the words in the prayers and songs indicate that this is on the singer's mind and is expressed verbally. The Blackfoot deem recognition of doing harm a necessary part of preparing for the hunt. Therefore, Naapi stories are crucial. They demonstrate that a major reason the Blackfoot need Naapi is to reconcile ourselves to the fact that we kill others to exist and that this is essentially who we are; this is *our* nature. Of course, we are not alone in that we kill to take care of ourselves. However, we are different from others (i.e., Bear, Mountain Lion) because when they do it, they are being true to *their* nature. That is their way. We need Naapi to remind us of who and how we are, so his stories define and affirm our identity while educating us about how to handle ethical dilemmas. Naapi's toils are exercises for the People, not for those giving themselves for the People. By his example, Naapi shows us who we are and why we do what we do and thus that we are fundamental to Blackfoot life. Reconciliation, gratitude, and offerings, which are the basis of ceremonies and prayers, are recognition of how People simultaneously justify and apologize for killing and taking; songs and prayers express our need to those we take with as much care and attention as is humanely possible under the circumstances.

The tragedy of so much attention being dedicated to "Trickster" figures as the antithesis of cultural and moral values is that little attention is given to understanding how such values have come about within Indigenous life-ways, as cultural mores strongly embedded in ecological aspects. Studies should consider the original physically embedded nature of the story to deal with matters of Naapi: the earth and the cosmos. Perhaps including them in Naapi stories makes Naapi's origins too "primitive," banal, or boring to merit the attention of scholars who wish to theorize the "higher" (i.e., "civilized") achievements of humanity. Scholarly study deems worthy the "achievement" of so-called cultural mores and moral universes, limiting them, of course, to human interaction. "Primitive" minds, which include non-human participants, that are recognized as grasping the physical realities about them are still considered somehow less sophisticated, theoretical, hypothetical, and philosophical. Purely theoretical approaches are unnecessary and even destructive to the whole of Naapi and his Algonquian/Algonkian relatives.

"Persons" in these traditions include other dimensions of our shared world, where Peoples' customs are based on the relationships that made themselves known when the People found themselves confronted with ecological constraints and spiritual realities. It was not usually necessary to bring down the entire system to know that one part of it was wronged or damaged. Naapi stories teach that rules for People were originally set by nature's limits. Naapi does not exemplify "clever" tricks or "unkillable" energies because he seeks to be the antithesis of everything ordered and good, nor is he the "imaginary hyperbolic figure" imagined in some academics' minds. Rather, *Naapi is the totality*, the sometimes overwhelming reality of ecological, social, spiritual, and emotional boundaries that simultaneously constrain and nurture People and to which the People must adhere. Such rules limit the potential destruction humans can wreak and still allow the environment and all those who live in and from it to survive. The People, in turn, also benefit, as we are not the only ones to consume other life forms, although Naapi stories focus on the destruction wreaked on every other life form by Naapi's wild or out-of-balance actions because People are the most dangerous.

Naapi is the veritable guinea pig, the canary in the mine. He gets to become imbalanced first to show us what we could become; he then calls out for help and we rescue him from the brink of disaster, time after time. Each Naapi story offers yet another opportunity to witness this cycle, and we People get to see ourselves again when we are forced either to see others rescue Naapi or to do it ourselves. This type of story invites us listeners—the People—to interrogate ourselves about what we would do in similar circumstances, with similar opportunities to abuse or take advantage. We have to consider the possibility that we may want to overdo it, reach too far, ask for too much, and then hoard it. Once we've gone that far, as far as Naapi does, what would we do to fix it or prevent it? How could it be different? How would we react to someone else who was breaking up the world? If we witnessed destruction, what responsibility would we have to fix it? Do we assume the right to rectify or rebalance inevitably destructive actions?

Naapi stories are based on a strict understanding that his interactions with the universe have bounced back on him. Rules delimiting humans' access to power to have an impact on the world are unintentionally discovered by Naapi when his schemes continue to backfire. Naapi's lessons—although learned vicariously by listening to stories about his adventures—are the truths before us throughout our lives and our interactions with nature and, most important, with ourselves. For the struggle is not whether we can live with others but if we can live with ourselves *and* others. Naapi presents the truth and consequences of our obscene excesses and of the destruction we cause, practicing on others and ultimately perfecting what we learn on ourselves. Failing to grasp the import of the opportunities to learn through his examples, we will succeed in destroying that which gives us life. Naapi stands before us, calling for help to fix whatever it is he has temporarily wrecked and usually on the brink of annihilating everyone. If we respond readily and responsibly in accordance with nature's rules, Naapi's destruction will be temporary, and he will reign only as long as he is tolerated. When the present conditions alternate, switch, shift, and adjust, thereby knocking Naapi out of his presumed position of setting a goal contrary to the rhythms of those already in place, those rhythms take over and reestablish themselves. Order reigns again. Soon enough, Naapi will resuscitate himself and chaos will take over again, but only for a while. So goes the way of nature.

Naapi will never be dead because we People have a propensity toward excess, which if left unchecked will revive him in both spirit and body. That is, if we succumb to selfishness, greed, ingratitude, or a host of other things Naapi stories teach listeners to reconsider, we become him. There is no "psyche" in nature, nor is nature remiss for omitting it. Naapi stories show us the potential for our own destruction: the misuse, abuse, and excess of others are ultimately suicidal acts, as these others are those on whom we depend. They also show how nature overcomes destruction through myriad chances for rebirth, regeneration, and renewal, just as we People are children of Naato'si, Ko'komiki'somm, Naapi, and others—all Beings that undergo visible regeneration: Sun every year, Moon every month, and Naapi daily, cycles that repeat for all time. We also share a characteristic ability to relearn, reconfigure, and renew ourselves. This is one of Naapi's most important teachings for the People.

Naapi is but one part of a long and complex series of Blackfoot creation stories, a characteristic he shares with other Algonquian/Algonkian and Plains Peoples' Tricksters. A major point of the many creation stories that exist among the Blackfoot and linguistically similar Peoples and among geographically proximate Peoples is that "the religion of these tribes (applying this term to their combined mythology and worship) resembles the language. It is in the main Algonkin, but includes some beliefs and ceremonies derived from some other source."[10] What this "other source," as referred to here and in other diffusionist theories, refers to is always some other human population. This theory assumes that there is a central place where certain beliefs or practices originate and that they are dispersed from there. The idea that a broad array of Indigenous Peoples, independent of one another, may have happened upon universal rules of earth, nature, or the environment by living within particular ecologies and that they discovered truths that are independent of human decision-making powers—even if these stories were subsequently shared—is simply not taken seriously. At the extreme of the "other" derivative sources are the teachings from aliens from outer space.

Understanding Naapi requires a broad consciousness, as observations of the natural processes are what give continued relevance to Naapi stories and to those of his contemporaries among other Plains and Algonquian/Algonkian Peoples. Blackfoot consider natural processes a source of information about sacred dimensions; thus when Naapi "travels," it is understood in a literal *and* spiritual way. Stories about Naapi's travels essentially represent Naapi, by his own definition, in a holy role that shows the opposite of that which is sacrosanct or spiritually pure. Naapi stories deal with considerations of material life and spiritual regeneration, and they are never exclusively about just one or the other. By revealing contrasts and contradictions in the virtuous or righteous or by being otherwise reflective of devout belief and pious living, Naapi is a teacher without equal. Knowing Naapi in this context unquestionably ties him to creative energies that are shared by other Blackfoot Peoples and to similarities in other Algonquian/Algonkian Peoples' creation stories and their concomitant practices and beliefs:

> In their view, as in that of the Ojibways, the Delawares, and other Algonkin nations, there were two creations—the primary, which called the world into existence, and the secondary, which found the world an expanse of sea and sky (with, it would seem, a few animals disporting themselves therein), and left it in its present state. The primitive creation is attributed to a superior divinity, whom they call the Creator (*Apistotokin*), and sometimes identify with the sun. After this divinity—of whom their ideas are very vague—had created the watery expanse, another deity, with the aid of four animals, of which the muskrat was the chief, brought some earth from the bottom of the abyss, expanded it to the present continent, and peopled it with human beings. This deity is commonly styled by them as the "Old Man" (*Napiw*), a name implying, as used by them, a feeling of affectionate admiration. He is represented as a powerful but tricksy [*sic*] spirit, half Jupiter and half Mercury. "He appears," writes M. Lacombe, "in many other traditions and legendary accounts, in which he is associated with the various kinds of animals, speaking to them, making use of them, and especially cheating them, and playing every kind of trick."[11]

Naapi is a vital Blackfoot creator/teacher who offers lessons that range from the construction of basic hunting tools to how to guard one's spirit from contamination and danger, all to ensure the continuation or regeneration of life. Naapi does not so much cheat or lie as he convincingly feigns to deceive, a necessity of survival in a world where one must eat and in which animals are often more perceptive than humans about potential danger and intrusion into their affairs. Naapi stories instruct humans to live effectively and successfully and to humbly accept that the world is not exclusively theirs. Hunters' beneficial or at least non-detrimental relationships with others are a prerequisite for living, given that socializing, eating, and surviving weather conditions are just some of their primary objectives. Naapi stories demonstrate and acknowledge animal wisdom and how to get around it while also respecting it. Such a goal necessarily involves a level of false impressions, since animals often detect People easily and quickly find ways to outsmart or outrun them. Naapi's ways cannot clearly be considered deceit, so this is a misnomer; they are an exercise in respecting an animal's desire to live while also finding a way to keep one step ahead of its awareness that the People want to kill it for food and use its body for shelter, tools, shoes, medicines, and similar items. In the end, if the animal's intention to remain alive enables it to escape, the People go without having basic needs met.

Finding a way to capture and kill animals quickly and without warning—otherwise known as Naapi's "tricks"—is also a way of keeping spiritually clean and is therefore deemed a worthy goal. Such a method might not only ensure success in hunting; it also obliges People to prepare for the act of killing another with prayers of thanks, offering, and exchange. Naapi's so-called deceiving of the animals, which drives them in ignorance to their death, is in this context an act of mercy and compassion, which contrasts with its interpretation as something "bad." Naapi doesn't shy away from his need to kill to live but rather teaches the People through his example how to make animals' imminent death less traumatic for them. "Tricking" them, in this framework, is a manner of preparing them physically, emotionally, and spiritually for what will ultimately be their death, and "looking ridiculous," as Naapi is prone to do, is part of this process; the focus is less on what Naapi does that could be viewed as absurd and more on what he accomplishes. Any "foolish" depiction of him usually results in his having made a fool of himself to achieve his ends, which he does quite well when he is successful at capturing game. Thus he is the opposite of a fool, since he is inadvertently smart enough to know how to use mere disguises to outwit others, which he's forced to do because they are so savvy. All his guile and getups communicate to the animals, and he often accomplishes his objectives, even if in story form it appears to be a result of a mistake or an accident. Naapi is a master model of how to conduct oneself in such a way that the animals will be obtained. Naturally, these lessons are meant to be interpreted by and applicable to other Peoples.

Many Naapi stories demonstrate how he misuses his powers of perception and perspicuity—excessively practicing, playing with, and applying them in misguided actions with the aim of duping People. Recall that Naapi moves others through his dances and words and songs, and this is how People stay alive. These examples are revealed as a clear misappropriation and dangerous use of knowledge, with Naapi as a prime negative exemplar, a model of precisely how not to be—but he gets the job done. Such reminders are replete in the Naapi story sequence.

Indigenous Peoples' oral traditions express an understanding of and have compassion for the distress humans cause animals and the rest of nature; the traditions show that feeding these nurturers is a way to compensate for the burden People place on the world and its extant organization. Naapi's stories and methods are also created to reduce these effects. Ironically, in spite of the negative reputation he has acquired, Naapi is really a conciliatory character. For instance, an animal that is forewarned of its impending death undergoes a change of chemistry in its body that doesn't just enable it to run faster or increase its sensitivity to its surroundings; the change also affects the quality of the food obtained by killing said animal by altering the taste and toughness, making its high level of fear come through in a "gamey" flavor. When animals are terrified at the time of death, it makes the meat less palatable. Indigenous Peoples the world over seek to mitigate or downplay the forewarning and frightening stage of the hunt or kill so that animals may go to their death unwittingly, which greatly reduces the time they have to become emotional or reactive before their death. Taste is one reason for caretaking during killing and ethical concerns are another, since the relationship between the two is not considered coincidental. On one level, Naapi's example demonstrates the Peoples' awareness that fear changes the quality of kills. On another level, the need for peace and resolution for those who may be killed is also considered, hence many offerings and prayers are made to and in honor of them.

Naapi is the first to originate the "games" or "tricks" devised to reduce the stress animals may suffer as they die so that killing will be less traumatic for both those killed and those who do the killing. These "tricks" are used to a good end and serve as a model for how to provide the best food for one's People. It is because of the dual nature of his work that the People say Naapi is simultaneously a destroyer and a creator, that he takes life in order to give it:

> In this being we recognize at once the most genuine and characteristic of all the Algonkin divinities. In every tribe of this wide-spread family, from Nova Scotia to Virginia, and from Delaware to the Rocky Mountains, he reappears under various names—*Manabozho, Michabo, Wetuks, Glooskap, Wisaketjak, Napiw* . . . everywhere with the same traits and the same history. He is at once a creator, a defender, a teacher, and at the same time a conqueror, a robber, and a deceiver. But the robbery and deceit, it would seem, are usually for some good purpose. He preserves mankind from their [*sic*] enemies, and uses the arts of these enemies to circumvent and destroy them.[12]

Naapi's complex character gives and takes, provides and denies, and elicits from communities of animal and plant Beings a willingness to be taken for the use of the People.

This apparent contrariness and these contradictions frustrate efforts to gain clarity about whether Indigenous Peoples consider Naapi part of the realm of the sacred. If operating from the view that being a creator of good things and providing for one's People's survival puts one in the "sacred" category, then yes, Naapi is sacred. This is true despite, and in part because of, his sacrilegious and disrespectful acts. If the focus of who he is revolves around acts that are meant to be precautionary or protective but are mistakenly taken literally as a model for the way to be, then efforts to understand him are doomed to continue to miscalculate his importance, and he would not be considered part of the "sacred" exemplars.

Naapi's complex nature continues to baffle academic and popular interpretations. For instance, "In Longfellow's charming poem, he is confounded with the

Iroquois hero, Hiawatha."¹³ Traditions around Naapi (and his counterparts) now even include Indigenous Peoples who would assume the best of him. Unfortunately, their reliance on Western-based models of scholarship as opposed to their traditional languages for interpretation makes Naapi incomprehensible. Judging from the review of the literature and the many Naapi stories considered for this book, the best way to evaluate Naapi stories is by *not* comparing him to other so-called heroes but by understanding his patterns as derived from nature itself. Algonquian/ Algonkian and specifically Blackfoot terminology that refers to Naapi in his many forms helps in such an effort. In his ethnological study of the Blackfoot, Horatio Hale encourages those who listen to Naapi stories to focus on the rhythms of nature, the patterns of the climate, the cycles of time, and the seasons instead of on a personality or attitude, a study of characteristics, or the sacred versus profane contrast. Hale conveys the value of such an approach to Naapi stories by presenting Daniel G. Brinton's work. In Brinton's view, Naapi's origin is found in a nature-myth, representing "on the one hand the unceasing struggle of day and night, light and darkness, and on the other that no less important conflict which is ever waging between the storm and sunshine, the winter and summer, the rain and clear sky." Napiw, the "Old Man," has, it seems, other names in the Blackfoot tongue. He is known as Kenakatsis [*sic*], "he who wears a wolf-skin robe," and Mik-orkayew [*sic*], "he who wears a red-painted buffalo-robe." These names probably have some reference to legends of which he is the hero.¹⁴ The names rephrase some of the expressions mentioned previously as referring to Naapi, and yes, they do connect to the stories about him and are also referents to seasonal signals the People attended to when Naapi was specifically "robed" in a particular way.

While still concerned about whether Naapi is any kind of "hero," Brinton importantly refers to Naapi's association with light as the "impersonation of light ... hero of the dawn."¹⁵ The power of the eastern sunlight that is referred to in many Trickster stories, of which Naapi stories simply comprise one family, is Brinton's focus: "From this direction came, according to almost unanimous opinion of the Indian tribes, those hero gods who taught them arts and religion, thither they returned, and from thence they would again appear to resume their ancient way. As the dawn brings light, and with light is associated in every human mind the ideas of knowledge, safety, protection, majesty, divinity, as it dispels the sprectres of night, as it defines the cardinal points and brings forth the sun and the day, it occupied the primitive mind to an extent that can hardly be magnified beyond the truth."¹⁶ These effects interact with meteorological changes of the elements, thunder and lightning, rain, wind, and the light in the atmosphere that intersects with the earth, the physical realm, and thus enters into the lives of the People.¹⁷ The range of expressions Naapi energy takes on includes blizzards (i.e., "charge storms"), and the rust remains in the form of iron ore at the bottom of basins where glaciers melted that match the young Buffalo calf with reddish fur.

These are precisely the types of details that are at the crux of how to use Naapi stories to interpret or forecast weather or other types of information contained in the stories. An extensive review of the ways these stories use language reveals that they are references to name changes as Naapi undergoes transformations. In this case, Naapi's names depend on the season, climate, or specific meteorological event. His present name describes key elements *at that time* and *in that place* to be on the lookout for when things transition. Red robes indicate warmer weather, since this is taken from the reddish hue of buffalo calf fur in the spring and summer. Wolf robe refers to winter weather, cold, snow, and blizzards. These meanings, of course, are not derived from or decoded based on one name or any single story; rather, they build on other stories and sociocultural references that orient the listener to know which cues to notice. As he appears in the stories, Naapi's name signifies the season in which the story is told, thus he may be called one thing during a particular time or weather condition and by another name during another season, spell, or set of conditions.

Such attention to detail is crucial for understanding Naapi's overall effect, since it reveals how precisely the Blackfoot language tracks his changes in large increments throughout the year and during smaller ones over the course of a day. Furthermore, it shows how the Blackfoot use Naapi stories to work into knowing, moving from micro-levels of personal awareness and experience to understand macro-level universal patterns about the landscape and seasonal weather changes in the homeland. Terms referring to Naapi indicate particular conditions; knowing what these terms mean recalls those conditions and hence the time of year the story takes place. All of these details are extremely important in terms of the information the stories convey. Keeping tabs on which terms are used and when in the telling of the Naapi stories helps listeners know what other details mean in the context of the stories being told. Studies of Blackfoot language use confirm what native Blackfoot speakers remark upon: it is practically impossible to know what Blackfoot terms mean outside the contexts in which they are used. It is essential to be mindful of this in trying to interpret Naapi stories. These examples of Naapi's name changes are only a few out of hundreds of examples of how the fluidity of name is the identifier of general situational fluctuations. It is said that People cannot control the weather, but Indigenous Peoples' pointed and precise details in stories such as these provide such an in-the-moment update on alterations in surrounding conditions that they give People a level of control over what to do in anticipation of or when things change.

In another example of this point, Naapi arrived after the original phase of creation, which is why he is sometimes considered a secondary creator. It is important to know what or who qualifies as a creator in Blackfoot cosmology to see that Naapi is, without doubt, also a full-fledged creator. The following is one explanation of the origin of the name of Naapi's creator:

> The name of the Creator, *Apistotokin*, . . . affords a good example of the subtle [*sic*] grammatical distinctions which abound in the Siksika, as in other Algonkin tongues. The expression "he makes," which, like other verbal forms, may be used as a noun, can be rendered in four forms, of varied shades of meaning: *Apistototsim* signifies "he makes," or "he who makes," when the complement, or thing made, is expressed, and is an in animate [*sic*] object. *Apistotoyew* is used when the expressed object is animate. *Apistotakiw* is the indefinite form, used when the complement, or thing made, is not expressed, but is understood to be inanimate; and, finally, Apistotokin, the word in question, is employed when the unexpressed object is supposed to be animate. By this analysis we gain the unexpected information that the world, as first created, was in the view of the Blackfoot cosmologists an animated existence.[18]

The "animated existence" here refers to the Blackfoot understanding that since Naapi himself was created by an animate and animating force, the same ability to give life was transferred to him. Naapi therefore can and does transfer life energy and thereby gives life to People, animals, land, weather—essentially, to all living Beings that inhabit or course through natural elements such as rocks, water, winds, plants, and animals. When Naapi stories describe certain processes that involve these powerful life forces, many include what non-Indigenous models of reality consider "inanimate" or reflective of meteorological or geological forces—for instance, such phenomena as winds, storms, floods, earthquakes, or blizzards. All of these types of forces occur in the Blackfoot homeland, and traditionally the People interpret them as actions and forces directly connected to the universe's creative forces and thus to Naapi energy.

Chapter 4

A Different Conceptual Order

The part-whole, general-specific relationship between the macro and the micro of the Blackfoot universe ties together items and topics that have a meaningful connection to the ancient Blackfoot. Encapsulated in the expressions "we are all related" and "all my relatives" (two of many similar expressions) are Blackfoot concepts and practices that tie cosmology to the People. The larger ontological and philosophical connections linking the actions of individual species of plants and animals are revealed through close inspection of the plants' appearance, habitat, growth patterns, structures, seasons, and interactions with other plants. Animal species' activities, migrations, reproductive seasons, and many recorded interactions with each other—including their feeding, lounging, resting, and running spots and paths—are marked and noted and related to the situation of constant exchanges between an animate earth and sky. The home of Blackfoot personhood is exemplified in the all-encompassing nature of these cycles within cycles, in which humans and nature itself are inextricably intertwined.

Naapi stories describe patterns occurring in the homeland and among the People in it. Place existed before People came and changed its condition and character, history, present, and future. Naapi stories illustrate how People may interact in place and indicate what they may not do. Traditional Algonquian/Algonkian and Blackfoot concepts at work in Naapi stories have modern equivalents in constructions of human rights, ethics, morality, philosophy, and humanity. The Algonquian/Algonkian paradigm incorporates a deep and intimate knowledge

DOI: 10.5876/9781607329794.c004

of nature into everything in which human rights are inseparable from considerations necessary for the People to survive as part of a natural universal network.
Blackfoot spiritual traditions, philosophy, and ontology incorporate these observations and teachings, which remain "the point" of much of Blackfoot ceremonial
life: the reduction of Peoples' negative impact in the universe consciousness in
Naapi stories.

Spirituality identifies moral and ethical boundaries that are meaningful and
necessary for the People. These are defined primarily through Naapi's interactions
with natural phenomena and forces at work in the universe, which are retold and
re-sung across generations to pass on lessons of the sources of our intellectual,
spiritual, and moral life; thoughts shape action, and reasoning and imagination
are linked with nature. Naapi stories' toponyms name special sites associated with
Naapi in landscapes that record and hold space for him to explain and interpret
their place and their personhood by relating his activities and to connect to the
living landscape through these shared stories. Blackfoot spiritual identity models
itself in relation to, and involves close affinities with, place and space to explain
metaphysics in the laws of reciprocity, connection, kinship, reincarnation, transfers, and offerings.

Naapi stories revolve around movement, specifically, points of transformation
between types of matter or in their locations or even the force of expression of their
direction of movement. Naapi's maladaptive and destructive behaviors are meant
to underscore the opposite; humans should be industrious, generous, caring, protective, and nurturing and possess other characteristics modeled by other Beings.
Cosmological movement, flora and fauna growth patterns, and climatalogical
rhythms are predicted and explained so thoroughly that ultimately no part of existence, visible or not, is excluded from integration into everyday and sacred settings;
rather, all that exists is accounted for in Blackfoot cosmology. It underscores characteristics, highlighting those most successful in absorbing the lessons demonstrated
all around and thereby making them a way of life.

Algonquian/Algonkian and Blackfoot ceremonial languages make special note
of indications that certain elements, shared space, or other Beings are affected by
changes brought by transformers. Naapi epitomizes adaptability, the skill to present a believable ruse so well as to earn respect, as Naapi models for generations of
Indigenous Peoples the range of knowledge of nature Plains Peoples have attained.
Power is one direct result of convincing changeability, and these understandings are
the basis for strict laws and social expectations for relationships between People;
they outline and define the nature of knowledge itself and of how to know how
to know. The intertextualities of Blackfoot life are brought by this forceful, highly
unpredictable, seemingly mischievous creator who is endlessly occupied making

new life and re-forming what already exists to the point that People officially recognize his influence on thought patterns, on explanations of the world, and on Blackfoot life practices and humanity.

Verbal play, like "opposite-speak," which this study regards as Naapi's key linguistic artform, also includes situational ironies to show human vulnerabilities. Each Naapi story reveals opposite-speak that varies, further complicating an already serious challenge to interpretation. Naapi's verbal play is a way to turn situations, perceptions, and roles inside out and upside down to reverse the expected order. Close observations of and participation in rhythms and cycles of natural surroundings and their concomitant systems and particular placing show Naapi's impermanence; he is not a particular animal, plant, person, anthropomorphic being, or static entity. Instead, Naapi is like the high point on a three-dimensional map, the area where the culminating point, the arc of the energy, the change in the direction or force of wind or a wave, occurs. Naapi is the highest or strongest point in the flow of processes, patterns, cycles, and living energies in multiple manifestations. Constellations, seasons, activities, elements, and structures form crucial relationships and interconnections that balance and continue life, in which he is a central or major driving force. Naapi's selfishness, insatiable appetites, rebelliousness, creativity, impatience, persistence, humor, presence, and longevity underscore his need to adapt and transform in the face of constantly changing conditions. He compels us to reflect on, recognize, and laugh at our own faults and foibles, as well as to discover our strengths—often through extreme tests, hardship, and near-death situations. Humor is key to Peoples' survival, just as it is for Naapi, which reflects ingenuity, imagination, and regenerative abilities derived from and integrated with nature. As a tool for self-awareness, it helps deal with even minor catastrophes. Interconnected stories and materials demonstrate fundamental recurring natures, cycles within cycles forming basic Blackfoot aesthetics, religious philosophy, and cosmography.

Howard L. Harrod deals with the Blackfoot language, noting that "Edward Sapir argued that Algonquin-speaking peoples were distributed as far west as the Pacific coast."[1] Similarities between stories are shared throughout the Plains and even among Plains People who do not share the language. Algonquian/Algonkian languages have similar stories, such as "How They Stole the Sun and Placed It," "How the Kiowa Became Paramount," and "White Crow Hides Away the Animals and Is Tricked by Sendeh and Spider Old Woman," which show how the Blackfoot share several features with the Arapaho, Kiowa, Cheyenne, Gros Ventre, and Crow.[2] Similarly, Blackfoot stories that feature "Old Man" (Naapi) are similar to other Plains Peoples' stories, and these are classified and summarized by Clark Wissler:

1, Old Man Series; 2, Culture Hero; 3, Ritualistic Origin Myths; 4, Moral and Entertainment Tales. A comparison of the myths of these groups with the published mythologies of the Arapaho and Crows indicates a very close relation between the mythologies of the Arapaho and the Blackfeet. Of eighteen myths in the Old Man Series, eleven have direct parallels among the Arapaho and five among the Crows. Of twenty-seven Moral and Entertainment Tales, ten have direct parallels among the Arapaho and two among the Crows. Of fourteen Culture Hero Tales, four have direct parallels among the Arapaho. Thus, out of fifty-nine tales, twenty-four were directly parallel to Arapaho and seven to Crow tales. All the Ritualistic Origin Myths seem to be peculiar to the Blackfeet, and may be regarded as their own contribution to their mythology.[3]

The categories and classification schemes created in the academic literature to organize and delineate Naapi stories from one another reinforce the cultural and academic paradigms within them, as well as their theoretical and linguistic limitations and expectations. In a throwback to times when diffusionist theories and structural linguistics arguments predominated in discussions of Indigenous Peoples' stories, these summaries and tabled comparisons were de rigueur. In them, similarities and differences among story versions, types, and styles abound, despite misnomers and misclassified stories. Unraveling and rediscovering Naapi's true meaning requires deconstructing the ideas behind these organizational schemes and reconstructing more appropriate ones. This process also entails reuniting and synthesizing stories for an overview.

HUMOR WITHOUT PROFANITY

Naapi stories are humorous nuggets that convey important ecological and social facts that the Blackfoot know influence the survival of all the People. However, the Blackfoot do not confuse humor or laughter with a lack of seriousness, which is often assumed by non-Indigenous collectors of these stories, who thus miss the point. These views are presented along the following lines: "Old Man [stories] are told by the Blackfeet for entertainment rather than with any serious purpose, and when that part of the story is reached where Old Man is in some difficulty which he cannot get out of, the man who is telling the story, and those who are listening to it, laugh delightedly."[4]

On one level, these stories are certainly meant to be humorous; Blackfoot use laughter as an instrument of reflection, making it a prime instrument for philosophical or meditative study. Naapi is not a buffoon, however, and while the sacredness of his character is debatable, his role as an early creator was traditionally viewed with great respect. The Blackfeet "name for the Supreme Being is *Na-pi-eu*. Its literal translation is the Old Man or, more respectfully, the Venerable Man. As his existence antedates that of the Indians,"[5] Naapi is a preexisting energy, just as all the elements of the universe predated the People. He, Sun and Moon, and others watch over the universe, a relative of all creation, the invisible spirit that infuses all of it and who is explained further throughout the corpus of Blackfoot stories and their accompanying songs and dances. The relative sacredness of Naapi's name or being should focus more on the sacredness of his teachings than on literal interpretations of his actions, a discussion taken up throughout this book.

Naapi stories tell about the way things are, and aspects seen as vulgar or indecent reflect conditions as the People see them. To Blackfoot speakers, the power of each utterance is so profoundly rooted in the culture and speech act customs and not simply in psychology, protocol, or etiquette that speakers are entrusted with a rather heavy responsibility to be accurate. Moreover, storytellers love to exaggerate and make things more dramatic and impactful, thus such details should be read as an element of truth telling:

> Profanity is not indigenous to the Blackfoot language . . . The Blackfoot Indian, in
> his primitive ignorance, regards the human body as a perfectly decent and inculpable member of the natural world; the Blackfoot does not see his body as a sexual
> fetish, and he considers neither any portion of his body, nor any of his bodily
> functions, nor any of the terms which describe those functions, to be in any way
> reprehensible. And since the Blackfoot does not take it upon himself to decide
> the relative purity of his neighbor's conception, or to determine in advance the
> post-mortem destiny of another person's soul, it was left to the super-culture of the
> White Man to elevate the Blackfoot Indian even unto the artful employment of
> profanity and imprecation.[6]

Blackfoot's capability to convey extremely precise speech means that speakers must make definite choices in their utterances, but the point of this excerpt is still well taken; when speaking a language that allows specificity to such a great degree, it is crucial to know the boundaries between what can be known and what one can say they know with certainty. There is only so much room for interpretation before the opposite of what is being stated takes over. This "opposite-speak" is a central feature of Blackfoot storytelling and of Naapi stories especially and is the source of much of their significance, influence, and especially humor.

Emphasizing Naapi stories' "entertainment" value further advances the false impression that these stories are important only for their ability to amuse or distract. While Naapi storytelling traditions do invite laughter, Naapi is nevertheless central in the People's ceremonial life. Naapi stories review some of the most important and serious considerations the Blackfoot hold dear, including laughter. Focusing solely on the humor, however, is to misunderstand and degrade their worth—they are so much more. Spotted Eagle, well-known for being very humorous in gesture and in mimicking sounds, told the serious story of how Naapi made the homeland and all the People in it: "The ancient Indian traditions of Old Man have left their impress in many geographical names of this region, as Old Man's River, Old Man Mountains, Old Man's Slide, and Old-Man-on-His-Back Plateau."[7] The Blackfoot still acknowledge this special link: "There are special places in Blackfoot territory where the ancient stories of our culture happened. This is where the Spirit Beings changed into human form and gave us our sacred ceremonies. These places provide physical evidence that the events really happened and are part of Blackfoot history. Sacred places connect the Blackfoot to our territory, are part of our identity and are the basis of our claim to this territory."[8] Specific formations, such as mountains, hills, valleys, and gullies, help the People study the cosmos and the earth's sustaining flora and fauna and recognize their unity. They are traditionally marked locations because their unique features help the Blackfoot as hunters and collectors of and participants in the surrounding cornucopia, both materially and spiritually.

These beings do not "turn into" humans in these places; rather, they become comprehensible to the People, a difference that represents more than a semantic differentiation. It points to a Blackfoot understanding of transformation and communication, wherein other Beings transform their usual mode of communication and use signs that are comprehensible to Blackfoot. As a "communicator," Naapi conveys messages between all of creation's Beings and the Blackfoot by changing from being unintelligible to an intelligent being worthy of respect and reciprocity. Thus in Blackfoot, "being" and "becoming human" mean learning to be intelligible and intelligent with regard to other Beings and to be understood by them. Transformation of all kinds is possible but is not registered unless it is noticed, since even spirits want to communicate, and these transformations are evidence that they do. The universe is speaking all the time, even though the People only get some of the messages some of the time.

Geological processes and formations that gave form to the Blackfoot homeland's riverbeds, mountains, plains, forests, caves, and glaciers and that create their own weather patterns also have their unique terrains and plants that work together to form the rhythmic rhyme and reason of nature. It is upon all this that traditional Blackfoot life has been, and in many ways continues to be, based. Naapi stories teach this through patterns of repetition, time, and climate. The next section deals with how all of these elements intersect in the homeland and the language.

NAAPI'S CYCLICAL TIME IN THE HOMELAND

Because they reflect cyclical time, many Naapi stories are ordered in accordance with the seasons. Prehistoric conditions are the context in which the earliest Blackfoot stories were conceived and are their source; they relate conditions identified by natural science and history, reaching back an unknown amount of time. Linguistic, atmospheric, geological, anthropological, and other information from several fields of knowledge contributes to a conversation between disciplines, which for this chapter has been drawn from a variety of documents, oral histories, and ceremonial practices, even though the stories in this study cannot represent the entire body of Naapi-based explanations of the earliest times or of how the People came to know and become part of the homeland. Those included do identify local weather patterns, animals, birds, geological formations, and other elements the Blackfoot traditionally valued for their traits and the lessons they could learn from them. Throughout the Blackfoot storied traditions, Beings with the power to signal transformations or portend changes in the environment or who transform themselves to adapt to the larger context or environmental conditions merit a story that details how to excel. Naapi's "Trickster" character demonstrates how he achieved and maintains this status using his strengths of adaptability and transformation, frequently changing so rapidly as to escape any definite identity—except, of course, as the ultimate transformer, transgressor, and boundary breaker, in which cases this identity is ephemeral. At the heart of this book is the Plains Peoples' homeland generally—and specifically that of the Blackfoot—and a search for the earliest references from myriad Naapi stories about this co-creator of the People's universe in manifestations of the atmosphere: mist, ice, fog, drizzle, hail, snow, rain, rainbows, creeks, rivulets, rivers, glaciers. Naapi's archetype is based on observations of these forms and his adaptability over an untold span of time, making him timeless, ever-present.

Naapi creates the original homeland, placing each animal family where it can successfully reside, where everything—water, plants, medicines, and shelter—the animals need is provided. Naapi and other creators have designed things to work similarly for People in this time and space. Naapi is the only element that can transform itself from gas to liquid to solid, to mist and fog and back; he can potentially be all of these things, albeit only one at once and in any given place. His constant changing presents dangers and benefits to all of life, as the forms he takes are unpredictable—his most predictable aspect. Naapi stories about weather and animal and plant cycles differ every time they are retold, but they are also mirrors of each other. As an example of opposites: winter to spring brings birds, berries, and engorged rivers. These cycles recur repeatedly but are never exactly the same.

Naapi as "elder brother," creator of a great life, together with his family, is revealed in linguistic turns that occur regularly in ceremonial prayers, where the Creator-"Trickster" phenomenon is expanded and which belie interpretations of Naapi as a part-human, part-sacred person, a mythical character, or a trope that destroys the integrity of his wholistic creation. Naapi's earthbound co-creator status was related by old-timers who referred to Naapi in very reverent terms. George Bird Grinnell and other non-Indigenous trappers, missionaries, and traders later tried to understand and explain Naapi with misinformed descriptions in English and French. The Blackfoot, however, who were in their eighties and nineties in the mid-1940s stated in interviews that before all the talk about Sun and the ceremony commonly and mistakenly known as the Sundance, Naapi and Naato'si shared the role of "creator." When Grinnell and others wanted an explanation of Naapi they could comprehend, the Blackfoot tried to show them that Naapi was white—not "white" in the racial sense but analogous to early morning light. Grinnell and others then converted this metaphor to mean what they presumed the Blackfoot meant in explaining Naapi.

Two centuries later, after much confusion about the origin of this supposed likeness, the fact that the Blackfoot originally drew a comparison to the white man's *behavior* and not his *color* is still lost. Ironically and egotistically, Western-based models' interpretations often understood this "confusion" to mean that Indigenous People thought they were all-powerful, like a god. The old-time Blackfoot protested this interpretation and claimed that Naapi's image as a "buffoon," which seemed interesting and entertaining to non-Indigenous people, garnered more attention than the more somber stories. Hence, the misleading stories eventually became more popular among non-Indigenous audiences. This curiosity, together with such listeners' desire to share them as entertainment, in turn generated more retellings, to the point that these "buffoon" stories became the norm—whereas Naato'si and more serious Naapi stories predominated in earlier times, before they were excised from the corpus of Naapi stories. Historically, then, the Blackfoot note that the abundant non-Indigenous interest in Naapi's clownish doings fueled their production and reproduction. Indeed, some so-called Naapi stories were told to collectors before the storytellers admitted they were not Naapi stories. As a result, as time went on, the tone and content of the stories became more ridiculous in response to the non-Indigenous desire for titillation. Ironically, this tendency also affirmed the non-Indigenous onlookers' insistence that these stories were not commenting on anything "real" or particularly sacred. This view fed back into the storytelling traditions, eventually convincing even some Blackfoot of their insignificance, especially those for whom the Blackfoot language was being erased. Without it the People would have no recourse but to wonder if what the white man wrote is correct. Meanwhile, at least in publication if not in the oral recounting, violent and overtly sexual episodes were still censured and condemned, thereby further reducing their popularity and any subsequent circulation and Indigenous interpretation. Judging from the collection of Naapi stories available for the current study, these restrictions on repeating the stories continue to inhibit serious study of this essential part of the traditional story collection.

Notwithstanding these challenges, specific linguistic and landscape associations that accompany Naapi offer alternative explanations about his origins, purpose, and role. Some of these include archenemies like "Red Old Man" (Blackfoot) and "Round Fat Man" (Cree), which are rocks, rock formations, buttes, and mountains. Other sources are Naapi's various names, including the Blackfoot name for "Rainbow," "Old Man," "Cold Maker," "White Old Man," "Short Red Robe," "Old Wolf Robe," "Wolf Robe," "Old Man of the Mountains"; "old" in all of these cases means "has been around a long time." However, these names should not be interpreted as "a long time *ago*" or "chronologically, as humans age," a distinction virtually undeveloped in the literature. A reference to Naapi's meteorological essence is found in "Cold Maker—which is the Blackfoot name for climate—also the Old Man,"[9] but only a partial aspect, since *all* the elements and forces that originate in or interact forcefully with Sky Beings are in stories that describe the "'atmosphere' as the Indians characterize it."[10] Naapi is also personified as "Sour Spirit"[11] in yet another reference to the fact that weather conditions are interpreted as his expressions. Indigenous People nonetheless aim to refer to him whenever possible with unoffensive terms, since he—like all living Beings—is responsive. This is also likely why the traditional Blackfoot never characterize images of Naapi; he encompasses the whole environment, not merely the atmosphere or sky realm. Any depiction can only possibly refer to a temporary state or to a few select conditions from myriad possibilities from a kaleidoscope of patterns within patterns.

A pervasive mistaken opinion about Naapi is concisely and precisely communicated by the direct comparison to Sun: "Primarily the Indians were sun worshipers, but they also had a lesser, mysterious, more homely deity whom they called Napi, the Old Man. Anything which the Indian could not understand was believed to be magic, and therefore the work of Napi."[12] Unfortunately, similar views continue to predominate, presuming to point out errors in Blackfoot judgment. Such attempts continue to relegate Naapi stories to marginal consideration under the rubric of myths, fairy tales, and other things deemed nonsensical. Researchers unable to comprehend the Blackfoot world make comments like this one, which follows a long-standing academic tradition of accusing Indigenous Peoples of being confused rather than the other way around.

Fear of the sacrilegious or obscene and of the ribald appearance Naapi occasionally presents was behind the initial impulse to limit and censor the retelling and distribution of many Naapi stories. Newcomers' "sensibilities" tainted the perception
of Naapi, encouraged ignorance, and rendered many incapable of comprehending
the stories at all. Even those who considered themselves good listeners and excellent storytellers struggled with what could be repeated, fearing its pornographic or
otherwise disturbing content. They epitomize this stance: "The foregoing legends
are all that the writer has learned thus far, which may with propriety be printed in
a public journal."[13] Many agreed with similar summarizations of the general viewpoint on whether to edit or exclude entire Naapi stories. Similarly inappropriate
judgments about propriety, decency, morality, and other factors were shared by
most early recorders of Naapi stories and by those retelling them. Such determined
resistance still plagues the conversation and understandably destroys Naapi stories
or scars them deeply. Ideas of what constitutes "proper" prohibit the retelling of
these stories, a legacy that continues.

Traditional Blackfoot views taught no shame regarding the body and its actions and
functions; all were considered according to the way they were made and what they were
made to do. As such, if a story referred to menstruation, flatulence, excrement, mucus,
tears, sex, birth, death, or any other human bodily functions, People did not censor or
omit it from the Naapi repertoire, although the topic would influence the choice of an
appropriate audience. The general position of non-Indigenous People—and increasingly that of Indigenous Peoples—excludes most such stories from Blackfoot story
collections. Such extreme censorship reduces the nucleus of traditional Blackfoot
Naapi stories and unequivocally damages their traditional sequence and continued
sharing. This also affects the Blackfoot who adopt the limits on what stories can be
told—often on instructions from clergy, who label them "obscene," "heretical," and
"profane." This effort to shame the stories out of existence has had a chilling effect on
the enjoyment of telling the traditional stories and has resulted in a virtual silencing,
which is only worsened by their classification as myth or legend.

Naapi's already complex self was increasingly complicated by rules prohibiting
speaking of him imposed on the Blackfoot by clergy, Indian agents, schoolmasters,
and a host of other administrators of Indigenous Peoples' lives. To the detriment
of scholarly study and cultural continuity, these stories' order, sequence, and logic
have been greatly affected by the limits imposed on repeating them. Many are missing from the oral traditions, and it is difficult to know how many will be known by
the younger generations, especially as the language is increasingly diminished and
meanings are lost. This is unfortunate because it means the loss not just of Blackfoot
knowledge of its Trickster figure in a semantic sense, as a living creator, but also the
loss for other Indigenous Peoples.

Researchers also create problems for a proper interpretation of Naapi by taking him and stories about him too literally, based on existing misnomers and inadequate interpretations and on the perception of him as a recently evolved phenomenon. Analyses of some of these stories, such as "Lone Woman" and "Lone Pine" (see the appendix), determined that Naapi did not and does not represent anything having to do with creation.[14] Such conclusions are common; many non-Indigenous record-ers interpret Naapi's actions as so ridiculous, irreverent, and outright disrespectful that he could not possibly be a representative of Creation. Naapi has had a vital role in the Blackfoot creation sequence with a complex identity from the start, where strict ideals such as "good versus bad" or "sacred versus profane" that exist in the non-Blackfoot and non-Indigenous ways of understanding the Blackfoot do not apply to Naapi. Trying to fit him into such rigid roles misses the point of his stories and does him a disservice because Naapi's sacred energy is the key to his Trickster energy. There are no valid separation arguments in this regard, since both have to coexist. Naapi's connection to the sacredness that abounds in nature is in its own way hallowed.

The Naapi stories that Cecile Black Boy collected from her People, the Small Robes band of the Aamsskaapipikani, show that the traditional Blackfoot consid-ered the earth-Naapi connection a very close one. Her interviewees link Naapi to other creation stories with, for example, Naapi as just one among many traditional oral knowledge forms; other stories focus on stars and planets, other sacred Beings' origins, and the origins of ceremonial knowledge. This reveals the closeness such stories maintained in the Blackfoot consciousness. Although Naapi has commonal-ities with other Blackfoot creators, it is widely acknowledged that he usually fails at managing or controlling sacred energy or knowledge: "Besides the numerous tales about Old Man's adventures, the Blackfeet related an unusual number of star myths and many myths about the origin of sacred rituals, 'the rituals themselves being in part dramatic interpretations of the narratives.' There were also many adventur-ous, historical, and military narratives."[15] Black Boy's records of her People's oldest stories about all aspects of their lives necessarily include this character with such a rich contribution to their history. Other authors' obsession with stories of war is a reflection of non-Indigenous Peoples' interest in the stories and not a true reflec-tion of Indigenous Peoples' corpus of traditional literature or of Black Boy's work. Understanding the difference between "warriors' conflicts" and connections to the larger genre of Blackfoot coup stories as a struggle to survive nature's vicissitudes first also relates to the Naapi creation story sequence. These erstwhile competitions help judge the relative significance, or lack thereof, of Naapi stories relative to these crucial yet complementary dimensions of Naapi.

Naapi's actions are in sequence and begin a cycle or multiple cycles of existence, as Naapi teases, pulls pranks, and torments those with whom he interacts throughout stories in which he is a main player. There is no separate "serious side of his creation" from Naapi's "foolish and spiteful deeds"; instead, these elements are considered in conjunction with the assertion that *each story has a moral*: "All Blackfeet knew of Napi, from the serious side of his creation to the foolish and spiteful deeds he performed, this is where we get our Napi stories. Napi stories have been passed down from generation to generation in the Blackfeet Nation up until today. Each family has their own interpretation of the various Napi stories, but in the final analysis each story has a common moral in the ending. One story might teach a lesson or prove a point; whereas, another story may tell of how a certain part of nature came to be."[16]

Some scholars nonetheless take seriously the need to reconsider the position that Naapi is a purely foolish character. Author Hugh A. Dempsey's letter to his friend and colleague John Ewers hints at why Dempsey thought this might be important:

> I know the trickster-creator phenomenon is widespread but I've limited my studies to the Blackfoot. This has led me to a number of conclusions, some of which may be tested and others not. First, I do not think that Napi was always perceived as the ribald, foolish and mischievous character as he is portrayed today. I believe that these were only some facets of a very complex character but over the years, as Christianity and European ethics have come to predominate, the more serious stories of Napi have been discarded and he was relegated to the role of a funny guy whose stories were told for enjoyment only. There are some indications that these other stories in the writings of Grinnell, Uhl[e]nbeck, and others. Also, I believe (and have had it indicated to me) that there was a certain order in which the stories were told. However, no one seems to agree now of the order of those that have survived. Yet if one analyzes them, there appears [*sic*] to be four clearcut periods: the creation of the world and the things upon it; the adventures of Napi with these creatures and things; the creation of people; and Napi's adventures with them and the teaching of them, concluding with the marriage of men and women at the Women's Buffalo Jump. If this is correct, then the stories of Napi would almost seem to be Ulysses-like, starting with Napi as an unformed being, gradually obtaining good and bad qualities which would ultimately be passed along to the people. When he finally engineered the first marriages, he established the final social structures in order for the Blackfoot to survive on their own, and he disappeared from the scene by changing himself into a pine tree. Does it sound far-fetched to you? The fact that the stories of Napi's funny adventures with animals are the ones which have survived made it hard to place emphasis on [those] other aspects of his character. But I don't know if the lack of other stories is because they have been forgotten or because they never existed. However, I am continuing my research and analyses and I'm beginning to think more and more that my approach may be valid . . . Your key period for field work was in the 1940s and mine was in the 1950s. Today,

there are only a handful of people that I could even ask about cultural matters and I suspect that my success rate with them would be less than five percent.[17]

Naapi stories deal with the context of the stories' longevity in the Blackfoot homeland, where they mean far more than what they had been limited to in previous deliberations that overemphasized prankster/clown portrayals. Naapi's historical and geographical ties to the stories offer reasons to rethink preconceived conceptions of him:

> According to Blackfoot mythology, the trickster/creator Napi, or the "Old Man," made the first people at the beginning of time. When he made men and women, they at first lived in separate camps, but he convinced them to unite, and the first marriages took place at Women's Buffalo Jump near the Porcupine Hills of Alberta. The antiquity of Blackfoot occupancy also is implied in the name of the Oldman River, one of the main watercourses through their hunting grounds. It is derived from the Blackfoot name *Napiotsi-kaxtsipi*, or "Where in the Old Man Gambled," and a boulder monument paying tribute to the event existed for many generations on the upper waters of the Oldman . . . The reference to the old man, of course, was to *Napi*, not a white man. It fits very well with an account of *Napi*'s journey north from what is now Wyoming after the Big Flood, creating animals, birds, humans, and natural features of the land as he traveled. He ended his journey at Women's Buffalo Jump where he turned himself into a pine tree.[18]

Positive movement in Naapi studies requires a return to the land and to the language of the land. One huge blind spot of too many interpretations of Naapi is the complete lack of any physical or geographical content or context. In Indigenous languages and understanding, no reality exists without placement within it, so Naapi stories are marked by place indicators; further, *where* stories take place is paramount to *when*. From an Algonquian/Algonkian or Plains Peoples' point of view, this is logical, since time is cyclical. Studies that regard all interactions as between humans are therefore useless for getting to Naapi's purpose because such strong ethnocentric analyses overlook the fact that humans are only one of many types of Beings. Most of Naapi's antics and actions are reminders about the needs, intelligence, and sensibilities of others and are meant to be taken in context, literally, to teach about the life of humans in the ecological context of the homeland.

THE POWER OF REFLECTIVE PRACTICE: NAAPI STORIES AND SPEECH

Trickster elements in Naapi's nature are why he is foundational to "Plains cultural values . . . Trickster, that enigmatic and fascinating figure which emerges within

North American Indian traditions."[19] In studying Trickster, "We shall not review the interesting and sometimes tortuous arguments about this figure which have emerged in the various traditions."[20] These seminal viewpoints explain why Naapi still has not received adequate respect in research; an excessive focus on the particulars of researchers' disciplines fails to attend to the insights available from Naapi. Consequently, it is worthwhile to discuss Harrod's brief summary of the history of arguments about Naapi's nature as a response to claims stated therein.[21]

To begin with, Harrod focuses on Daniel G. Brinton's *Myths of the New World* (1896), which seeks to unite the seemingly contradictory aspects of Naapi's Trickster image: "According to Brinton, the Algonquian trickster figure emerged as a consequence of the influence of late accretions upon an original conception of a noble light deity. By a process of negative evolution, the god of light becomes the Great Hare of the trickster cycle."[22] It is curious that James Willard Schultz's (1926) work reflects this idea, as it is not clear that the Blackfoot ever communicated this perspective to him. Linguist Franz Boas "took the position that trickster elements in the oral traditions were probably the oldest strata."[23] Like other students of Blackfoot life, Boas's unfamiliarity with the physical context in which Naapi stories still occur meant he did not immediately present them as stories about the struggle to justify or legitimate Peoples' need to take others' lives, to take just one example. Boas's and other researchers' focus on Naapi stories does not see these stories as addressing ethical questions involved when, for instance, humans necessarily eat animals, consume plants, and take from the land so they can live. Lacking this important context and interpreting the stories without them, Boas saw only the Naapi who arrives "originally a self-centered, amoral character. As human thought developed, however, there evolved the notion of a culture hero who brought good things to humans. Furthermore, contended Boas, the more highly developed the oral traditions, the greater degree of separation between the figure of the trickster and the figure of the culture hero."[24] Harrod subscribes to the idea that Indigenous Peoples who did not differentiate Naapi from a proper culture hero—or at least so that others could understand the distinction—had less advanced intellectual achievement, and he presents the argument about the difference between "trickster" and "hero" in this light: "In the less sophisticated traditions, the Janus-like aspects of the trickster's personality are comingled."[25]

Unfortunately, the argument about the progression of Indigenous thought overshadows what Naapi represents while introducing quandaries for studies of Naapi that have nothing to do with him and are even contrary to his nature. Discussing Paul Radin's *The Trickster* (1956), Harrod states that "Radin also took the position that these materials represented a very ancient stratum . . . Radin developed a psychological interpretation which viewed the trickster as a representation of primal human mentality, appearing in its undifferentiated state. In the career of the trickster we see the human psyche struggling toward differentiation, and thus full humanity."[26]

Naapi stories are not measuring the progression toward humanity *as a move away from* an animal awareness or state, nor are they a psychological trope created to assist Peoples' removal from animals or animal nature. Naapi, in fact, celebrates the opposite; the stories are dialogues in which we the People become animal and in which the animal is us, and then because Naapi becomes us, this viewpoint switches back and forth again and again. This storytelling technique of switching the identity of the central character back and forth between participants in the story and of alternating the first-person dialogue and speech forms that predominate at each turn places the listener in the unique position of being able to inhabit more than one viewpoint during the telling of just one story. Add to this the fact that over the course of many Naapi stories the listener is able to inhabit the juxtapositions and contradictory viewpoints of all involved so that the listener is hearing Naapi's words spoken in the first person, as if the listener may actually be speaking those words. At another point, Naapi is speaking from the perspective of those he is interacting with, thus allowing the listener to become, so to speak, those Beings as well. The end result as we are listening to these stories is that we the People speak from the perspective of the animal, plant, or wind to us and in response as the animal back to us as the People—humans. Naapi's dialogic story form demonstrates how communication between animal and human is being made so that the animal understands why the human must take its life.

This is what is meant by the term *opposite-speak* in this study. This style of communication, which characterizes the speech of the frequently unwilling participants in Naapi's activities, allows all parties to show themselves. It can also be a situational opposition that is highlighted in the story, which is used to focus on self-reflection. Animals, plants, the planets, and winds show intentions, feelings, thoughts, and the like. These stories accomplish this task of self-reflection for the teller and for the listener; each can occupy different participant roles, which place speakers where they can empathize, have compassion for, and show mutual respect for others and vice versa for listeners. All Beings are included in these exchanges at the core of Naapi's teachings.

Radin, as summarized by Ricketts presented original ideas in his survey about the Trickster before he fell more in line with Jungian ideas.[27] He found and emphasized similarities between "the structure of popular belief, whereas the culture hero and the conception of a high god were the consequence of the activities of religious professionals, a class of shamans."[28] This position reiterates the sacred-profane distinction that certain sacred or holy concerns of priests were not the same as those of humble everyday people:

In developing his position, Ricketts uses the distinction between shamanistic activity and popular belief to argue that the trickster figure actually represents not the religiosity of priestcraft but the religious sensibilities of humanism. "The trickster may best be understood as the personification of all the traits of man raised to the highest degree. Man is sexual; the trickster is grossly erotic. Man is driven by hunger; the trickster will do anything to obtain a meal. Man is slow to learn from his mistakes; the trickster repeats the same blunders again and again. Man's lot is hard in this world, yet life has its pleasures and joys also; the trickster is continually being buffeted about, but he also has his fun and he always comes up laughing."[29]

This distinction makes no sense in Blackfoot because, as discussed previously, the so-called priests or highest echelons of ceremonialists in Blackfoot society know and tell of Naapi. They work in a field and specialize in knowledge that recognizes his contributions and participation. Naapi embodies these exaggerated behaviors and reflects what one looks like doing them, but the point of Naapi's episodes is to show us, the People, how we can damage other Beings first; as a result, we in turn destroy ourselves. Telling or listening to Naapi stories is an exercise in ethical and moral considerations, an act of reflexive meditation as "another" becomes us and vice versa. The "othering" of distance and dissociation does not occur in Naapi stories because of the way language is used. Naapi story lessons are not limited to quotidian concerns of mortals; they are on the highest level of spiritual and metaphysical aspects of Blackfoot life.

The many manifestations of hunger, for example, are a central theme of Naapi stories because hunger is a reality of all life, not just in its physical manifestation but in all of its forms, including spiritual and emotional. If Naapi demonstrates hunger's more extreme and obvious forms, he does so so that the People may learn from his episodes and antics to reserve control and prepare for the presence of all types of hunger in their lives. A major theme is to be prepared and ready for hardship and to plan for cooperation and companionship, however defined. Developing counterpoints and strengths against adversity is another part of the practice of these stories.

Laughter is also a central theme of Naapi stories. It should not be mistaken for simple humor, although on one level it is. It also is a reflection of wit, intelligence, and extreme vigilance, as in being awake or sensitive and sensible in the world. Laughter teaches the ability to detect irony, satire, jest, and, most important, the reversal of identity and fortune that befalls Naapi. It manifests itself often when Naapi acts in a manner opposite to what an appropriate and judicious response would be, which results in reversals contrary to expectations and lots of opposite-speak. The full meaning of this is explored in myriad examples found throughout Naapi stories.

Another theme is the ability to detect others' weaknesses, which is one of Naapi's greatest strengths. In his skillful practice it sometimes amounts to Naapi pandering to Peoples' vanity or to their assumed powers, among other human foibles. This is another dimension of his keen attentiveness and observation; seeing our weaknesses, so obvious to others, causes us to engage in a certain amount of self-conscious pondering. This intense awareness, it is hoped, encourages us People to see more of our true selves, even the parts that are the toughest to accept. Naapi's best teaching moments occur when he demonstrates these machinations, as they provide opportunities for us, the People, to see ourselves and how we can so easily be undone by our own insecurities, arrogance, and gullibility. We should laugh at the absurdity and potential for spitefulness, ruthlessness, or any number of unkind, wasteful, or egregious acts Naapi engages in, which the stories caution against doing through Naapi's oppositional example.

This is the opposite of yet another distortion of Naapi's intended effect, such as when "[Åke] Hultkrantz assigns the figure of the trickster to the category of 'myths of entertainment,'" a view based on the separation of Blackfoot "good" versus "bad" characters epitomized in the contrast between Naapi the degenerate and other, higher, better powers.[30] Harrod compares Hultkrantz's views to those he held previously:

> Hultkrantz took the view that the high god of American Indian mythology could be distinguished from the culture hero/trickster figure . . . The supreme being often plays little part in the creation, the most active role being taken by the culture hero. The culture hero has been evolved, through the story-teller's art, into the trickster, who is the "degenerate symbol of the evil and distorted in existence" . . . In his activity as culture creator and transformer, the culture hero may exhibit more noble qualities, but in other cases he may intentionally bring into being conditions which are harmful to humans. Hultkrantz continues: "More than any other mythological figure he has thus come to represent the somewhat capricious, dangerous, often malevolent aspect of the supernatural" . . . The trickster may also represent a tendency in human experience which incorporates the comic within the experience of the sacred but perhaps not with the intent that Hultkrantz indicates, which is "to ease the pressure brought on by the tense and solemn atmosphere."[31]

Hultkrantz critiques Naapi as if he were a representative of the supernatural, a category that does not exist in Blackfoot cosmology. Naapi's humorous dimension is borne out of our reflection on how insane, foolish, and self-important we look when we see ourselves in him, as he teaches us to laugh at ourselves and see our feebleness as People. Naapi is no mythological figure, nor is he a supernatural; he occupies the space and the force of the powers of the universe, which express themselves in the earthly, physical, and very tactile realness of life. This is one reason the stories present his many distresses so fully; he is hungry, angry, impatient, conniving, suspicious, scheming, jealous, dishonest, and unbelievably selfish—all things we People also feel. Through Naapi's example, we learn that we are no better than our own ability to overcome these infirmities, these sicknesses of the soul. Naapi stories do not refer to existence as "evil and distorted" except insofar as People, as demonstrated by Naapi's actions, maintain the potential to make it so.

Harrod also discusses Sam Gill's work on Trickster and his connection to moral principles as guiding human action by representing humans' desire to be free of morality and able to live without harm or restraint.[32] In this framework, Naapi is a Trickster who lives "characterized by gastronomic and sexual excesses that violate the normative structure of most societies. The trickster, however, is represented as being unable to violate the morals of society without consequence. He violates the rules, but he usually suffers in the aftermath of the expression of his boundless desire."[33] Gill believes that Trickster is literally the embodiment of "the human struggle against the confinement felt by being bound to place, even within the obvious necessity of such definition in order to prevent chaos."[34] To repeat, Naapi is not these things. Harrod maintains that the Trickster role is about emphasizing the "importance of the restraint and structure which are given to human life by the presence of moral principles and a shared moral ethos."[35]

One of the deep-seated yet vital assumptions grounding most misinterpretations of Naapi is that the Blackfoot assume that the world is created by humans, for humans, and practically only about and for humans. Terminology such as "humanism" pervades a world in which the People assume center stage of all things in life. In contrast, Indigenous Peoples' perspectives regard the entirety of creation as the foundation on which social and societal rules and customs are built. In the Blackfoot universe, Naapi stories guide People so they do not upset the inherent balance of the environment by killing or taking beyond necessity, which is correctly understood to be a true source of death. Whatever moral customs and practices derive from the understanding and application of ecological principles become core Naapi teachings, since Blackfoot interpret these stories as simultaneously ecological and social. Naapi stories' real grounding for teaching lies in their biological, spiritual, cosmological, physical, and social sustainability features, which by extension encompass and express the imperative for moral and social mores. The ultimate meanings of Naapi stories is not a human-on-human debate or a contest concerning social rules or customs or what Western-based theories refer to as moral or ethical laws; they deal with the matter of laws established by nature, which no amount of human engineering or ingenuity can alter permanently, although we can destroy them. We know this because Naapi tries to alter nature through many schemes and fails repeatedly. Naapi stories, based on these well-known and established regulations and limits, teach People about potential ecological disasters, population decline, extinction, global warming, and other horrors by going before us—which we court by our carelessness, selfishness, lack of foresight, and disrespect for nature's limits. Telling these stories through Naapi's perspective and mistakes allows People to preview such disasters—albeit on a small scale—so they first learn and then continue to obey the rules of the natural world. We can thereby, it is hoped, avert our own early or unnecessary demise by controlling our impulsive and meager-minded selves. This is why a theme that runs through many Naapi stories concerns the destruction of a food source, a first-degree crime. Naapi violates humans and, by following his antics from one episode to another, it is apparent that the rules that govern human interaction are based in rules similar to those he has needed to learn from plants, animals, and weather Beings and not coincidentally. Episodes in which he injures People occur *after* he has barely survived episodes of a similar sort with these other Beings in nature. The Naapi story order reveals how he learns first from others so that he may learn to operate and conduct himself appropriately in the world of the People. Wisdom is the result of awareness and is derived from the same source.

The Western obsession with polar opposites and the inability to reconcile the fact that Naapi and other "Trickster" figures are perpetrators of reprehensible acts solely to show listeners the clear lines of what is considered most sacred to a community are why structuralist analyses have been introduced and accepted as a way to understand Beings like Naapi: "Claude Lévi-Strauss interprets the trickster as a figure who performs a mediating function between polar opposites, such as human and animal; as such this figure is typically ambiguous and equivocal."[36] Naapi, however, bridges mutual comprehension between Beings because they are *not* considered opposites; rather, their similarities are underscored: they care about their young, they need to eat, they want warm and protective shelter, and they work together to help each other. These are just a few ways Naapi stories remind us, the People, to keep compassion and the "humanity" of these other Beings in mind as we take what we need—and no more. Plains Peoples' cosmologies are expressed through creators like Naapi *on the assumption of similarity, not the certainty of opposition.*

In another view, "Volney Gay interprets Trickster as the 'antithesis of the culture hero who provides order out of chaos, form out of emptiness, and laws and customs from disorder and lawlessness.'"[37] This stance also presents an opportunity to discuss the fact that Naapi does not so much create order out of various types of disorder but instead provides humans with examples of what happens when he—and, by extension, the People—violates the order that already exists. It is the flip side of what's already there; Naapi's "lawlessness" does not create "order." Alternatively, like water that covers a pebble thrown into it or an avalanche that has completed its slide, the way the water and earth resume their march, their natural movement, *is* the order. This is simply reaffirmed in Naapi's attempts to alter order to his liking and whim; it rejects him and leaves him disappointed that it has its own rhythms and he is mostly, although not completely, powerless to change the inherent nature of those rhythms, even if he can change some details temporarily. What he fixes more permanently is left alone because it works better that way, more in line with nature's imperatives. This is true even if his original intention was seemingly to vent his anger or mete out vengeance.

Again, unfortunately, work that remains consumed by considerations of human limitations apparently demonstrated by Naapi's violations offers no insight into the environment's role in revealing truths the People use to organize society. Naapi is in no way an "imaginary hyperbolic figure." To the contrary, he is the nature of our nature, as earth, animal, and ourselves. Just as the landscape and the temperature, the shapes of water and ice continue to change, so will Naapi always be involved in "playful disguises and shape-changing," as these are simply ways the Blackfoot and other Algonquian/Algonkian Peoples convey the reality of the cosmos and the cycles that pervade it.

Finally, the Trickster figures of the Northwest Plains Peoples contribute "to the preservation of certain specific cultural values which form the moral universes of these peoples. Trickster performs this function, among others, through playing the role of a negative moral agent, through whose action the normative moral order may be viewed. Other horizons of meaning surround these trickster figures, some of which seem interpretable through stories such as have been described. The main point of this analysis, however, is to emphasize the role which Trickster has in maintaining, through oppositions, the shared moral universe of the people."[38] This view interprets Trickster

> as representing the polar opposites of the cultural values we are interested in examining. In this sense, Trickster's acts will be understood as functioning to reinforce the normative social order, or at least to suggest what it is, precisely by striking and often obscene oppositions. In sum, Trickster embodies a deformed world, a world opposite to that which is envisioned in the creation narratives. From this point of view, Trickster may be interpreted as a negative moral agent, of being vicious as compared with [of] virtuous character. We can approach these traditions through an examination of the value oppositions that are evident in Trickster's behavior: reciprocity/non-reciprocity, generosity/stinginess, truth/deception, kindness/brutality, and bravery/cowardice.[39]

This view of Trickster is in error because it is antithetical to the conclusion that Naapi embodies the same world that gives People sustenance and life. Naapi's is not by any means a twisted or sick world but instead a welcoming, nurturing, and life-sustaining world, albeit with caveats and strict rules. Naapi lives in it, as do we, because it is a generous and compassionate universe, but it also demands acute self-awareness. Naapi shows us how *not* to be. Rather than being depicted as a twisted or immoral soul in a twisted and immoral world that he "embodies," Naapi's stories show how he mirrors us; he plays us at our worst so that he may forewarn us, guide us, prevent us from the most horrible elements and capacities within ourselves first. Simultaneously, of course, he shows us the potential for our best, our most generous thoughts, kind traits, and potential self-sacrifice for the good of the community.

HIERARCHY WITH LEADERS NO "LONE WOLF": BLACKFOOT LANGUAGE AND LIFE

Blackfoot linguistic structures' unique ability for expression allows grammatical features to reflect the observed natural world. Naapi stories about animals relay that ability, across several species in most herds and many flocks. Someone takes the lead in the community, and many communities are founded according to some hierarchical gradation among its members. The traditional Plains Peoples learned this from close-up observation and intimate knowledge of the animal world, and the truth of it finds expression in the Blackfoot language and linguistic forms, in mirroring ideas about living beings. Examine, for example, the description in the following excerpt; when a "pack" or a "herd" of animals replaces the spots where grammatical structures are mentioned, one can see similarities between Blackfoot social and animals' hierarchies:

> In Blackfoot, it is the egocentricity hierarchy which determines discourse promi-
> nence. First person ranks highest in prominence, second, third, fourth, and fifth
> person follow. Only by moving out of a certain position in this hierarchy and into
> another can participants change their obviation status. This option, however, for the
> reasons outlined above, holds solely for non-speech-act participants; the position of
> first and second person in the hierarchy, on the other hand, is fixed and their obvia-
> tion status is thus unchangeable. As a result, an entirely free switching into or out
> of [a] discourse-prominent position is possible for a participant only with a clause
> whose valency slots are exclusively occupied by non-speech-act participants . . . the
> Blackfoot obviation system is, in its handling of participants, superior to Indo-
> European subjectivization: not only patients . . . can advance to proximate position,
> but virtually any participant, regardless of its semantic role, can do so if it is included
> in the valency of a transitive verb and if an inverse construction is used.[40]

Blackfoot speakers include spatial-relational aspects of grammar in speech, since the language places a speaker physically in context with the valency of a transitive verb, which encompasses consideration of physical relationships in space. Storytellers recounting Naapi's activities and character speak as participants in the physical setting where the Naapi events occur. Blackfoot speakers also constantly include their own and their addressees' relationship to each other and to others, physically placing participants in the practice of speaking:

> The preservation of obviation statuses, however, is anything but the rule in Blackfoot discourse. On the contrary, repeated switching from proximate to obviative marking (and vice versa) is extremely common for participants in Blackfoot narratives . . . The giant is introduced into discourse as an obviative, then becomes the center of attention, which is manifested in proximate marking, and, as soon as he is about to disappear from the scenery, in words, is about to fade away from the mental screen of the speaker, [he] is again coded as an obviative. It is clear that here the notion of some abstract, pragmatic deixis is being expressed, coinciding both with Uhlenbeck's ideas about obviation placing the participants of a clause at different stages of "closeness" to the *ego*, as well as with the concept of foregrounding, i.e. discourse prominence. Such regular switches in marking would not occur if the proximate and obviative were notionally empty categories and functioned as purely grammatical reference-trackers.[41]

One effect of the ability to mark location in telling a story or in having a discussion is that it results in the recognition of membership, acknowledgment, and witnessing that comes from multiple sources and places them in their respective locations vis-à-vis the speaker. Algonquian/Algonkian languages' stratification of speakers and conversation participants into a hierarchy is elaborated on by Uhlenbeck in his description of what Regina Pustet terms the valency possibilities and requirements of the Blackfoot language. It is also found in what Uhlenbeck refers to as "the important distinction of centrifugal and centripetal forms, a distinction . . . which . . . in none of the Algonquian languages is so clearly discernible as in Blackfoot."[42] The distinguishing feature of these forms, as seen in the following description, is of marked movement through space:

> I call centrifugal those transitive animate forms which represent the action as withdrawing from the first person's self, centripetal, on the other hand, those whereby the action is represented as approaching the first person's self. To the feeling of the Algonquians, the other persons are at different distances from the centre, the Ego, so that the second person is nearer to the Ego than the third person, whereas the fourth and the fifth persons are still more removed. Forms with the first person as acting

subject and another person as patient, and those where the action is ascribed to the second person with respect to the third or fourth, or to the third with respect to the fourth or fifth, and to the fourth person with respect to the fifth person, are centrifugal, whereas those forms which express an action of any other person with respect to the first, or of the third or fourth person with respect to the second, or of the fourth person with respect to the third, are centripedal.[43]

It is difficult to distinguish the singular speaker from the hierarchy of the social circles in three Algonquian/Algonkian languages: Ojibway, Cree, and Blackfoot. They share the propensity to include and attach other speakers' involvement to the speech of one individual:

> There is a peculiarity in the pronoun especially observable in the Ojibway, Cree and Blackfoot languages, namely the *double first person plural*. This has already been explained under the *exclusive* first person plural and *inclusive* first person plural. As this is a highly important distinction, which ensures definiteness of expression, I shall repeat the explanation in another form . . . In the *exclusive* first person plural *Nitstunan*, a person speaking do[es] not include the second persons, that is the persons addressed. This exclusive plural includes only the first and third persons, viz.:—He and I; or, They and I. The *inclusive* first person plural or second first person plural *Kistunon*, includes the persons addressed, and not the third persons, viz.:—Thou and I; or You and I. Great care must be exercised in grasping intelligently and thoroughly this distinction, as it is very extensively used in the language, especially in the verb.[44]

As mentioned in the discussion of diexsis and spatial orientation, direction and location in space figure rather largely and specifically in Blackfoot. The language integrates spatial and social relations into grammar to create acute distinctions and strict relationships.

The expression "Lone Wolf," which has become a symbol for an outcast or loner, represents someone not deemed a viable Blackfoot community member. As such, it does not really exist in Blackfoot grammar or concept, since the idea of a singular figure contrasts with community and, as far as Blackfoot are concerned, no living entity survives outside of community. Wolf packs, herds, flocks, and other pairings and groups are loyal to one another as members of communities, as are human communities of People. Therefore, a Lone Wolf is perceived on a spiritual, social, physical, and grammatical level as the antithesis of creation and regeneration. By extension, this is also possibly a symbol of all that is literally wrong, dangerous, or simply unproductive.

As Blackfoot stories are shared, the emphasis of the act requires at least one listener; to convey stories about the People requires additional interactions at yet another level. At the very least this doubles its effect, since the storytelling event recapitulates the first action, the original instance of the happening, and then re-creates another in Blackfoot. A Lone Wolf does not live long. Just like Wolves, People ideally live within a moving, growing, changing, and viable community. Blackfoot grammatical forms replicate this preference: "In Algonkian, transformations from inanimate to animate are possible by use of grammar. An ashtray is regarded as an inert object until it is used, and then it partakes of motion; it becomes animate. Similarly, a lone person is felt to be an inactive thing, inanimate; but a plural number of persons conveys a strong sense of animateness."[45] As this book is based on a review and exploration of Naapi's many adventures, the requirement that he understand that the fundamental nature of life is to get along with and to assist and be helped by others becomes progressively clearer. Naapi is not alone, and neither are the People. We are all born to someone and into the family that is the matrix of life on earth, upon which Naapi travels, dances, and talks to us.

A DIFFERENT CONCEPTUAL ORDER

What if the questions an Indigenous linguistics model prioritizes can only be answered by listening to wind, water, and sound as the bases for animate/inanimate, sound versus silence, aspiration versus none? What if the life force that Naapi imbues is in conflict with, or maybe just not imagined in, the models for understanding the energy that inhabits a variety of life forms in the Algonquin/Algonkin linguistic studies based on Indo-European-based models of interpretation? "What if we do not seek their thoughts, because our thoughts, words, and languages are responding to a different conceptual order?"[46] We are asked to think about how we understand linguistics and the ways we can study Indigenous languages that use it. In his beautifully crafted editorial statement about using foreign tools to study Indigenous philosophy, the African philosopher Nkiru Nzegwu explains: "The dominant view of philosophy installed a regime of truth that limits what philosophy could be. But what if that view is no longer ascendant? What if we step outside its influences that for decades have exerted control on our thoughts, imagination, and beliefs? Seriously, what if we forgot about Descartes, Spinoza, Locke, Berkeley, Hume, Kant, Hegel, Marx, Hussel, Heidegger, and all those famous names? What if we do not seek their thoughts, because our thoughts, words, and languages are responding to a different conceptual order? How would we philosophize and engage our world—water, wind and sound?"[47] The same questions could be raised about the positions and values in the way Naapi and his escapades have been studied. Just as there are surely differing ideas of what constitutes philosophy, as well as different sources consulted for understanding, insight, and knowledge, the same is likely true for Indigenous languages. Models built on other traditions and applied to "minority languages" still maintain the options and perspectives available to their origins, and they become the basis from which others are identified and described. Maybe the words are different *intentionally*. Despite inherent limitations, there are many unknowns and questionable conclusions about Indigenous languages that can be better addressed by considering not just the grammatical but also the cultural and social aspects of language use. Many features of Blackfoot language use can increase our understandings and broaden the takeaway message about ultimate meanings in that language.

PARTICIPANTS AND PARTICIPATION

The Algonquin/Algonkin languages decide on eligibility for consideration as a "contributor" to an exchange or interaction, based not just on Beings who employ verbal forms of expression; indeed, to participate in an exchange, the main criterion is to be *present* for it. That presence may be physical or non-physical (i.e., as in spirits or invisible energies), and participants' actions may or may not be verbal. Broadening the category of who can be included as an interlocutor, even without a verbal contribution, is essential to understanding the ancient Blackfoot use of language. As such, when considering inverse inflection and obviation—for example, conversational participant rankings—discussions of personhood, patients, and the valencies of the verb (i.e., its options for participants) must necessarily be based on a wider concept of participation if the verb is to be understood in Indo-European languages. For instance, in Blackfoot this structure refers to situations when the action of a verb returns to a recipient or when a participant outranks an agent (of the action). To discover how these exchanges are met in Blackfoot by what is potentially a multitude of possible actors requires a broader concept of "person" (e.g., first person, second person, third person) for grammatical analyses to be reflective of the *intent* or meaning of the expression.

ANIMATE AND INANIMATE

In Blackfoot, "The coding of the second, non-agentive argument of the transitive verb also involves a differentiation between animate and inanimate"[48] The animate/inanimate distinction is such a foundational aspect of Algonquian personhood marked in the grammar of the language that it determines the role of the obviation and subjectivization by adding a dimension of the unknown to the use of grammatical structures. The very need for the use of obviation and inverse inflection may have to do with how the Blackfoot use language to clarify potential ambiguities created by the need to allow for the unpredictable and indeterminate in life and thus in the language used to describe it. Obviation and inverse inflection are two sides of the same coin, so to speak; they work together to organize actors'/participants'/patients' activity. Since there is much that cannot be known or named in the Blackfoot experience of the world, much less accurately described, this grammatical habit could be founded on an imperative to "leave room" for this reality in spoken Blackfoot. As such, "silent syllables" (i.e., voiceless yet articulated phenomena) may be likewise "holding a place" for meaning that is determined by the context at the moment the speaker is speaking, which is generally not available outside a context. This is another way of saying that speakers' meaning may be rendered or derived *in that moment in time*, but it cannot be determined as an abstracted, distanced-from-setting sorting thing. It is thus possibly also time-sensitive and has an expiry beyond the meeting that occurs when it is expressed. This participant-making technique moves, establishes, and reorganizes participants' actions/energy around space vis-à-vis speech and physically expressed (sounded and not) intents. It also accounts for and allows for energies that do not use verbal expression and may make no sound at all.

Recall that:

1. Obviation is an integral part of inverse inflection and is a grammatical pattern of suffixes.
2. Inverse inflection marks person on transitive verbs, which is accomplished by the special mechanism of participant role model ascription known as inverse inflection.

If the person-ranking system in Blackfoot centers on hierarchical ordering around the ego, with first person occupying the prominent role in an interaction, second person the next, and so on, a corollary to this is that depersonalization employs distance- and/or proximal-making techniques that move conversational participants to, alternately, the foreground or background in speech activities (e.g., to second- and third-person roles).

ENERGY AS ACTOR

The grammatical rules that govern Blackfoot speech do not just order the speaker in forms that represent seemingly automatic restrictions, artifacts, or vestiges of language forms that present things that just *are*, which speakers unthinkingly inherit just because they are raised speaking the language. To the contrary, grammatical structures, rather than just being the rules that somehow unconsciously govern speech patterns, *might be intentional* and made to correspond to a Blackfoot way of seeing the world, where space is occupied by energies wherein even so-called empty space has energy and therefore the capacity and potential, if not immediately identifiable agents, for action. That is, rather than accept the idea that language just is and speakers use it without conscious acknowledgment of all that it is doing, what if throughout the progressive development of the use of the Indigenous language, unknowable generations of its speakers selected or preferred certain expressions because they involved, in some perhaps even remote way, a choice to highlight something? This is the idea behind the question raised earlier about African philosophy but which could apply to the study of Indigenous languages as well, which is that over countless generations of speakers, might not the Peoples' values, cares, preferences, in short, any question of material import, find their way to influence the grammar? This is what is meant by the idea that different linguistic structures are intentional; they accomplish a meaningful distinction or possibility for speakers.

SOME EXAMPLES

To demonstrate the point of raising the question of whether intentionality is a potential framer of language forms, we can deconstruct some Blackfoot expressions such as "go to," "cut with," "come from," and "work for."[49] In context, obviation and its double reference to people/actors/participants is meaningful: it is used to control, identify, and define unknown and ambiguous energies that inhabit things such as a person's mind, wind currents, and the forces that live in the cardinal directions. When we look closely at the types of energy that obviation allows for, it is generally used to capture references to *space and time*;[50] thus prefixes refer to locative, directional, comitative, benefactive, and causative and to source and instrumental action. All of these are caused by energy. Blackfoot speakers have no issue with double referring to these potential agents and patients because they all work to rearrange action in space and time, a priority for Blackfoot speakers because it satisfies the need to signal recognition of both the unknowable and the unknowability of the unquantifiable while simultaneously keeping options open for non-human agents. The agent/experiencer roles can be modified on the spot through the application of obviation and inverse structures. Unknown energies occupy a main protagonist role regarding agency, and Algonquian/Algonkian languages express this cultural priority grammatically.

INVISIBLE WITNESSES AND RESPECTFUL DISTANCES

Algonquian/Algonkian oral traditions rely on actors/witnesses in interlocutor considerations, so the structural organization of speech also incorporates this understanding. To explore Blackfoot "participation" in speech contexts is to see how grammar reflects the priorities of the speakers' need to have action in space organized. These emphases may be meta-linguistic. Witnesses are one way to address essential concerns such as truth, validity, recall, accuracy, and other important components of speech. Speech acts in Blackfoot organize the contribution of each participant; thus "oblique participants" are crucial to grammatical expression of the mysterious, unknown, indeterminate non-physical energies that flow about and that influence peoples' thoughts and words (e.g., English "spirits"). These are the ephemeral, ethereal, metaphysical, universal energies that are accounted for in Blackfoot and Algonquian/Algonkian expressions that describe Indigenous interpretations and concepts of ultimate reality. In addition, these grammatical expressions allow for the inclusion of what in English we might refer to as "bystanders" to action. Blackfoot acknowledges their presence in grammatical expressions that not only are *not* directed at them but that also *do not expect* a verbal response from them. Their role is nonetheless indispensable to Blackfoot concepts of reality, since respect for unseen energies determines what grammatical expressions are allowable and under what circumstances. For example, saying certain things may rouse, call, concern, upset, or offend unseen energies (which are considered inanimate objects in English), so watching what one says in this regard is an essential part of learning to speak Blackfoot. Participation can be defined as action, which can be expressed by listening, being present, acknowledging others' views, and bearing witness—none of which involve the use of words.

The degree to which Blackfoot speakers regard grammatical correctness has a lot to do with how well speakers account for non-verbal participants. The idea that distancing (e.g., "proximate," "obviation") is inherently part of obviative and inverse use can be supplemented with the awareness that Blackfoot speakers must understand how to avoid offending unseen energies. Some of the need to create distance in Blackfoot has to do with not casually or accidently calling upon or directly referring to a plant, animal, moon, or wind, for instance, since this should only be done intentionally and with care. Euphemisms are often used to complete phrases and expressions that are purposefully designed to avoid possible offense. Multiple actors are all potential participants, since they all imply energetic though unseen power.[51] Blackfoot speakers need to be aware of how the "nearest" (i.e., proximal) Being is determined. To know this, speakers have to weigh the relative considerations regarding space, time, spirit, emotion, volition, and similar elements of unseen participants to account for physical, social, emotional, and spiritual realities. All of these exist without speech yet not without response from some entity who is not physically apparent, at least not at that moment, so participation is constantly fluctuating.

Constantly evolving facts and situations allow for movement of energy. The first, second, third, and fourth persons identified by researchers (e.g., Frantz, Uhlenbeck, Pustet) represent one way Blackfoot distinguishes witness levels' distance from firsthand experience. Firsthand experience assumes grammatical prominence, with other places following. It is also a way to account for and take responsibility for what is being said. The grammatical forms host relative status changes by many possible participants who, it is taken for granted, all have agency. Calling on the participation of one or another of these participants (e.g., by using second- or third-person forms) depends on the relative emphasis the speaker wants to convey. In Blackfoot, the order of the grammar has to be fluid enough so speakers can exercise this freedom to be precise in that exact context. Blackfoot discourse prominence highlights the cultural value of prioritizing firsthand experience. It also takes advantage of certain opportunities and limitations the brain has for retaining facts/memory to make the most of storytelling and memorized verbally conveyed facts.

BACKGROUNDING, IMPERSONALIZATION, AND DEPERSONALIZATION

These phrases (e.g., benefactive, directional, locative, and others such as time) are often translated into a best approximation of what is available in English, which is most often a passive construction (e.g., Uhlenbeck). For all the aforementioned reasons, this unfortunately creates totally unsatisfactory translations. It is possible that Algonquian/Algonkian languages created a system to speak about action and agency precisely because these constructions are reflective of, for instance, the Blackfoot need to relate the "what" to the "how" while ensuring that the grammar holds a place for myriad possibilities. The grammatical rules adhered to could exist because essential priorities require their role as energetic participants, directly or indirectly, in action. Converting these expressions into passive constructions destroys the core meaning Algonquian/Algonkian speakers intend to convey, which is that an agent is involved; passive constructions depersonalize action, causing the main protagonist (i.e., energy) to lose strength, focus, intention, and the like, and to lose the point. The power behind the story is thus lost and, ultimately, so is the purpose of telling the story itself.

One example of this type of confusion is an excerpt from a Naapi story that references Coyote's eyes with "he gave that coyote his eye back,"[52] where it is difficult to determine the referent. One is apparent in English, but it is not what the Blackfoot story intended. Similarly, another Naapi story excerpt is translated into the English expression "there was a state of being happily blown about,"[53] which is also confusing. The -op construction seems to eliminate all valency-bound participants (recall that "some words may be animate or inanimate, according to their meaning")[54] and leads to the conclusion that it refers to coyote. Although the story is ostensibly about coyote (i.e., Naapi), the Naapi story style is meant to place the listener/reader in the equivalent of a narrator's stance regarding expressions that are about all of us and yet about no one in particular. So the story can, through the Blackfoot grammar (when it is not translated), tell what is happening to Coyote as Coyote *and* as narrator. This means that "zero-valency" constructions are in fact the opposite: Blackfoot valency is impermanent but not without person, meaning that valency (i.e., person) is changeable: "The preservation of obviation statuses, however, is anything but the rule in Blackfoot discourse. On the contrary, repeated switching from proximate to obviative marking (and vice versa) is extremely common for participants in Blackfoot narratives."[55] This speaks to the movement of the agent and to its respective fluctuating power.

SPEAKING OF A PLACE IN THE WORLD

It is difficult to claim to stick to strictly linguistic concerns in translation/interpretation because there is no such thing. Purely linguistic analyses lack the contextual information necessary to make determinations about grammatical tendencies and rules, which renders them unable to fully capture what speakers mean by the use of certain forms. This can be remedied by references to oral traditions that underscore particular themes, names, processes, Beings, or, in the case of this book, the creation of grammatical categories that match the desire for or insistence on leaving room for ambiguity, for multi-valent options. This may stem from the Blackfoot People's regard for the sacred, for all of the things humans cannot control. The Blackfoot language, through the obviation system, allows for a "popping in," if you will, of other-than-human action even as it allows known agents to take part in the action being spoken about. When creating stem forms, when it is clearly and specifically known who/what actors are involved, they are named. It is thus possible to identify which participants are doing what, with the caveat that this is so far as we know or it can be known. Ambiguities of agency/force/source/benefactor are all ways to recognize semantic understandings and practical/physical realities about energy. That is, they articulate uniquely Blackfoot ways of interacting with the metaphysical considerations at the heart of grammatical stipulations.

Fusional forms add to the complex of Blackfoot expressions because they create yet another opportunity to consider such questions as the following: Where is energy? How does it move? How does it affect people? How does it alter and adapt itself? New, unexpected, entirely unheard-of expressions are created on the spot to address these questions. Space/deixis concerns are also behind grammatical choices in Blackfoot: "It is clear that here the notion of some abstract, pragmatic deixis is being expressed."[56] Where they remain unexpressed in verbal form, they nonetheless influence the rules for living and language. Rather than define the unexpressed as "semantically empty," what if we considered that they refer instead to a host of possibilities that are imminently available but as yet undefinable *if* called into action by speech? What if the indescribable is just that until it is given form in expression, when at that point it is named? Blackfoot allows for the immediate inclusion of the constantly evolving. The obviative and inverse reflect Blackfoot considerations in which "thoughts, words, and languages are responding to a different conceptual order"[57] that defers to subjectivity, chance, and the unseen's participation in everyday life and in the order of the universe. Like other Indigenous peoples, the Blackfoot consider sacred energy to be ever- and all-present, unpredictable, and expressed in multiple and varied forms that are multi-valent Beings. If they are being spoken about or to, they have agency (from the Blackfoot perspective), so depending on the context, their valency varies. The Blackfoot language structure accounts for this as it honors the life force inherent in many Beings and as it mediates our communications with them.

THE METAPHYSICS OF NAAPI MATTERS: THE APPLICATION OF THE EPHEMERAL

The Naapi characterizations and features introduced in this book are found throughout the Naapi story genre. Indeed, a multitude of stories explain how he achieved his Trickster moniker, a principal focus of scholars of Indigenous Peoples across academic disciplines. Naapi and his equivalents in other Indigenous traditions nonetheless continue to elude any definite identity or clear placement within a single academic discipline, thus giving rise to many different representations depending upon the lens of these disciplines, from religion to psychology to linguistics and others that address his Trickster-brother existence. This problematic is fitting, as Naapi is an exception in academe as the ultimate transformer. His most notable attributes are the conflation of his mutability, unpredictability, adaptability, and refusal to adhere to rules combined with amazing tenacity. The inability to fit his diffuse nature into any discipline perfectly or firmly is part of his allure and his most significant teaching. Adaptability is a greatly admired and valued characteristic, for it ultimately determines success.

Drawn from the earliest references to Naapi, these stories present the multiple forms he takes, often simultaneously, and reveal his power as a co-creator of the Blackfoot universe. The evolution of his characteristics is reviewed, with a focus on how Naapi maintains his status as the epitome of the earth's and life's changeability. The logic, language, and explanations in Naapi stories about the sources of life and how to maintain them are at their core the accumulated knowledge of countless generations of the People's observations of nature's cycles. Naapi story forms mirror these processes and model their manner of unfolding. The stories are therefore similar with every telling although never exactly the same: nature's cycles repeat, are re-created, reproduced, and retold, but they are always different. This book is therefore a linguistic, historical, geographical, archaeological, ecological, and anthropological "dig" through countless generations of Naapi stories.

Understanding Naapi's paradigm—which is capable of ever-new creations and stories with infinite possibilities for renewal—as an interpretative prerequisite requires knowledge of how nature is integrated into Blackfoot and other Indigenous Peoples' lives and how stories of it make art in origin stories that describe with incredible finesse and accuracy the lived natural world. They include the balance between life and death, planetary cycles, wind direction and forces, and the qualities needed for life to continue, such as pinpointing the precise conditions and places where it can do so. Naapi stories are therefore real, for they entail universal truths relating to the essence of life as it is presented to and interacted with by the Blackfoot. There could be more stories in the genre and certainly many more have been lost that show these patterns.

Blackfoot thoughts, reasoning, and imagination mirror the intimately linked natural world through Naapi, the "elder brother," a common ancestor and creator of life. Naapi is not, however, a part-human, part-sacred mythical character or a trope, although his actions help People understand their humanity. The Naapi-filled storied landscape identifies Naapi's actions and highlights locations with which he is originally connected, underscoring his descriptive and discursive patterns. These places are not easily distinguished or identified, and they require analysis, reflection, meditation, and observation, among other things, to be thoroughly understood and applied.

Naapi abounds in the intertextualities of Blackfoot life as forceful yet highly unpredictable power with multiple favorite hangouts, contests with rivals, and other forceful actions that result in relatively destructive and yet not entirely unpredictable creative consequences. Initially, Naapi often attempts to trick others or to get them to help him or otherwise be of service to him. Once he solicits help, he prefers to let others do the heavy lifting or deal with nuances, as he cannot be bothered. Then, when he gets what he wants, he is stingy and refuses to help or share with others. Ultimately, then, he tricks himself, since what he destroys or hoards eventually becomes bounty for everyone else. These episodes go on during the all-consuming and endless task of creating the land, animals,

People, and weather and shaping the cycles that define the patterns and forms of everything else. Naapi's defining characteristics include his unbounded, rash, impatient, shortsighted, selfish, voracious, appearance- and appetite-obsessed behavior. Yet he also seeks fun and work shortcuts, as he abhors hard labor or attention to detail and thinks he knows better than others, so he ignores their advice. His most important contribution is in ways to use language that helps People learn to see themselves, living the landscape and acknowledging kinship to Naapi and his influence on story forms, thought patterns, explanations of the world, and their humanness.

Naapi's verbal play and other artistic forms are found in our interpretations of his behavior and are integrated into the thought and art based on close observations of natural surroundings and their concomitant systems and particular placing in the world. They invite participation in rhythms and cycles, which are captured in story as characteristics that are the essence of his survival and of ours as well. In telling stories of Naapi's actions, we sort of tell on him and on ourselves; through him we reflect on and laugh at our own foibles and faults. Realizing that humor is key to survival, we can reflect on how our ingenuity, imagination, and regenerative abilities are derived from and integrated with defeat and death and also punctuated with surprising opportunities for laughter.

In a bit of a reversal created by the employment of opposite-speak and soliloquies, story outcomes outline the principal relationships, processes, and universal laws of nature that are established by Naapi as models for humans that mirror cycles described throughout the natural sciences and social sciences and particularly metaphysics, albeit in Blackfoot terms, that collectively describe the metaphysics of life, just as the Blackfoot testify that they are given to the People by Naapi. These original forces are created to be re-created in myriad ways in the visions and visual arts of the People: lodge, drum, beadwork, robe designs, face paintings, and the oral tradition and story arts include expressions of Naapi's creative powers. Derived from descriptions of material arts in Naapi stories, this story-language is unique and significant in its ecologically based approach to Naapi's formally transferred sacred and religious art and how these designs are given to the People. Cycles-within-cycles ecological systems are foundational to the oral tradition. They employ a methodology that interconnects stories with demonstrative, fundamental, recurring natures—a basic tenet of Blackfoot aesthetic and philosophy, or life-way. Together they provide the basis for the ideals and models of behavior identified by the People as preferable because they are life-sustaining.

Naapi is rooted in movement or changes in states or conditions. Specific points of transformation among types of matter, animals in certain locations, or the structure of elements, for instance, are key. For example, if it is acknowledged that the large boulders called *erratics* that are distributed throughout the Plains are moving over time, explanations for this are offered in Naapi stories. Furthermore, the temperature at which glaciers begin to melt and the routes their runoff takes are noted and explained in Naapi story. Changes of the colors of leaves, the budding of flowers, and the popping of berries are similarly contextualized. Moreover, when clouds make rain or wind causes dirt to whirl, when blizzards hit or adjustments occur in current environmental conditions, such as when rainbows appear, Naapi stories note, condense, and synthesize these conditions. These stories record change and thus predict outcomes.

Like other Tricksters, Naapi teaches People to observe that all beings leave traces on the earth and all mark memory and place, which is why they are included in Indigenous Peoples' oral traditions. Long-standing observations of nature are incorporated into Indigenous Peoples' comprehension of the cosmological order of the universe in which People actively participate; a few characteristics separate those who are most successful at adapting lessons demonstrated in nature into their way of life. Close observation of cyclic environmental truths shows that constant change is the way of things, sometimes arriving without warning. Naapi exemplifies maladaptive and destructive behaviors to be shunned and avoided because they are detrimental. Naapi stories simultaneously demonstrate how People may emulate the industrious, generous, caring, protective, and other favorable and admired characteristics of those who assist Naapi. Every Trickster story works at many levels of interpretation. Each story has various lessons, many of them offered simultaneously as a sort of double entendre. The immediate, physically apparent reality, on the one hand, and the larger ecological, social, and cosmologically relational level, on the other, exist concurrently.

FUTURE AND PREDICTABILITY: THE POWER OF
OPPOSITIONAL ENERGY AS CHARACTER BUILDER

These stories involve recurring past patterns that foresee expanded reality and are included in the most sacred Blackfoot oral traditions and settings. Consideration is made for the animals, plants, meteorological factors, and other-Person creation that are traditionally appreciated for their power to transform and adapt themselves. These creators share in shaping the world and are esteemed for their survival and the details of how they overcome odds and thrive. A main focus is on how each specifically contributes to the world's well-being.

The body of Naapi stories incorporates Indigenous Peoples' eons-old observations into a kind of shorthand, a central crux that unifies multiple art forms associated with knowledge composed of untold generations of observations. Some

Naapi stories notice instantaneous changes and make special note of those that indicate elemental, spatial, or other Beings affected by the changes described therein. Others are more longitudinal. Naapi's power as a transformer is in change that can "trick," which really means to catch off guard. His homeland jaunts are basically roundup time, collections of scientific, social, and spiritual rules of the traditional homeland that are much the same in other homelands, hence their powers as universally recognized storied paradigms. Naapi's behaviors practically compel a response as he communicates to future generations of Indigenous Peoples a range of knowledge about the workings of the earth, exemplified by his power to constantly and immediately change, constantly shifting and altering the forms he takes in unexpected ways and posing a potential danger to People who depend on a degree of constancy.

Naapi's single predictable aspect is fickleness, which encompasses multiple forms of life-giving forces within a single concept or phenomenon whose sudden, volatile, and irrepressible changes are potentially deadly. Naapi is, however, simultaneously a gifted life giver; his stories, reflecting the natural patterns after which they are modeled, repeat similar patterns and topics of birth, growth, and death—reflecting natural cycles and their important, reiterative, and lasting patterns. The Peoples' thoughts, reasoning, imagination, and definitions of knowledge stem from how stories flow through the land with starting points and special sites for certain incidents attributed to and named by Naapi.

While artistic depictions are lacking (outside of story), linguistic, geological, and geographical clues do exist. Some animals' ability to adapt to the weather by changing colors with the seasons is also accounted for, as is the knowledge that certain animals are able to compete with and kill People. Specific strategies animals use to hunt or, alternatively, to evade hunters are also noted. The pacing and scheduling of animals' migration routes and their esteemed value to humans are conveyed, and animals' hunting strategies and bird migrations, as pacesetters, mapmakers, and world developers, are established and their stories embellished with all the details about the ways they help Indigenous Peoples.

Naapi's ostensibly contradictory nature has spawned a multitude of studies that have produced little conclusive evidence about what he constitutes. Nevertheless, countless Blackfoot have contributed to the retelling of Naapi stories for centuries, and they still do in order to know how to live:

> From within the mists of their ancient origins, the peoples of the Blackfoot
> Confederacy tribes, Kainai, Pikuni, Siksika, have always referred to their tribal
> genes . . . This story, as well as other stories, was passed on through an oral tradi-
> tion. Storytelling, both of legends and of authentic historical facts, constituted the

Blackfoot people's life-purpose education system. Tribal elders were the custodians of tribal folklore, history and cultural values. Each storyteller, elders and adults, had his or her favorite introduction, always based on the natural environment. They used examples set by all life forms—human and animal—of how each cared for their young. These stories are examples of life's responsibilities and our rapport with nature and our environment. Old Man or Napi was half-spirit, half-man. He could speak to nature and to animals, the elders said, but he was also a trickster. He was very mischievous—greedy, deceitful, bad-tempered, vain—everything discrepant to a human being. These stories were told to teach people how not to mistreat each other! They also explain how certain animals, birds, or plants were translated into their unique characteristics. There is a moral or lesson to be learned from the storytellers' interpretation of a story. If the legend or historical account is beneficial to the people, the emphasis is always on cultural maintenance and innovations. If the story is traumatic, the moral or lesson is always on individual and group survival, both in terms of physical and psychological survival. The . . . legends . . . and historical accounts . . . were so much a part of Blackfoot life-purpose education.[58]

As discussed previously, Cecile Black Boy, a member of the Small Robes band of the Aamsskaapipikani (Southern Peigan/Blackfeet), a Pikuni, documented Blackfoot stories. She explains that "there are a lot of things to show what he had done and they still show the way they are told, such as these few I am writing."[59] Many of the first stories Blackfoot children learned were about Naapi, told in Blackfoot. It is hoped that this book can contribute to the continuation of the life of Trickster energy.

Appendix

Selected Naapi Stories

All of the stories referred to directly in the book are presented here. Several versions of the first story, "Person's Face," are offered as examples of the types of confusion and variables at play in any interpretation of these stories. For each of the other stories, one version is presented.

1. PERSON'S FACE

[Naapi's face at St. Mary's] "When Napi left these boys. After telling them that he was running a race to get some eagle tail feathers, after he had gone over a hill, he raced up a deep coulee which led to the mountains, until he come to two large lakes. He looked around and wondered what he was going to do to get away from the people that were after him and going to kill him. Then he thought to himself, 'I believe, I will go way up on this mountain, north side of this lower lake, and change myself into a dog and turn to stone and that way these people will not kill me.' So he goes up there, and after he finally climbed up on this high mountain he laid down on his stomach, facing east. He thought, 'This is the way I am going to lay and turn myself into a dog, then into a stone.' He laid there a long time and thinking, 'If I stay here, and if they see a dog form they surely will come and ruin the stone, for they will know that I have changed myself into a rock.' So he got up and thought, 'I will go farther back and higher up in the mountains and stay there and watch for them to come looking for me.' He goes way back up higher to the highest mountain and

DOI: 10.5876/9781607329794.c005

stands there in the side of the mountain, with just his face sticking out. There are times that this face looks like it's moving around. This tells how he was peeking and watching for the people to come in sight, looking for him. He turned into a rock and today he is still there. If you go up there you will see the face of Napi looking Northwest from the lower lake, on the north side of the upper lake, after he had left the first mountain he had come to, and where he was laying, on his stomach think- ing how he would lay, if he did turn into a rock. When you look at this mountain it also looks like a dog laying there on his stomach facing eastward. The people never did find him after that or knew what became of him. After the white men come up here to our mountains and given each mountain a name. There was one man by the name of Hugh-Monroe that went with these men, as a guide, took them to these two big lakes and showed them this dog mountain and the face. They called this dog mountain Almost-a-Dog Mountain and they named this face St.-Mary's face. So now both of these lakes are called St. Mary's Lakes; one is the Upper St. Mary's, and the [other is] lower St. Mary's. This Hugh Monroe was familiar with these mountains and lakes and had known where this face was, that's why he took these men over there."[1]

[Going-to-the-Sun] "If one were standing on its summit, 9584 feet above sea level, he would look almost straight down nearly one mile into St. Mary Lake. The unusual name has no connection with the height of the mountain or its imposing cathedral- type architecture. It is an inaccurate translation of an Indian name. Many years ago, according to the Indian legend, the Sun Father sent his representative, Sour Spirit [i.e., Napi] to the Piegans and Blackfeet to teach them all the useful arts—how to make a tepee, tan the hides of the wolf and elk, from which to manufacture mocca- sins and clothing, and other useful things. He showed them how to make bows and arrows that would kill the elk, deer and buffalo, and assure them plenty to eat. Sour Spirit lived with them a long time, but was finally called back to the lodge of his father in the sun. In order that his good work and teachings would not be forgotten, he caused the likeness of his face to be placed on the side of this mountain. It may be seen here today in the form of a great snowfield, the outline of which strongly resembles an Indian face with the head dressed in a war bonnet. Ever since that time the Indians have called it 'Mah-tah-pee-o-stook-sis-meh-stuk,' which means 'The mountain-with-the-face-of-Sour-Spirit-who-has-gone-back-to-the-sun.'"[2]

[Going to the Sun] "By the head of Upper St. Mary's Lake looms a mountain whose contemplative face looks like it might belong to an ageless old man who is always looking towards Sun. This is the imposing Going-to-the-Sun Mountain. The Blackfoot name for it is Matapi Ostuksis, meaning Person's Face. Unfortunately, no legend for either name has been recorded. Apikuni (writer James Willard Schultz) says that he named the mountain after one of his old Blackfoot friends told him that, were he still physically able to, he would like to 'go up on that mountain to fast and pray and visit the Sun.' Certainly the mountain was a popular place for the spiritual vision quests that men used to take. Since vision seeking often involved complete surrender of one's spirit to Sun, the mountain was very sacred to those who used it for 'going to the Sun.'"[3]

[Sour Spirit] "The superb peak, Going-to-the-Sun, undoubtedly the finest peak in the Park, commemorates the highly important personage of the Blackfeet— 'Sour Spirit.' 'Person's Face' is the real Blackfeet name of this mountain; but from an imperfect telling or interpretation of the legend by the Indians, or an imperfect understanding of it by white men, the name 'Going-to-the-Sun' originated. The name should be 'Mah-tah-pee O-Stook-sis' on the charts to-day if given in Indian, and 'Person's Face' if given in English. According to the Indian lore, Sour Spirit was a great benevolent spirit and mystic creator, who, in the long ago, descended from his Lodge of the Sun and came to earth to show the Blackfeet how to do all things that they needed for their comfort in daily life. He showed the Indians how to shoot with bow and arrows; how to tan hides; how to build tepees; and how to trap buffalo in the 'pound,' thus killing a herd at a time. Sour Spirit had great supernatural powers, and [the ability] to do many magic and wonderful things with the greatest ease. He returned to the Lodge of the Sun when his work of teaching was finished. Going-to-the-Sun Mountain, when seen from the plains east of the peak, shows a gigantic face on its front like the face on a silver dollar. This stone face, the Indians say, is the likeness of Sour Spirit, who turned to stone when his spirit returned to the Sun's Lodge, and the face on the mountain was left for all men to see who may doubt the story of Sour Spirit and his deeds. In other words, Sour Spirit in the flesh turned to stone and left his face on the mountain to show that he had been here; his spirit then returned to the Lodge of the Sun. Hence the Indian name, Mah-tah-pee O-Stook-sis Meh-stuck, literally Person's-face Mountain, which to the Indian conveys this idea: Sour Spirit-Person's face-who-went-to-the-Sun; or in English: The face-of-Sour-Spirit-who-went-to-the-Sun-after-his-work-was-done Mountain."[4]

[Going to the Sun] ". . . right where Blackfoot legend pointed to the Indian prophet Going to the Sun through the luminous curtain of light that drapes each sunset"[5] "Napi, pursued by people who wanted to kill him, ran over a hill and up a deep coulee into the mountains. There he came to two lakes, now called Lower St. Mary Lake and Upper St. Mary Lake. At the Upper lake he said to himself, 'I believe I will go up on that highest mountain and change myself into stone.' In a crevice in the mountain he lay down, with just his face peeking out, and turned himself into a rock. He is still there. You can still see Napi's face on Going-to-the-Sun-Mountain. At times the face seems to be moving around, just as if Napi were peeking out and watching for people to come looking for him."[6]

2. LONE WOMAN

"As he wandered on his journey he kept beckoning in different directions, so that if any one saw him he would receive help and find his people. A woman saw him throwing his arms about as if desiring some one to come to him, and at once she went and asked him what he wanted. He said, 'Take me to the place where the people are.' She took him and led him along by means of a stick, the woman going in front and Napioa following. He was afraid that she might leave him, so he tied a bell to her dress, that he might follow her should she try to escape. Nothing eventful happened until they crossed a river, when he inquired, 'Are there any buffalo to be seen?' The woman answered, 'Yes, there are some at the river now.' He told her to point his arrow toward the buffalo, that he might shoot one. She did so; but he missed the buffalo, and then he shouted that the arrow did not belong to him. Again he commanded her to point the arrow in the right direction; but the buffalo were not killed, and again he asserted that the arrow did not belong to him. After several attempts he shot a buffalo, and then called out, 'That was my arrow.' He bade the woman skin the animal, cut up the meat, and bring it to the camping ground. While she was doing this he said that he would put up the lodge. He sought the lodge-poles; and as he brought them one by one, he failed to find those that he had already placed on the ground. He had quite a number of lodge-poles arranged here and there, but owing to his blindness he could not collect them. When the woman returned she asked him why he had so many poles, and none arranged in their proper places. 'That you might choose the best ones,' he replied. Thus was Napioa ever crafty, never allowing any one to say that there was anything wrong with him. The lodge being prepared, and supper ended, Napioa went to sleep. As he lay with his hair drawn over his eyes, the curiosity of the woman tempted her to lift the hair that she might see his face. As she slowly lifted his locks she gazed into the empty sockets from which his eyes had been torn, and suddenly seized with terror, she fled from the lodge and sped her way through the darkness. Napioa heard the bell, and springing from his grassy bed, pursued her, guided by the ringing of the bell. She ran in different directions; but he was fast gaining upon her when she tore the bell from her dress, and as she threw it one way she ran in another direction, and thus escaped from the wiles of Napioa."[7]

3. LONE PINE

"Napi Turns to Lone Pine Tree. A long time ago when men were first made and put on earth, they did not get married. The women lived off alone and killed their own buffalo to eat and made clothes for themselves. They made moccasins and made teepees out of skins. They went right along and lived by themselves. The men lived by themselves to one part of the country. They were lazy and they did not know what to do. They took the hide off of the shank bones and tied them together and used them for their moccasins and they did not make clothes for themselves, they just wore breech-cloth out of skins, and feathers on their heads. One day Napi told all the men, 'Let's go and find the women and all get married to them.' They went all over till they found the women. Way out here on Milk River. At a place we call Women's Buffalo Falls. The women had just got through killing buffalo and were all busy cutting their meat and drying it. When all the men lined up on a hill right by the camps Napi yelled out and said, 'Say, you women, who is the Head Woman of your camps?' The Head Woman jumped out and the other women told him, 'Here she is.' He told them, 'All of us men come to ask you women for marriage. We thought it would be nice to all get married, so that we could help one another; the men folk will go out and get food for you while you women stay home and tan hides and make clothes for us.' So they Head Woman said, 'Yes,' and all the women said, 'yes' too. He told them, 'I am the Head Chief of the men folks. I will ask the Head Woman to come up and choose me for her husband.' This Head Woman was all dirty, she did not even wash her hands, because she jumped out in a hurry, she was still cutting meat and her hands were bloody and her dress was the same way and her hair not combed. She went up there to get Napi. She start to take a hold of him by the arm, when he noticed how dirty looking she was. He jumped out of the way, and told her, 'No, I don't want you. I want the Head Woman.' This Head Woman told him, 'Alright,' and then she went back to the camps and cleaned up and called all the women together and told them, 'Now, I am going back up there, and pick a man for myself. And you all watch out for that man that refused me; I don't want any of you to get him. We will just let him stand there all alone and he can turn into a pine tree. I want every woman to pick a man for herself, and that one that refused me is an odd number. All the men will be all taken down here, and he will be the only one left for making me so ashamed, to refuse me.' This Head Woman was all cleaned up and her hair combed up nicely. She started up again. When Napi seen what a beautiful woman she was, he knew that she was not coming for him. He jumped over to the direction that she was going, but no, she went and picked another man and took him home. Then all the women rushed up there and got all the men and took them to their camps, and poor Napi was left up there all alone. This Head Woman told him, 'You can just stay here for the rest of your days and turn to a pine tree.' Sure enough that evening Napi kept a kicking on this hill, and made a steep bank on one side of it. The next morning he had turned a pine tree. So every after, everybody knows this place, on Milk River and the lone pine tree was old Napi. The tree is still there."[8]

4. WHEEL GAME

"Old Man Gambles. Far up in the north there is a place known as Old Man's Gambling-Place. There is where Old Man played the game of the arrows and the rolling wheel. Once when he came to this place, he found some people playing at the game. He joined them, and lost his robe and moccasins. As soon as he took them off, the robe became back-fat, and the moccasins buffalo-tongues. As the winner had not use for such things, he gave them back at once. The Old Man put the tongues on his feet, and they became moccasins, and, putting the back-fat on his shoulders, it became a robe. So he gambled again and again, always with the same result."[9]

5. SLIDING PLACE

"Napioa is the Secondary Creator of the Indians. There are two kinds of stories told concerning him. One class reveals him in the character of a good man, and the other class as a bad man. He is not, however, a man, but a supernatural being, able to perform deeds which no human could perform. The Indians do not know the manner of his birth, nor the place from whence he came. He is still living in a great sea away to the south. He made his home for a long time at the source of the Old Man's River, in Alberta, where may be seen the lake from which he drank, the stones which he threw along the ground when he was sporting, and indentations in the ground showing where he lay. At the Red Deer River there is a high ridge, where there is a land-slide, down which Napioa slid as a toboggan slide."[10]

Notes

PREFACE

1. Divisions of the Peoples' bands known collectively as Siksikaítsitapiiksi: Kainaa (Blood), Siksiká (Blackfoot), Aapatohsipikani/Skiniipiikani (North Peigan), and Aamsskaapipikani (Southern Peigan/Blackfeet) are all "Real People," meaning Indigenous People. These are some of the groups of bands that constitute the Blackfoot Confederacy that straddles the US-Canada border. This book does not discuss the non-Blackfoot-speaking members, since it is about the Blackfoot and Algonquian/Algonkian languages. Depending on the source, it is alternately referred to by the collective terms *Blackfoot* or *Blackfeet* or sometimes by other terms that refer to one of the smaller specific groups of the larger community. For simplicity's sake, this study uses the term *Blackfoot* to refer to the People, language, and culture and the term *People* to refer generally to Indigenous People or, alternatively, to a specific Indigenous community (e.g., Crow). The term *Beings* is used to refer to invisible entities or energies as well as other living, visible beings such as plants, animals, and other People. The Blackfoot language is called Niitsí'powahsin, which includes various terms used to describe the Blackfoot-speaking Peoples in the citations discussed and refers here (in the ways MacLean means) to the language/culture of the Niitsítapisini, the Niitsítapi, Siksikaítsitapi, the Blackfoot People. Analysis of the Blackfoot language begins with his description of the term that unites all the people, which was recorded over a century ago as "*netsepoye,* i.e., the people that speak the same language" (John MacLean, *The Blackfoot Language*, vol. 5: *1895–96*, Transactions of the Canadian Institute [Toronto: Printed for the Canadian Institute by Murray Printing Company, 1898], 129), but

Nitsí'poyi is the proper spelling, although it would normally not be used as a stem alone, the way the author does in his quote.

2. Donald G. Frantz and Norma Jean Russell, *Blackfoot Dictionary of Stems, Roots, and Affixes*, 2nd ed. (Toronto: University of Toronto Press, 1995), 305.

3. Frantz and Russell, *Blackfoot Dictionary of Stems, Roots, and Affixes*, 305.

4. Jeffrey E. Davis, *Hand Talk: Sign Language among American Indian Nations* (Cambridge: Cambridge University Press, 2010).

1. WHO IS NAAPI? SIGN AS FIRST LANGUAGE

1. I first introduced this version of my interpretation of Naapi at the Folklore and Mythology Symposium held at Harvard University, Cambridge, MA, February 12, 2009. My presentation publicly introduced a discourse about Naapi (the Blackfoot/Niitsítapi) "Trickster" that shifted from critiques of Naapi in fundamentally literary, philosophical, or religious discussions to one that revisits the origins of his original "Elder Brother/Friend" Creator aspect in the Blackfoot language. As I developed these first ideas for this book, I presented an initial sketch as "Spiritual Identity as Collaborative Process between Body and Place: Some Algonquin Examples" for the panel The Dynamics of Body, Place, and Subjectivity in the Study of Religion, American Anthropological Association, 112th Annual Meeting, Future Publics, Current Engagements, Chicago, IL, November 20–24, 2013.

2. Walter McClintock, *The Old North Trail: Life, Legends and Religion of the Blackfeet Indians* (Lincoln: University of Nebraska Press, 1910; Lincoln: Bison Book Printing, 1968), 337.

3. Personal communication, Arthur Westwolf, 2016.

4. This territory is bounded on the west side by the Rocky Mountains and is located between the Yellowstone River to the south, northward into Canada as far as the South Saskatchewan River, and as far east as the Medicine Hat area of Alberta, Canada, and the Badlands of Montana in the United States.

5. George Bird Grinnell, "A Blackfoot Sun and Moon Myth" *Journal of American Folk-Lore* 6, no. 20 (January–March 1893): 44.

6. Grinnell, "Blackfoot Sun and Moon Myth," 44.

7. John MacLean, "Blackfoot Mythology," *Journal of American Folk-Lore* 6, no. 22 (July–September 1893): 168.

8. MacLean, "Blackfoot Mythology," 168.

9. Shelagh M. Nolan, "Indian Legends of Alberta," *Canadian Cattlemen* 10, no. 4 (1948): 229.

10. (Sister) Annette Potvin, "The Sun Dance Liturgy of the Blackfoot Indians," MA thesis, Department of Religious Science, University of Ottawa, Canada, October 14, 1966, 39–40.

11. Jack Holterman, "Seven Blackfeet Stories," *Indian Historian* 3, no. 4 (Fall 1970): 39.

12. Nolan, "Indian Legends of Alberta," 201.

13. Nolan, "Indian Legends of Alberta," 201.

14. Nolan, "Indian Legends of Alberta," 201.

15. Donald G. Frantz and Norma Jean Russell, *Blackfoot Dictionary of Stems, Roots, and Affixes*, 3rd ed. (Toronto: University of Toronto Press, 2017), 317.

16. Quoted in Mark Elbroch, *Mammal Tracks and Sign: A Guide to North American Species* (Mechanicsburg, PA: Stackpole Books, 2003), 754.

17. William M. Edwardy, "The Sign Language," *Harper's Weekly* 11–17 (1888): 0874ad.

18. William Tomkins, *Indian Sign Language* (New York: Dover, 1969), 59.

19. Elbroch, *Mammal Tracks and Sign*, 71–73.

20. John MacLean, *The Blackfoot Language*, vol. 5: *1895–96*, Transactions of the Canadian Institute (Toronto: Printed for the Canadian Institute by Murray Printing Company, 1898), 137.

21. MacLean, *The Blackfoot Language*, 5: 137, 139.

22. *The American Heritage Dictionary of the English Language*, 4th ed. (Boston: Houghton Mifflin, 2006), 479.

23. Eugene Green and Celia M. Millward, "Semantic Categories in the Names of Algonquian Waterways, International Congress of Anthropological and Ethnological Science, 9th [International Congress], Chicago, 1973," in *Approaches to Language: Anthropological Issues*, ed. William C. McCormack and Stephen A. Wurm (The Hague: Mouton, 1973), 419.

24. Green and Millward, "Semantic Categories in the Names of Algonquian Waterways," 420–423.

25. Green and Millward, "Semantic Categories in the Names of Algonquian Waterways," 423–424.

26. Green and Millward, "Semantic Categories in the Names of Algonquian Waterways," 424.

27. Regina Pustet, "Obviation and Subjectivization: The Same Basic Phenomenon? A Study of Participant Marking in Blackfoot," *Studies in Language* 19, no. 1 (1994): 65; original emphasis.

28. Donald G. Frantz, "Person Indexing in Blackfoot," *International Journal of American Linguistics* 32, no. 1 (January 1966): 51.

29. C. C. Uhlenbeck, *Some General Aspects of Blackfoot Morphology: A Contribution to Algonquian Linguistics*, Afdeeling Letterkunde, Nieuwe Reeks, Deel XIV, no. 5 (Amsterdam: Johannes Muller, 1914), 51.

30. Frantz, "Person Indexing in Blackfoot," 51.

2. NAAPI'S NAME

1. Edward F. Wilson, *Report on the Blackfoot Tribes*, Drawn up by the Rev. Edward F. Wilson and supplementary to that furnished in 1885 by Horatio Hale, Report of the Fifty-seventh Meeting of the British Association for the Advancement of Science held at Manchester, August–September 1887 (London: John Murray, Albermarle Street, 1888), 186. [He prefaces these stories with the following statement: "Chief 'Big Plume,' another minor chief in the Blackfoot camp, gave me the following information. I have put it down word for word as it was interpreted to me" (185).]

2. James Willard Schultz, *Sinopah, the Indian Boy* (Boston: Houghton Mifflin, 1913), 71.

3. Philip Godsell, ed., Robert Nathaniel Wilson Papers/Manuscript, vols I and II (M4421 and M4422), Glenbow Museum and Archives, Calgary, Alberta, 1958.

4. Schultz, *Sinopah, the Indian Boy*.

5. Richard Lancaster, *Piegan: A Look from within at the Life, Times, and Legacy of an American Indian Tribe* (Garden City, NY: Doubleday, 1966), 229–230.

6. Canon [S. H. Middleton?], "Legend and Folklore of the 'Inside Lakes': Here Is Told How Waterton Lakes Were Formed by Supernatural Powers Long Ago" [as told by Mountain Horse], *Canadian Cattlemen* 21, no. 8 (August 1958): 24.

7. Lesley Wischmann, *Frontier Diplomats: Alexander Culbertson and Natoyist-Siksina' among the Blackfeet* (Norman: University of Oklahoma Press, 2004), 249.

8. George Bird Grinnell, *Blackfoot Lodge Tales, The Story of a Prairie People* (New York: Charles Scribner's Sons, 1923), 258.

9. Clark Wissler and D. C. Duvall, compilers and translators, introduction by Alice B. Kehoe, "Old Man Gambles," in *Mythology of the Blackfoot Indians* (Lincoln: University of Nebraska Press, 1995), 10.

10. Anthropologist Alice B. Kehoe states that Keith Seele, an Egyptologist philologist who visited Chewing Black Bone every summer, taking down texts in Blackfoot, told us that the name is "Bone" singular, not "Bones." Also, Clark surely did not get this paragraph directly from C.B.B. Personal communication, January or February 2017.

11. Ella E. Clark, *Indian Legends from the Northern Rockies* (Norman: University of Oklahoma Press, 1966), 218–219: "Chewing Blackbones, an elderly grandfather, recalled a fragment of one version of the end of *Napi*'s days—spent in what is now Glacier National Park. (Because he could tell the old tales only in the old Blackfoot language, his fourteen-year-old grandson had to ask a middle-aged neighbor to interpret for us)" (219).

12. S. H. Middleton, *Kainai Chieftainship: History, Evolution, and the Culture of the Blood Indians and Origin of the Sun-Dance Indian Chiefs: Ancient and Modern* (Lethbridge, Alberta: Lethbridge Herald, 1952), 49.

13. James Willard Schultz, *Signposts of Adventure: Glacier National Park as the Indians Know It* (Boston: Houghton Mifflin, 1926), 182.

14. Schultz, *Signposts of Adventure*, 182–183.

15. James Willard Schultz, "The Old Man Punishes a Thief," in "Life Among the Blackfeet, Eleventh Paper—Folk-Lore," *Sportsman Tourist, Forest and Stream; A Journal of Life, Travel, Nature Study, Shooting, Fishing, Yatching* . . . 22, no. 2 (February 7, 1884). https://www.biodiversitylibrary.org/item/134145#page/33/mode/1up.

16. Godsell, ed., Wilson Papers, appendix II, vol. II, "Appendix: In the original R. N. Wilson Manuscript there were at the end a number of items, unnumbered, and on different sized sheets, stapled in five separate parts, numbered with Roman numerals from I to V. Since most of these are enlargements of the general text and explanatory, in instances, of material therein, they have been assembled herein as Appendices, Nos. 1 to 5, which was no doubt the original intention of the writer. P. H.G.," 1958, 326, 346.

17. Anonymous, "The Torture Ordeal at the Blackfeet Sun Dance," *Harper's Weekly* 34, no. 1773 (December 13, 1890): 975.

18. John MacLean, "Social Organization of the Blackfoot Indians," *Transactions of the Canadian Institute*, Toronto, Canada, 4 (1892–1893): 251.

19. Robert H. Lowie, *The Crow Indians* (Murray Hill, NY: Farrar and Rinehart, 1935), 253.

20. J. B. Tyrrell, ed., *David Thompson's Narrative of His Explorations in Western America 1784–1812, Part I* (Toronto: Champlain Society, 1916), 362.

21. Tyrrell, *David Thompson's Narrative*, 362.

22. Clark Wissler, *North American Indians of the Plains*. Handbook Series 1 (New York: Museum of Natural History, 1912), 102.

23. Grinnell, *Blackfoot Lodge Tales*, 263.

24. Kenneth E. Kidd, "Blackfoot Ethnography: Being a Synthesis of the Data of Ethnological Science with the Information Concerning the Blackfoot Indians Contained in the Writings of the Explorers, Travellers, and Traders from the Time of First Contact to the Year 1821," master's thesis, Department of Anthropology, University of Toronto, Trent University, Peterborough, Ontario, Archaeological Survey of Alberta, Manuscript Series 8, Alberta Culture Historical Resources Division, 1937, 184. [Editor's note: Seven Blackfoot Indians who supplied me with information concerning the customs of their people are referred to in the text by the letters A., B., C., D., E., F., and G. Only B. and D. were able to converse in English. Of these, A. is one of the three leaders of the Tobacco Society as it is organized at present. He is somewhat past middle age, intelligent, and responsive. Mr. E. Curtis refers to him in *North American Indian* 18: 193 by the name "Whitehead Chief," 184.]

25. Kidd, "Blackfoot Ethnography," 176–178.

26. Mike Mountain Horse, *My People the Bloods*, ed. with an introduced by Hugh A. Dempsey, Glenbow Museum and Blood Tribal Council (Calgary, Alberta, Canada: Glenbow-Alberta Institute and Blood Tribal Council, 1989), 54.

27. Jessica Donaldson-Schultz, Montana State University Special Collections (Coll. 2336, File 19 2, WPA Gros Ventre History), informant: Takes A Prisoner, woman, 94 (oldest in tribe), collected by Fred Gone, November 17, 1941, 19.

28. Donaldson-Schultz, Verification of Takes A Prisoner's Story on Gros Ventre Legends, informant: John Buchman, collected by Fred Gone, November 17, 1941, 21.

29. Clark, *Indian Legends from the Northern Rockies*, 217–218.

30. Philip Godsell, ed., Wilson Papers, Part II, vol. I, "Myths and Legends," Glenbow Archives, Calgary, Alberta, Canada, 1958, 21.

31. James Willard Schultz, *Blackfeet Tales of Glacier National Park*, Western History Classics (Helena, MT: Riverbend Publishing in cooperation with Montana Historical Society Press, 2002 [1916]), 89.

32. Schultz, *Blackfeet Tales of Glacier National Park*, 89.

33. Schultz, *Blackfeet Tales of Glacier National Park*, 89.

34. Wilson, *Report on the Blackfoot Tribes*, 198.

35. Clark, *Indian Legends from the Northern Rockies*.

36. Walter McClintock, *The Old North Trail: Life, Legends, and Religion of the Blackfeet Indians* (Lincoln: University of Nebraska Press, 1910; Lincoln: Bison Book Printing, 1968), 335.

37. McClintock, *The Old North Trail*, 338.

38. McClintock, *The Old North Trail*, 337.

39. McClintock, *The Old North Trail*, 337.

40. McClintock, *The Old North Trail*, 337.

41. McClintock, *The Old North Trail*, 337–338.

42. MacLean, *The Blackfoot Language*, 5: 155.

43. Hugh A. Dempsey, *Charcoal's World: The True Story of the Canadian Indian's Last Stand* (Calgary, Alberta: Fifth House, 1998), 119.

44. Alika Podolinsky Webber, *The Rod and the Circle* (Washington, DC: Smithsonian Institution, 1984; revised, 1986), 120 [Smithsonian Library, Call #E98 S7W37 1986 SOA]. Cites Marguerite Mackenzie's letter to A. Cooke, September 29, 1981.

45. George Bird Grinnell, "Old Man Stories," in *Blackfeet Indian Stories* (New York: Charles Scribner's Sons, 1926 [1913]), 156–157. Republished as George Bird Grinnell, *Pawnee, Blackfoot, and Cheyenne: History and Folklore of the Plains* (New York: Charles Scribner's Sons, 1961), 150–151.

46. Wilson, *Report on the Blackfoot Tribes*, 199.

47. Bruce Haig, ed., *Southern Alberta Bicentennial: A Look at Peter Fidler's Journal, 1792–93 — 1992–93, Journal of the Journey over Land from Buckingham House to the Rocky Mountains in 1792 &3*. HRC Limited Edition Series (Lethbridge, Alberta: Historical Research Center [HRC], 1990).

48. Claude E. Schaeffer Papers, Series 3, n.d., Glenbow Archives, Calgary, Alberta, Canada, n.p.

49. Truman Michelson, "[Review of] Original Blackfoot Texts," *American Anthropologist, New Series* 13, no. 2 (April–June 1911): 330. [Original Blackfoot Texts, by C. C. Uhlenbeck. Ver d. Kon. Akad. Van Wetenschapen te Amsterdam, Afd. Lett., n.r.d. 12, no. 1 (1911).]

50. Agnes C. Laut, "The Glacier Land of the Blackfeet," *Travel* 46, no. 3 (January 1926): 7.

51. Claude E. Schaeffer Papers, Series 4, Blkft, M-1100-157, Field Notebooks, I Blackfoot, File Folder 1, Yellow Kidney (no interpreter mentioned), February 27, 1950, Glenbow Archives, Calgary, Alberta, Canada, 7–8.

52. Claude E. Schaeffer Papers, Series 3, Myths—Questions.

53. James Willard Schultz, with illustrations by George Varian, *The Danger Trail* (Boston: Houghton Mifflin, 1923).

54. Hugh A. Dempsey, letter to John C. Ewers, John Canfield Ewers Papers, Series 1 Correspondence, Box 7, September 7, 1992, National Anthropological Archives, Smithsonian Institution, Washington, DC, 1.

55. C. C. Uhlenbeck, *Original Blackfoot Texts from the Southern Peigans Blackfoot Reservation Teton County Montana*, with the help of Joseph Tatsey, collected and published with an English translation, Verhandelingen der Koninklijke Akademie van Wetenschappen te Amsterdam, Afdeeling Letterkunde, Nieuwe Reeks, Deel XII, no. 1 (Amsterdam: Johannes Muller, 1911), 94.

56. Godsell, "Myths and Legends," 21.

57. C. C. Uhlenbeck, "Some Word-Comparisons between Blackfoot and Other Algonquian Languages," in *International Journal of American Linguistics*, ed. Franz Boas and Pliny Earle Goddard with the assistance of Dr. Rivet, Edward Sapir, William Thalbitzer, and C. C. Uhlenbeck, 3, no. 1 (July 1924–1925), 103–108. Published by University of Chicago Press. https://www.jstor.org/stable/1263163.

58. Uhlenbeck, "Some Word-Comparisons between Blackfoot and Other Algonquian Languages," 105. See description of abbreviations: "Oj. *misk-*; Cree *mik-*; Fox *meckw-*; Men. *maqkik, maqkiu* red (*maqki* blood); Passa. *mkw-* red; Nat[ick] *mus-qui, mishque, msqui* (it is) red" (105).

59. The 49th Parallel marks the border between the United States and Canada. In the Blackfoot homeland, at this point the rivers travel northward, and stories say Naapi went north when he finished making the life and land for the Blackfoot and headed into what are now north Canada, the Northern Territories, and the Arctic and Polar regions.

60. MacLean, *The Blackfoot Language*, 5: 155.

61. Donald G. Frantz and Norma Jean Russell, *Blackfoot Dictionary of Stems, Roots, and Affixes*, 3rd ed. (Toronto: University of Toronto Press, 2017), 493.

62. Brian O.K. Reeves, "Culture Change in the Northern Plains: 1000 BC–AD 1000," Archeological Survey of Alberta Occasional Paper 20, Alberta Culture Historical Resources Division, Edmonton, Alberta, 1983, 45.

63. Reeves, "Culture Change in the Northern Plains," 45.

64. F. V. Hayden, "Contributions to the Ethnography and Philology of the Indian Tribes of the Missouri Valley," Part II, Article III, chapter V [Vocabulary of the *Sik-si-ka'* or Blackfoot Language], in *Transactions of the American Philosophical Society* XII–35 (Philadelphia: C. Sherman, Son, 1863), 266.

65. Hayden, "Contributions to the Ethnography and Philology of the Indian Tribes of the Missouri Valley," 266.

66. Hayden, "Contributions to the Ethnography and Philology of the Indian Tribes of the Missouri Valley," 270.

67. Stuart J. Baldwin, "Notes: Blackfoot Neologisms," *International Journal of American Linguistics* 60, no. 1 (January 1994): 71.

68. Baldwin, "Notes: Blackfoot Neologisms," 71.

69. Hayden, "Contributions to the Ethnography and Philology of the Indian Tribes of the Missouri Valley," 271.

70. Anonymous, "Art. II.–1. Archaeologia Americana: Transactions and Collections of the American Antiquarian Society," vol. 2 (Cambridge: Printed for the Society at the University Press, 1836), 573. 2; *Inquiries Respecting the History, Traditions, Languages, Manners, Customs, Religion, &c., of the Indians Living within the United States* (Detroit: Printed by Sheldon and Reed, 1823), 64; *North American Review (1821–1940)* XLV, no. XCVI (July 1837), APS Online 34–59, this quote is on 46–47. "The rules of the transition, to which we have adverted, will perhaps impress themselves more distinctly, by the following additional forms, in which, as above, the transitive particles of the Odjibwa are added to English words."

Declension of Pronouns for Tense.
I, Nee, or *Nin*; in compound words often N.

I-gee.	*I was–had–did.*
I-guh.	*I shall, or will.*
I-guh-gee.	*I shall, or will have been.*
I-gud.	*Let me.*
I-dau.	*I may, or can.*
I-dau-gee.	*I may–can–or might have been.*

Exchange the letter N for K in the second person, and O in the third, on the whole declension is formed.

Adjectives.
Inanimate form.   Animate form.
Beautiful-ud.   *Beautiful-izzi.*
Bad-ud.   *Bad-izzi.*
Soft-un.   *Soft-izzi.*
Hard-un.   *Hard-izzi.*
Strong-un.   *Strong-izzi.*
White-un.   *White-izzi.*
Black-au.   *Black-izzi.*
Red-au.   *Red-izzi.*

"These forms are respectively equivalent to *It is*, and *He is*, and are thus employed by the Indians, who separate perpetually, in their language, the two great departments of nature, characterized by the presence or absence of vitality" (46–47).

71. Anonymous, "Art. II.–1. Archaeologia Americana," 48–50; original emphasis.

72. Uhlenbeck, "Some Word-Comparisons between Blackfoot and Other Algonquian Languages," 107. See description of abbreviations: "Oj. *oma* here; Cree *oma* (inanimate) this. Cf. also Oj. *mi* so, it is so" (107).

73. C. C. Uhlenbeck, *Some General Aspects of Blackfoot Morphology: A Contribution to Algonquian Linguistics*, Afdeeling Letterkunde, Nieuwe Reeks, Deel XIV, no. 5 (Amsterdam: Johannes Muller, 1914), 26.

74. Hugh A. Dempsey, letter to John C. Ewers, John Canfield Ewers Papers, Series 1 Correspondence, Box 7, June 27, 1992, National Anthropological Archives, Smithsonian Institution, Washington, DC, 3.

75. For simplicity, in this section only, Old Blackfoot will refer to the variety described by Donald G. Frantz, *Blackfoot Grammar*, 3rd ed. (Toronto: University of Toronto Press, 2017), and Donald G. Frantz and Norma Jean Russell, *Blackfoot Dictionary of Stems, Roots, and Affixes*, 3rd ed. (Toronto: University of Toronto Press, 2017). Modern Blackfoot will refer to the variety spoken by the consultants. This is the distinction used by the consultants when asked about the differences between the forms.

76. Certain speakers omit the suffix *-wa* under as yet undetermined conditions. And many young speakers never seem to use it.

77. Sheena Van Der Mark, "The Acoustic Correlates of Blackfoot Prominence," Calgary Working Papers in Linguistics 24, University of Calgary, Calgary, Alberta, Canada, Fall 2002, 211–212, emphasis added.

78. C. C. Uhlenbeck and R. H. Van Gulik, *An English-Blackfoot Vocabulary, Based on Material from the Southern Peigans* (Amsterdam: Akademie van Wetenschappen, 1930).

79. Lancaster, *Piegan*, 204.

80. Lancaster, *Piegan*, 204.

81. Roxanne DeMarce, ed., *Blackfeet Heritage: 1907–1908, Blackfeet Indian Reservation, Browning, Montana,* (Browning, MT: Blackfeet Heritage Program, 1980), 273.

82. Lancaster, *Piegan,* 204–205.

83. J.P.B. Josselin De Jong, "Introduction," in *Blackfoot Texts: From the Southern Peigans, Blackfoot Reservation, Teton County, Montana, with the help of Black-Horse-Rider, Collected and Published with an English Translation,* Verhandelingen der Koninklijke Akademie van Wetenschappen te Amsterdam, Afdeeling Letterkunde, Nieuwe Reeks, Deel XIV, no. 4 (Amsterdam: Johannes Muller, 1914), 3.

84. De Jong, "Introduction," 4.

85. C. C. Uhlenbeck, *A New Series of Blackfoot Texts from the Southern Peigans Blackfoot Reservation Teton County Montana,* with the help of Joseph Tatsey, collected and published with an English translation, Verhandelingen der Koninklijke Akademie van Wetenschappen te Amsterdam, Afdeeling Letterkunde, Nieuwe Reeks, Deel XIII, no. 1 (Amsterdam: Johannes Muller, 1912), 248.

86. Uhlenbeck, *A New Series of Blackfoot Texts from the Southern Peigans Blackfoot Reservation Teton County Montana,* 248.

87. Uhlenbeck, *Some General Aspects of Blackfoot Morphology,* 5.

88. Uhlenbeck, *Some General Aspects of Blackfoot Morphology,* 5.

89. Uhlenbeck, *Some General Aspects of Blackfoot Morphology,* 5.

90. Uhlenbeck, *Some General Aspects of Blackfoot Morphology,* 6.

91. Uhlenbeck, *Some General Aspects of Blackfoot Morphology,* 5–6.

92. Uhlenbeck, *Some General Aspects of Blackfoot Morphology,* 6.

93. Truman Michelson, "[Review of] Original Blackfoot Texts," *American Anthropologist,* New Series 13, no. 2 (April–June 1911): 329.

94. Claude E. Schaeffer Papers, Series 5-1100-166, BLKFT Field Notes 2, Dicker Sanderville, George Bull Child, in addition to handwritten notes from other sources, n.d., Glenbow Archives, Calgary, Alberta, Canada, n.p. These are Schaeffer's explanations of preferred pronuncitation:

α = u in but
â = a in fall
Є = e in Messer
x = palatal voiceless fricative
X = guttural non-palatized voiceless fricative.

95. Hugh A. Dempsey, letter to John C. Ewers, John Canfield Ewers Papers, Series 1 Correspondence, Box 6, September 11, 1956, National Anthropological Archives, Smithsonian Institution, Washington, DC, 1–2; original emphasis.

96. Jean Lessard, O.M.I. (Anthropology, University of Ottawa), letter to Linguistics Department, Smithsonian Institution, Washington, DC, John Canfield Ewers Papers,

Research and Subject Files, Series II, Box 2, July 25, 1949, National Anthropological Archives, Smithsonian Institution, Washington, DC, 1.

97. Lessard, letter to Linguistics Department, July 25, 1949, 1.

98. Regina Pustet, "Obviation and Subjectivization: The Same Basic Phenomenon? A Study of Participant Marking in Blackfoot," *Studies in Language* 19, no. 1 (1994): 46.

99. Pustet, "Obviation and Subjectivization," 46–47; original emphasis. Pustet continues: "Some of the transitive verb stems are obtained by means of prefixes such as: *is(i)st-, (i) p-*: locative; *itap-*: directional; *ixp-, oxp-*: comitative; *ixt-, oxt-*: source, instrumental; *moxt-*: benefactive, instrumental, cause; (Only the major meanings of the prefixes are given.) Many of the Blackfoot transitive verb stems, however, are not morphologically derivable, but are fusional forms . . . Such instances of suppletion contribute a great deal to the enormous complexity of the Blackfoot lexicon" (47).

100. Michelson, "[Review of] Original Blackfoot Texts," 327.

101. Michelson, "[Review of] Original Blackfoot Texts," 329.

102. Michelson, "[Review of] Original Blackfoot Texts," 329.

103. Michelson, "[Review of] Original Blackfoot Texts," 330.

104. Uhlenbeck, *A New Series of Blackfoot Texts from the Southern Peigans Blackfoot Reservation Teton County Montana*, v (preface).

105. Uhlenbeck, *A New Series of Blackfoot Texts from the Southern Peigans Blackfoot Reservation Teton County Montana*, vii (preface).

106. Uhlenbeck, *A New Series of Blackfoot Texts from the Southern Peigans Blackfoot Reservation Teton County Montana*, vii (preface). "In the same way I would prefer now to write *matsipaskauki* instead of *matsipaskauoki* (obt p. 22). But in the corresponding forms of *-o-* stems and *-u-* stems I continue to write *-auop, -auoki*, because there the *-o-* is nearly always clearly pronounced."

107. Uhlenbeck, *A New Series of Blackfoot Texts from the Southern Peigans Blackfoot Reservation Teton County Montana*, vii (preface).

108. Uhlenbeck, *A New Series of Blackfoot Texts from the Southern Peigans Blackfoot Reservation Teton County Montana*, vii (preface).

109. Uhlenbeck, *A New Series of Blackfoot Texts from the Southern Peigans Blackfoot Reservation Teton County Montana*, vii (preface).

110. Uhlenbeck, *A New Series of Blackfoot Texts from the Southern Peigans Blackfoot Reservation Teton County Montana*, vii–viii (preface).

111. Uhlenbeck, *A New Series of Blackfoot Texts from the Southern Peigans Blackfoot Reservation Teton County Montana*, viii (preface).

112. Zenon Pohorecky, "Saskatchewan Indian Heritage: The First Two Hundred Centuries," the Extension Division, University of Saskatchewan, Saskatoon, 1970, 37.

3. MYTH, LEGEND, AND NAAPI

1. Philip Duke, *Points in Time: Structure and Event in a Late Northern Plains Hunting Society* (Boulder: University Press of Colorado, 1991). See also Alice B. Kehoe, "Ceramic Affiliations in the Northwest Plains," *American Antiquity* 25, no. 2 (October 1959): 237–246.

2. John C. Ewers, R. N. Wilson Manuscript, John Canfield Ewers Papers, Research and Subject Files, Series II, Box 13, n.d., National Anthropological Archives, Smithsonian Institution, Washington, DC, n.p.

3. The mapping of these sites is a subject for another book, since it is too extensive to be covered here.

4. Richard B. Roeder, "Charles M. Russell and Modern Times," *Montana: The Magazine of Western History* 34, no. 3 (Summer 1984): 7.

5. Lena Russell, "Bob Black Plume Lectures Students at Levern School on Indian Culture," *Kainai News*, March 15, 1969, 14.

6. Osborne Russell, *Journal of a Trapper: In the Rocky Mountains between 1834 and 1843* (Santa Barbara, CA: Narrative Press, 2001), 197.

7. Ives Goddard, "The West-to-East Cline in Algonquian Dialectology," *Actes Du Vingt-Cinquieme Congres Des Algonquinistes*, ed. William Cowan, Carleton University, Ottawa, Canada 1994, 187.

8. Goddard, "The West-to-East Cline in Algonquian Dialectology": "B *iipiimma* 'he entered' (*piit* 'enter' (imperat.) < (early) PA* *pi mwa* 'he enters' (displaced by PA *pi ntwike wa*): PA *pi mwa* 'he takes a sweatbath' . . . (14) B *ikimm*-TA 'show kindness to, bestow power on, care for' (*ikimmiiwa* 'he bestowed power on him') < (early PA* *ketem*-TA (*keteme wa* '*he takes pity on him'): PA *ketem-, ketema k-* 'pitiful, poor' (an initial), e.g., in F *keteminawe wa* 'he takes pity on him, blesses him with power' . . . Assuming that the Blackfoot verb in (13) can indeed continue PA * *pi mwa*, it reflects what must have been the original meaning 'enter.' This original meaning is also required to explain the transitive derivative PA *pi nta wa* 'he puts it inside' . . . originally 'cause to enter" (188–189).

9. Goddard, "The West-to-East Cline in Algonquian Dialectology," 189.

10. Horatio Hale, "Ethnology of the Blackfoot Tribes," *Popular Science Monthly* 29 (May–October 1886): 1, 3.

11. Hale, "Ethnology of the Blackfoot Tribes," 208–209.

12. Hale, "Ethnology of the Blackfoot Tribes," 209.

13. Hale, "Ethnology of the Blackfoot Tribes," 209.

14. Hale, "Ethnology of the Blackfoot Tribes," 209.

15. Daniel Garrison Brinton cited in Horatio Hale, "The Origin of Language and the Antiquity of Speaking Man: An Address before the Section of Anthropology of the

American Association for the Advancement of Science," delivered in Buffalo, NY, *Proceedings of the American Association for the Advancement of Science* 35 (Cambridge: John Wilson and Son, University Press, 1886), 13.

16. Daniel Garrison Brinton, *The Myths of the New World: A Treatise on the Symbolism and Mythology of the Red Race of America* (New York and London: Leypoldt and Holt, and Trubner, 1868), 91–92.

17. Daniel G. Brinton, *American Hero-Myths: A Study in the Native Religions of the Western Continent* (Philadelphia: H. C. Watts, 1882).

18. Hale, "Ethnology of the Blackfoot Tribes," 209–210.

4. A DIFFERENT CONCEPTUAL ORDER

1. Howard L. Harrod, *Becoming and Remaining a People: Native American Religious Traditions on the Northern Plains*, 3rd ed., Studies in Anglican History (Tucson: University of Arizona Press, 1995). See discussion of Native American languages in Edward Sapir, "Time Perspective in Aboriginal American Culture," *Geological Survey of Canada* 13, Anthropological Series (Ottawa, 1916): 81.

2. Ermine W. Voegelin, "Kiowa-Crow Mythological Affiliations," *American Anthropologist*, New Series 35, no. 3 (July–September 1933): 470–474.

3. Summarized in George Grant MacCurdy, "Anthropology at the New York Meeting with Proceedings of the American Anthropological Association for 1906," *American Anthropologist*, New Series 9, no. 1 (January–March 1907): 168–169.

4. George Bird Grinnell, "Old Man Stories," in *Blackfeet Indian Stories* (New York: Charles Scribner's Sons, 1926 [1913]), 156–157. Republished as George Bird Grinnell, *Pawnee, Blackfoot, and Cheyenne: History and Folklore of the Plains* (New York: Charles Scribner's Sons, 1961), 151.

5. John Mason Brown, "Traditions of the Blackfeet," *The Galaxy: A Magazine of Entertaining Reading* 3, January 15, 1867, 157.

6. Richard Lancaster, *Piegan: A Look from within at the Life, Times, and Legacy of an American Indian Tribe* (Garden City, NY: Doubleday, 1966), 164–165.

7. Walter McClintock, *The Old North Trail: Life, Legends, and Religion of the Blackfeet Indians* (Lincoln: University of Nebraska Press, 1910; Lincoln: Bison Book Printing, 1968), 338.

8. Blackfoot Gallery Committee, *Nitsitapiisinni: The Story of the Blackfoot People* (Buffalo, NY: Firefly Books, and the Glenbow Museum: Key Porter Books Limited, 2001), 50.

9. Agnes C. Laut, "The Struggle for the Life of the Blackfeet," *Travel* 46, no. 5 (March 1926): 20–21.

10. Anna B. Mesquida, "The Door of Yesterday: An Intimate View of the Vanishing Race at the Panama-Pacific International Exposition," *Overland Monthly and Out West Magazine* 46, no. 1 (July 1915): Proquest 0_002.

11. Mathilde Edith Holtz and Katharine Isabel Bemis, *Glacier National Park: Its Trails and Treasures* (New York: George H. Doran, 1917), 192–194.

12. Gerald L. Berry, "The Whoop-Up Trail: Early Days in Alberta . . . Montana," Occasional Paper 9, Lethbridge Historical Society, P.O. 974, Lethbridge, Alberta, Canada, 1995, 7.

13. James Willard Schultz, "Life among the Blackfeet, Fourteenth Paper—Folk-Lore," *Forest and Stream: A Journal of Outdoor Life, Travel, Nature Study, Shooting, Fishing, Yachting*, 22, no. 8 (March 20, 1884), https://www.biodiversitylibrary.org/item/134145#page/141 /mode/1up. These represent all the stories he has collected to this point and printed in the series of his papers 1–14.

14. Edward F. Wilson, *Report on the Blackfoot Tribes*, Drawn up by the Rev. Edward F. Wilson and supplementary to that furnished in 1885 by Horatio Hale, Report of the Fifty-seventh Meeting of the British Association for the Advancement of Science held at Manchester, August–September 1887 (London: John Murray, Albermarle Street, 1888), 198–199. These are some of his erroneous arguments and mistranslations: "We know the legend of the origin of horses at a recent historical foundation, so we may also conclude that this story of the women and their choice of husbands, coupled with the rejection of *Napi*, had its origin in some actual occurrence of perhaps not very remote date . . . If there ever was a camp of Indian women with whom no men were found, we may be tolerably sure that they were the survivors of a war in which all the fighting men of their tribe had been slain. The band of Kootenais, who formerly dwelt east of the Rocky Mountains, was certainly not dislodged by their Blackfeet enemies without a desperate war, in which, as a natural and almost inevitable result, the men would be killed—perhaps in a fight at a distance from their homes—and women, who were left at home, would be afterwards made prisoners, and would become the wives of the conquerors. Such events are of common occurrence in Indian history. The liberty given to the captive women, when once received as members of the Blackfoot nation, of choosing their own husbands would be entirely in accordance with Indian sentiments and habits. That these women should despise and reject *Napi*, the peculiar and rather ridiculous divinity of the Algonkins [*sic*], and should introduce the worship of their own glorious sun-god, is intelligible enough. Thus we can see how a tradition as improbable on its face as the coming of horses out of the salt water may represent an actual event which has deeply affected the language, religion, and character of the Blackfoot nation . . . I may venture to add that Mr. Wilson's carefulness in preserving these native stories—however trivial they might at first seem—precisely as they were received by him deserves particular acknowledgment" (199–200).

15. Ella E. Clark, *Indian Legends from the Northern Rockies* (Norman: University of Oklahoma Press, 1966), 219.

16. Rides at the Door, Darnell Davis, writer-compiler, *Napi Stories* (Browning, MT: Blackfeet Heritage Program, 1979), 7.

17. Hugh A. Dempsey, letter to John C. Ewers, John Canfield Ewers Papers, Series 1 Correspondence, Box 6, May 29, 1984, National Anthropological Archives, Smithsonian Institution, Washington, DC, n.p.

18. Colin F. Taylor and Hugh A. Dempsey, *With Eagle Tail: Arnold Lupson and 30 Years among the Sarcee, Blackfoot, and Stony Indians on the North American Plains* (Toronto: Key Porter Books, 1999), 52, 55.

19. Howard L. Harrod, *Renewing the World: Plains Indian Religion and Morality* (Tucson: University of Arizona Press, 1992), 178.

20. Harrod, *Renewing the World*, 178.

21. Harrod, *Renewing the World*, 178. The Trickster figure in Plains oral traditions, as well as elsewhere in North American Indian traditions, is an enigmatic being and has occasioned much scholarly debate. One set of problems has to do with the association, in the same figure, of creation and the bringing of culture and obscenity, humor and malicious behavior. Although we cannot completely solve these issues, it will be helpful to review some of the major dimensions of the discussion.

22. Harrod, *Renewing the World*, 178.

23. Cited in Harrod, *Renewing the World*, 178.

24. Harrod, *Renewing the World*, 178.

25. Harrod, *Renewing the World*, 178.

26. Harrod, *Renewing the World*, 178.

27. Mac Linscott Ricketts, "The North American Indian Trickster," *History of Religions* 5, no. 2 (December 1, 1966): 327–350.

28. Harrod, *Renewing the World*, 178.

29. Harrod, *Renewing the World*, 178–179.

30. Harrod, *Renewing the World*, 179.

31. Harrod, *Renewing the World*, 179.

32. Sam Gill, *Native American Religions: An Introduction* (Belmont, CA: Wadsworth, 1982), 28.

33. Harrod, *Renewing the World*, 179.

34. Harrod, *Renewing the World*, 179.

35. Harrod, *Renewing the World*, 179.

36. Harrod, *Renewing the World*, 179.

37. Harrod, *Renewing the World*, 179.

38. Harrod, *Renewing the World*, 180.

39. Harrod, *Renewing the World*, 180.

40. Regina Pustet, "Obviation and Subjectivization: The Same Basic Phenomenon? A Study of Participant Marking in Blackfoot," *Studies in Language* 19, no. 1 (1994): 54.

41. Pustet, "Obviation and Subjectivization," 62–63.

42. C. C. Uhlenbeck, *Some General Aspects of Blackfoot Morphology: A Contribution to Algonquian Linguistics*, Afdeeling Letterkunde, Nieuwe Reeks, Deel XIV, no. 5.(Amsterdam: Johannes Muller, 1914), 51.

43. Uhlenbeck, *Some General Aspects of Blackfoot Morphology*, 51.

44. John MacLean, *The Blackfoot Language*, vol. 5: *1895–96*, Transactions of the Canadian Institute (Toronto: Printed for the Canadian Institute by Murray Printing Company, 1898), 148; original emphasis.

45. Zenon Pohorecky, "Saskatchewan Indian Heritage: The First Two Hundred Centuries," the Extension Division, University of Saskatchewan, Saskatoon, 1970, 38.

46. Nkiru Nzegwu, "Editorial: Water, Wind, and Sound: Philosophy in a Different Key," *Journal on African Philosophy* 13 (2016). See Africa Knowledge Project (https://www.africaknowledgeproject.org) for original research on Africa and the African Diaspora.

47. Nzegwu, "Water, Wind, and Sound," 1.

48. Pustet, "Obviation and Subjectivization," 40.

49. Pustet, "Obviation and Subjectivization," 46.

50. Pustet, "Obviation and Subjectivization," 47; for example, Pustet's list is on page 47.

51. Pustet, "Obviation and Subjectivization." This comment refers to the list on page 47 and potentially to other similar expressions not included here.

52. Pustet, "Obviation and Subjectivization," 46.

53. Pustet, "Obviation and Subjectivization," 59.

54. Uhlenbeck, *Some General Aspects of Blackfoot Morphology*, 6.

55. Pustet, "Obviation and Subjectivization," 62.

56. Pustet, "Obviation and Subjectivization," 63. See pages 62–63 on this point.

57. Nzegwu, "Water, Wind, and Sound," 1.

58. Russell Wright Sr. (Elder, Siksiká [Blackfoot] Nation), "Forward"; Matthew Many Guns, *"Napi* and the Mice," in *Aakaitapitsinniksiists* (*Siksiká* Old Stories), *Siksikai'powahsin/Siksiká* Language Series Kit Level II (Gleichen, Alberta, Canada: The Siksiká Nation, 1994), 4.

59. Cecile Black Boy, "Napi Stories: Legendary, Napi," in Informants: Old Indians (Browning, MT: Museum of the Plains Indian, April 2, 1942), 1–2.

APPENDIX: SELECTED NAAPI STORIES

1. Cecile Black Boy, "Napi Stories: Naapi's Face at St. Mary's Lakes," in *Tribe: Blackfeet Indians* (Browning, MT: Museum of the Plains Indian, 1942), 1–2.

2. Mary Roberts Rinehart, *Glacier National Park* (St. Paul, MN: Great Northern Railway, circa 1922), 15.

3. Adolf Hungry Wolf, *Good Medicine in Glacier National Park* (Golden, British Columbia, Canada: Good Medicine Books, 1971), 20.

4. Mathilde Edith Holtz and Katharine Isabel Bemis, *Glacier National Park: Its Trails and Treasures* (New York: George H. Doran, 1917), 192–194.

5. Agnes C. Laut, "The Struggle for the Life of the Blackfeet," *Travel* 46, no. 5 (March 1926): 22.

6. Ella E. Clark, *Indian Legends from the Northern Rockies* (Norman: University of Oklahoma Press, 1966), 219.

7. John MacLean, "Blackfoot Mythology," *Journal of American Folk-Lore* 6, no. 22 (July–September 1893): 168–169.

8. Cecile Black Boy, "Napi Stories: Napi Turns to Lone Pine Tree," in *Informants: Tribe: Blackfoot* (Browning, MT: Museum of the Plains Indian, August 22, 1941), 1–4.

9. Clark Wissler and D. C. Duvall, compilers and translators, introduction by Alice B. Kehoe, "Old Man Gambles," in *Mythology of the Blackfoot Indians* (Lincoln: University of Nebraska Press, 1995), 24.

10. MacLean, "Blackfoot Mythology," 68.

Index

Aamsskaapipikani (Southern Peigan/Blackfeet), 33–34, 38–39, 54–55, 67
Aapatohsipikani/Skiniipiikani (North Peigan), 67
Above White Man, 37
abuse, rules against, 6
accents, notating, 65
actions, 47, 59, 73, 122; context of, 26–27; and space, 25–26
actors, as interlocuters, 120–21
adaptability, adaptation, 124, 128
affirmation, 47
agency, 47, 120, 122
air, 13, 46
Algonquian/Algonkian languages, 7, 39, 56, 91, 116, 118, 122, 148(n8); in ceremonial context, 95–96; "to be" in, 47–48; creation stories, 87–88; history of, 81–82; knowledge of nature in, 94–95; Naapi's name in, 42, 46–47; numerals, 49–51; whispered vowels in, 58–61
aliases, Naapi's, 43–47
allegory, Naapi as, 79
Almost-a-Dog Mountain, 131
aloneness, 47
alter egos, Naapi's, 43–47

ancestors, 46, 125
animacy, animate, 12, 24–25, 28, 51, 93, 94, 118–19; as focus of speech, 62–63; of Naapi, 45–46, 59
animals, 12, 13, 14, 50, 73, 75, 94, 108, 114, 128; killing, 84, 88–90; and seasonal cycles, 100–101
animate/inanimate distinction, 47–48, 53, 55, 118–19, 144–45(n70); grammatical classification and, 51–52, 56; plants and botanical terms, 57–58
Apistotoki, 44
"Appendix A: Blackfoot Syntax and Morphology" (Van Der Mark), 53
archaeology, and Blackfoot creation stories, 81
arrogance, 6
associations, stories told in, 10–11
atmospheric processes, 74
auditory absorbers, 61
awareness, wisdom and, 112

"Backbone of the World" (Rocky Mountains), 79
Badger, 50
balance, 15, 125; pairs/counterparts, 49–51
be, to, 47–48
Bear, 85

111–12; People and, 13–14, 16, 85–86; violating order of, 112–13
Nez Perce, 44
Niitsi'powahsin, 59
non-Indigenous Peoples, 122; mischaracterizations by, 31–37, 38–39, 40–41, 42, 101–6, 113–14; stories collected by, 77, 97
North Peigan, 67
nouns, 24–25, 64; animate/inanimate, 51–52, 53, 55, 56–57; final whispered vowels in, 58–61
numerals, 49–51
Nzegwu, Nkiru, 117

obviation, 118–19, 123
Ojibway, 55, 88, 116
Old Man Mountain, 99
"Old Man of the Mountains," 102
Old-Man-on-His-Back Plateau, 99
Old Man's River, 99
Old Man's Slide, 99
"Old Man" stories, 96–97, 99, 102
"Old Wolf Robe," 102
opposite-speak, 5, 6, 12, 76, 82–83, 96, 98, 108, 126
order, 6; natural, 112–13
orenda, 55
orthography, 63; gutturals in, 59–60; Uhlenbeck's, 66–67, 68–69
Other, and self, 6

pairs, 49–51
participants/participation, 118; listening as, 61–62; in speech contexts, 121–22
People(s)/Person(s), 12, 15, 17, 44, 46, 61, 110, 116; action and context, 26–27; and Naapi, 76, 87; and natural world, 13–14, 16, 85–86, 94–95; philosophical and intellectual life of, 77–78; rights to food and shelter, 83–84; stories of, 39–40
personal forms, in Blackfoot, 54
personhood, 17, 76, 95
person indexing system, 28
"Person's Face" stories, 130–32
Person's-face Mountain, 132
perspective, switching, 84
philosophy, 4, 17, 117–18; humor and, 97–99; Naapi's, 80–81
phonemes, sound duration, 64–65
phonology, 82
Piegans, 44

place(s), 12, 13, 15, 25, 47, 76, 99; and People, 94, 95; in stories, 4, 5, 83
Plains, 24
Plains Peoples, 75; creation cycle, 73–74; stories, 96–97; Trickster and, 112, 151(n21)
Plains Sign Language, 4, 17–18; participants of, 61–62
planets, 108, 125
plants, 12, 13, 14, 75, 108; animate/inanimate, 57–58; in Naapi stories, 73, 84; and seasonal cycles, 100–101
"Plays Wheel Game," 43
Porcupine, 50
power, 95; of Naapi, 3, 9, 110–11
prayers, 85
prehistory, 74, 75
presence, 118
profanity, 98
pronunciation, and silent vowels, 66, 67
protohistory, 74
proximity, and Beings, 121
Puster, Regina, 115, 122

Rabbit, 4
Radin, Paul, *The Trickster,* 107–9
"Rainbow," 102
Raven, 4, 50
reality, 121
reciprocity, 6
red, and death, 44
Red Crow, 37–38
Red Deer River, 38, 135
red earth, 38
Red Old Man (Blackfoot), 102
regeneration/resurrection, 10, 63; as theme, 87–88
relationships, 17, 50, 73
resolution, community role, 6
rivers, 24, 26, 27, 44–45
rocks, as ancestors, 46
Rocky Mountains (Backbone of the World), 79
"Round Fat Man" (Cree), 102
rules, grammatical, 122
Running Wolf (James White Calf), 54
Russell, Charles M., 78–79

sacred, sacredness, 99, 112, 123; Naapi as, 90, 97–98
sacred-profane distinction, 108–9